LATINO IMAGES IN FILM

Texas Film and Media Studies Series
Thomas Schatz, Editor

The publication of this book was assisted by
a University Cooperative Society Subvention Grant
awarded by the University of Texas at Austin.

LATINO IMAGES IN FILM

STEREOTYPES,

SUBVERSION,

RESISTANCE

Charles Ramírez Berg

UNIVERSITY OF TEXAS PRESS
AUSTIN

Chapter 5 was previously published in Chon A. Noriega, ed., *Chicanos
and Film: Representation and Resistance*, pp. 29–46 (Minneapolis: University of Minnesota Press, 1992). Copyright 1992 by the Regents of the University of Minnesota. Reprinted courtesy of University of Minnesota Press.

Chapter 6 was previously published as "The Margin as Center: The
Multicultural Dynamics of John Ford's Westerns," in Gaylyn Studlar and
Matthew Bernstein, eds., *John Ford Made Westerns: Filming the Legend in
the Sound Era*, pp. 75–101 (Bloomington: Indiana University Press, 2001).
Reprinted courtesy of Indiana University Press.

Chapter 7 was previously published as "Immigrants, Aliens, and Extraterrestrials: Science Fiction's Alien 'Other' as (among *Other* Things) New
Hispanic Imagery," *CineACTION!*, no. 18 (Fall 1989): 3–17.

Chapter 8 was previously published in Yolanda C. Padilla, ed., *Refle-
xiones 1998: New Directions in Mexican American Studies*, pp. 69–101
(Austin: Center for Mexican American Studies, 1999). Reprinted courtesy
of CMAS Books.

Chapter 9 was previously published in Chon A. Noriega and Ana M.
López, eds., *The Ethnic Eye: Latino Media Arts* (Minneapolis: University of
Minnesota Press, 1996). Copyright 1996 by the Regents of the University of
Minnesota. Reprinted courtesy of University of Minnesota Press.

Library of Congress Cataloging-in-Publication Data
Berg, Charles Ramírez, date
    Latino images in film : stereotypes, subversion, and resistance / Charles
Ramírez Berg.
        p.   cm. — (Texas film and media studies series)
    Includes index.
    ISBN 978-0-292-70907-2 (pbk. : alk. paper)
    1. Hispanic Americans in motion pictures. 2. Hispanic American motion
picture actors and actresses—United States—Biography. I. Title.
II. Series.
    PN1995.9.H47 B46 2002
    791.43'6520368—dc21   2002003438

    doi:10.7560/709065

To my parents:

My mother,
Hortensia Ramírez Berg,
and
my father,
Gerald Ellsworth Berg

They gave me everything:
life,
unconditional love,
and
the best of two cultures

CONTENTS

ACKNOWLEDGMENTS

No book is written alone. Because the writer's words arrive on the page with the help of many others, I want to acknowledge all those who supported and assisted me in this project. Chon Noriega has long been a friend and an enthusiastic supporter of my work, and as the editor of several anthologies, he first commissioned two of these essays. Over the years, in numerous conversations on these topics, I have benefited from his ideas on the subject of Latinos in the movies and from his editorial comments and suggestions. He is a generous scholar and one of the key reasons that Latino media studies is booming. I have likewise profited from the insights and generosity of friends and scholars working in the same area, especially Ana López, Kathleen Newman, Federico Subervi, and David Maciel. They have all been wonderfully helpful and unselfish colleagues who shared their time, resources, and ideas freely.

My interview with Robert Rodríguez would not have been possible without the help of his producer and wife, Elizabeth Avellan, who first interceded on my behalf. Of course, I must also thank Robert, who took time from his busy schedule in the midst of editing *Spy Kids* to talk to me about his films and his career. I will ever be in the debt of these two gracious filmmakers.

I am lucky to know and work with Tom Schatz, surely one of the best historians of Hollywood cinema. As chair of the Department of Radio-Television-Film where I teach, he has been a tireless champion of this book and of my teaching. In his capacity as editor of the Texas Film and Media Studies Series, he assisted me tremendously in the shaping of this book throughout its production. At the University of Texas Press, I was also helped by humanities editor Jim Burr, whose editorial guidance was invaluable.

At the University of Texas Center for Mexican American Studies, I have been steadfastly supported by former heads Rodolfo de la Garza (he first hired me to teach at the University of Texas at Austin, and it is to him that I owe my career), Gil Cárdenas, David Montejano, and the present director, José Límon. In addition, I have been inspired by the collegial and scholarly spirit of the faculty associated with the center, especially the inspiring example of the late Américo Paredes and the rigorous scholarship of José Límon and Richard Flores. They all set a very high standard for Latino cultural studies. I am also greatly indebted to Victor Guerra for his keen editorial assistance on the essay on Mexican American border documentaries.

It is impossible to credit the many students whose perceptions and original ideas led me to consider films I didn't know and to reconsider films I thought I knew. They will never know how much I have profited from their stimulating input over the years; all I can do to show my gratitude is to give them my sincerest thanks here. One graduate student, Ke-Ming Lin, helped by reading chapters of the manuscript and by providing technical assistance with the frame enlargements from two films, *Falling Down* and *Six Days, Seven Nights*.

Thanks also to Luis Reyes, who graciously provided movie stills from his archive to help illustrate this book.

This book was partially funded by a fellowship from the National Endowment for the Humanities, and it could not have been completed without that assistance. In order for me to take a full year off from my teaching duties with the NEH fellowship, the central administration of the University of Texas gave me supplemental funding, and I would like to thank then Vice-Provost Ricardo Romo for helping me secure those funds. The final piece of the funding puzzle that made the year's sabbatical possible was a matching grant given me by the best boss a college teacher ever had, Dean Ellen Wartella of the College of Communication. In movie terms these supportive administrators were the executive producers of this book, and it exists because of their unfaltering belief in me and in my research. It is moving, heartening, and humbling to receive such unquestioning confidence and support from administrators like them.

I want to thank my older brother, Gary, for taking me to my first movie (I think it was *Cinderella*) all those years ago. That's what started it all. Gary also found a rare Lupe Vélez film that helped me in my research.

Finally, I would like to thank my family—my son, Charles; my daughters, Anne-Marie and Christina Feliz; and my wife, Cecilia—who helped me weather the book-writing storm. Each of them modeled behavior that encouraged me as I worked on this project. Charles taught me the value of gentlemanly behavior, quiet determination, and sustained hard work. Anne-Marie's originality and ingenuity showed me that there's always a new way to see old things. Christina inspired me with her infectious optimism and cheery confidence. Cecilia's strength of character propped me up time and again. Over the years, she never once questioned my desire to write or to watch movies, even before those activities led to a full-time, tenure-track teaching job.

I am blessed to have such wonderful people around me on a daily basis. They support me in the single most important way—by believing in me. They give me love, patience, and understanding, and best of all, they make me laugh. There is no way to thank them adequately except to say thanks and I love you all—more than you'll ever know.

Austin, Texas
October 2000

INTRODUCTION

ORIGINS OF THIS STUDY

The University of Texas at Austin, where I teach, happens to be an orientation center for the Fulbright Scholars Program. Every summer, scores of foreign students from around the world and in various disciplines begin their graduate study in this country by coming to campuses like the University of Texas for an introduction to U.S. higher education and American culture. After several weeks here, they go on to their respective universities across the country to commence graduate work.

On several occasions I have had the opportunity to give lectures to these students on the topic of this book, the representation of Latinos in Hollywood movies. During one of these talks, in August 1988, just as I was about to list the characteristics of the *bandido* stereotype, something stopped me. Instead of describing the Mexican bandit myself, I asked them if they could. Immediately several hands went up, and in a matter of seconds the group sketched a vivid verbal picture of *el bandido*. Try it yourself and see if you don't come up with the same image they did, composed of these familiar details: the dark, sweaty, unshaven face (scar and gold tooth optional); the *bandoleras*, the bullet belts crisscrossed across his chest (creating an "X-marks-the-bandit" visual sign); the wide-brimmed sombrero; his weapons of choice (dagger and *pistola*); the ubiquitous bottle of tequila; the antisocial attitude (whose limited range stretches from the lecherous leer to the scornful scowl); the violent, criminal, generally pathological behavior (he is a bundle of hostility waiting to erupt).

Where had that image come from? In prompting their description, I had not cued them by mentioning a specific film, actor, or scene; nor had

1

I shown a photograph or film clip (I did that afterward). And yet they rapidly accessed the stereotype from some mental image database and precisely rendered it. My guess was that one prominent source for the image they so accurately recalled was the media, primarily the globally dominant U.S. media, and specifically—though not exclusively—Hollywood movies (no doubt Italian and Spanish spaghetti Westerns, which reactivated the stock *bandido* image, also shaped some of their responses). This study investigates the cinematic sterotyping process that, I believe, in large part made it possible for those Fulbright students— and, I would venture to guess, most of us—to describe the Mexican *bandido* so immediately, effortlessly, and exactly.

Latino Images in Film grows out of more than a decade of teaching, writing, and lecturing about stereotyping in movies in general and of the depiction of Latinos in Hollywood film in particular. I began researching this topic when I was asked to teach a course called "Chicanos and Film" for the University of Texas Center for Mexican American Studies in 1987. Though the course was on the books, it had not been taught for some time; I had no former teacher to advise me, and course materials and syllabi were nonexistent.

Forced to start from scratch, I soon realized that I was dealing with two main topics: stereotyping and a smaller subset of that subject, Hollywood's representation of Latinos. On stereotyping, I was faced with a confounding wealth of literature, mainly in the social sciences, psychology, and sociology. I wanted to begin my study with a basic understanding of terms, so I needed a handy explanation of stereotypes and the process of stereotyping. But what I discovered was that these concepts meant different things to different researchers in different fields. Initially bewildered, I nevertheless kept working to see if I could synthesize a theory of stereotyping that I could then apply to films. The result of that theory-building forms the first section of this book.

Concerning Latino movie imagery, on the other hand, there was a scarcity of information. Allen L. Woll's short but useful history, *The Latin Image in American Film*, provided a worthwhile introduction.[1] There was also Arthur Pettit's insightful look at Latin images in literature and film,[2] and a collection of essays, *Chicano Cinema*, edited by Gary D. Keller.[3] Clint Wilson and Felix Gutiérrez's practical study, *Minorities and Media*, focused on the portrayal of four main groups in the mass media: Asians, Native Americans, African Americans, and Latinos.[4] Beyond that, there were a few articles, and several stirring Chicano filmmaking manifestos, which used Hollywood's stereotyping of Latinos and the studios' closed-door policy toward young Chicano writers, directors, and producers as the basis for their emerging film aesthetic. And that was it. Clearly there was a lot of critical and historical work yet to be done on Latino stereotypes in the movies.

Happily, that work has begun. Since 1987 there has been an impressive boom in the study of the representation of Latinos in the media, a boom that I am happy and proud to have participated in and contributed to. As far as the scholarly analysis of Latino imagery in film goes, the landmark work was Chon Noriega's editing of the first anthology of Chicano film criticism, *Chicanos and Film: Representation and Resistance* in 1992.[5] This was followed by another key anthology, this time with a broader, pan-Latino focus, *The Ethnic Eye: Latino Media Arts,* edited by Noriega and Ana López in 1996.[6] Several other important anthologies and books soon followed.[7]

In addition, there is a lengthy and growing list of important articles by, among others, Carlos Cortés, Rosa Linda Fregoso, Lilian Jiménez, Christine List, Ana López, David R. Maciel, Kathleen Newman, Chon Noriega, and Federico A. Subervi-Vélez.[8] However, none of these books or articles, unquestionably significant and impressive as they are, addresses Latinos in film from quite the same vantage point as I do in this book. *Latino Images in Film* is meant to serve as an introduction to the operation of stereotyping, to analyze how it functions in film, and then to apply that knowledge to the critical analysis of the depiction of Latinos in U.S. cinema.

WHY STUDY STEREOTYPES?

Or, rather, why study stereotypes anymore, now that "images of" analysis has long since been actively pursued but then declared passé in film criticism and theory? Because my own research indicates that there are still important benefits to be gained from it. One of the most significant is the fact that studying stereotypes takes one back to the social sciences, and that provides a way to connect film criticism with lived experience. Social scientific research is empirical; it bases its conclusions on the experiences of individuals and social groups. On the other hand, film theory is of necessity ontological and conceptual; it seeks to grasp the essential nature of the film medium. Film criticism is interpretive: informed conjecture on the significance of a text. Neither is empirical in the scientific sense, which leads to a stumbling block in much of film theory and criticism, namely, how to connect philosophical and critical speculation with the lives that people actually live. Beginning with sociological and psychological studies on stereotyping, based as they are on ethnographic studies, surveys, lab experiments, and other empirical investigation methods, then, provides me a way to make one type of film-society link. Through the social science lens, stereotyping in film can be seen as a graphic manifestation of the psychosocial process of stereotyping in society in general.

However, the movement away from "images of" analyses in film studies is, in my estimation, a correct one. The study of representation in the media must be more than simple content analysis, a game of "spotting the stereotype," cataloging it, then bemoaning Hollywood movies for their pernicious imagery. It has to branch out in at least two directions. First, film representation needs to be understood within a social and historical context. The images of Latinos in American film exist not in a vacuum but as part of a larger discourse on Otherness in the United States. Beyond their existence as mental constructs or film images, stereotypes are part of a social conversation that reveals the mainstream's attitudes about Others.

The case of Latino stereotyping in mass media involves a discursive system that might be called "Latinism" (a play on Edward Said's Orientalism): the construction of Latin America and its inhabitants and of Latinos in this country to justify the United States' imperialistic goals. Operationalized externally as the Monroe Doctrine and internally as Manifest Destiny, U.S. imperialism was based on the notion that the nation should control the entire hemisphere and was willing to fight anyone who disagreed. For centuries, the precepts underpinning the Monroe Doctrine have been used as a rationale for U.S. interference in the internal politics of Latin America. On the whole, Hollywood endorsed North American dominance of this hemisphere, and as often as it depicted that hegemony uncritically, movies helped to perpetuate it.

In the United States, especially in the Southwest, Manifest Destiny meant taking land from Mexico, displacing Mexican landowners, subjugating Tejanos, Hispanos, and Californios (Texans, New Mexicans, and Californians of Mexican heritage), and exploiting them as cheap and expendable labor. In order to rationalize the expansionist goals laid out by the Monroe Doctrine and Manifest Destiny, Latinos—whether U.S. citizens, newly arrived migrants from the south, or Latin Americans in their own countries—needed to be shown as lesser beings. Movie stereotyping of Latinos, therefore, has been and continues to be part of

4

an American imperialistic discourse about who should rule the hemisphere—a sort of "Monroe Doctrine and Manifest Destiny Illustrated."

The second way that the analysis of Latino representation in the movies must move beyond superficial content analysis is by looking at the deep structure of Hollywood cinema. That is, we need to investigate how standardized cinematic techniques, the accepted norms of "good" filmmaking (including the star system, casting, screenwriting, camera angles, shot selection, direction, production design, editing, acting conventions, lighting, framing, makeup, costuming, and mise-en-scène), all contribute to the totality of the image we call a stereotype. Furthermore, we need to explore the narrative function that stereotypes play within classical Hollywood films and their purpose in various popular genres. This general trajectory—from stereotyping in general to stereotyping in film to the significance of Latino imagery in three genres (social problem films, Westerns, and science fiction films)—forms the first two parts of this book.

The third part looks at some ways that Latino filmmakers have tried to break with this pattern of representation through self-representation. And here is another example of how the in-depth study of stereotypes can help us analyze those films: surely one good way for us as critics to judge the efficacy of Latino filmmakers' anti-stereotyping aesthetic is to know the detailed workings of Hollywood's stereotyping apparatus that so many of them were reacting against.

QUESTIONS OF TERMINOLOGY

I use the terms "Latino," "Latin American," "Chicano," and "Mexican American" quite a bit, and I should explain what I mean by them. "Latino" is the umbrella term for people of Latin American descent that in recent years has supplanted the more imprecise and bureaucratic designation "Hispanic." Thus Cuban Americans, Puerto Ricans, Mexican Americans, and any people who trace their ethnic roots back to Central or South America are considered Latino if they live in the United States. Those citizens of Central or South America I refer to as Latin Americans, or by their specific nationality. However, when speaking of the stereotypes developed by Hollywood, I have used the term "Latino stereotypes" to mean both U.S. Latinos and Latin Americans. I do this for the sake of convenience and to emphasize the fact that Hollywood did not differentiate between these two broad groups in its stereotyping imagery. As far as Hollywood was concerned, U.S. Latinos and Latin Americans could all be lumped together as people with identical characteristics; as such, they could all be uniformly depicted stereotypically as bandits, harlots, Latin lovers, and so forth. And if Hollywood made no distinction between Latinos and Latin Americans, it certainly could not be expected to make finer distinctions, between, say, Mexicans (citizens of Mexico) and Mexican Americans (citizens of the United States).

"Chicano" is the term made popular by the Mexican American civil rights movement in the 1960s and 1970s; as an ethnic self-identifying label, it implied pride as well as activism and oppositional politics, much as the term "Black" did for African Americans during the same period. It is still used in this context, when referring to the movement or to ourselves as Mexican Americans, particularly by those of us who lived through that period. Our children, however, tend to prefer the term "Mexican American." In this book I have tried to use "Chicano" when I mean more politicized filmmaking and criticism, and "Mexican American" when referring to our more recent creative and critical practices. Thus Luis Valdez, who began his creative work by producing radical theater in support of the unionizing efforts of César Chavez, is referred to as a Chicano filmmaker. Robert Rodríguez, though he is also interested in correcting, countering, and avoiding stereotypes, belongs to a different generation of filmmakers. He was probably influenced more by Alfred Hitchcock, John Woo, and Steven Spielberg than by the Chicano movement or early Chicano filmmakers, and I refer to him as a Mexican American or Latino filmmaker.

I prefer the terms "Latino" and "Chicano" to terms like "Latina/o" and "Chicana/o," which refer to both genders. I do so because I mean "Latino" and "Chicano" as the name for the entire group, both men and women. In this, I agree completely with Chon Noriega's position, which he elaborated in his introduction to *Chicanos and Film*. It is worth quoting him in full:

In Spanish, nouns are gender-identified through an "o" or "a" suffix, with a distinction between *Chicano* (male) and *Chicana* (female). When used alone, the male form, *Chicano,* denotes both male and female. The use of *Chicano* in such a context, however, tends to present the same problems as the word or suffix "man" does in English: it provides convenient cover for an essentially male discourse. Various alternatives have been proposed, the most popular being Chicano/a. Like many *Chicana* feminist critics, however, I use *Chicano* as a cultural and political self-designation vis-à-vis the dominant culture, but (I hope) avoid the implicit male emphasis usually given the term. Also, at times I make a clear distinction between *Chicano* and *Chicana* critical and cinematic practices.[9]

At times I will similarly make the same distinction. For example, when I refer to Lourdes Portillo's film *The Devil Never Sleeps* as "Chicana film noir" in Chapter 8, I specifically mean a feminist variation on familiar Hollywood film noir genre themes made by an activist Mexican American filmmaker.

There is also the question of what to call members of the U.S. social dominant. "White" is the oft-used term, but as much as possible I shy away from using it because doing so, in my mind at least, reifies crude and essentialist racial categories—white, black, brown, yellow. As Richard Dyer has so convincingly shown, the idea of an essential white category (and by implication any racial classification) is a convenient— and divisive—social construct.[10] I use the term "Anglo" instead—not because it is any less problematic denotatively, but it seems to me to be less charged connotatively.

Finally, there is the problematic term "American cinema," which is commonly used when referring to U.S. films. But the United States is not America, only part of North America. A more accurate term might be "North American cinema," but, again, that excludes Canada and, depending on how one defines it, Greenland, Mexico, and the Carribean. The most accurate term to speak of the totality of this nation's filmmaking, both Hollywood and independent films, is "U.S. cinema," and I use that term sometimes, although it has the disadvantage of being both cumbersome and not in common usage. Despite my qualms about it, then, "American cinema" is the term generally accepted and widely understood, and if I use it here it is for convenience, and not in any way to disparage, discount, or dismiss the cinematic traditions of other North and South *American* countries.

ORGANIZATION OF THE BOOK

Latino Images in Film began as a slightly different project. At the urging of several editors, I originally intended simply to compile the articles I had written on Latino stereotypes in American film over the years, especially since some of them are difficult to find. Once I began, however, I realized that I needed to elaborate, refine, and develop some of my ideas, particularly regarding my theorizing of stereotyping in Hollywood film. I also realized that my taxonomy of six familiar Latino stereotypes did not tell the full story of Latino imagery in American cinema. There were some fascinating exceptions to the rule, Anglo filmmakers in the Hollywood system, like Richard Brooks in *Crisis* (1950), who managed to avoid stereotypes. In addition, there were certain wily Latino performers, like Lupe Vélez, Gilbert Roland, and José Ferrer, who found ways to subvert Hollywood's stereotyping machinery.

The resulting book, then, is a mix of new and old. It is composed of four new theoretical chapters that form Part 1. Also new is the book's extensive interview of the most successful Latino director in Hollywood history, Robert Rodríguez, in Chapter 10. Having written an essay (which appears here as Chapter 9) about his first two films, his student-short *Bedhead* (1990) and *El Mariachi* (1992), I wanted to follow up and talk about the rest of his career. Specifically, I wanted to know how he thought he could balance his ethnic pride with mainstream moviemaking success. Finally, I conclude with a newly written look at the present state of Latino images in American cinema. It considers the current "Latin boom" in U.S. entertainment and contrasts it with an earlier one in the 1920s. Seeking to evaluate the significance of the recent rise of Latinos in the movies, it draws a comparison with the ascent of another denigrated ethnic group—the Irish—in classical Hollywood cinema.

This new material appears along with five essays (Chapters 5–9) on Latino representation that I have written over the past thirteen years. In the present context, these essays serve as case studies looking at Latino representation in various film genres. Three of the essays appear in Part 2, which looks at Latino images in three classical Hollywood genres—the social problem film, the Western, and the science fiction film. Two more essays, one on Chicano border documentaries and another on Robert Rodríguez's early career, appear in Part 3, the Latino counterimagery part of the book.

How much did I alter these previously published works? On the whole, I opted for minor revisions that would bring them up-to-date with current critical literature, rather than larger-scale rewriting or reconceptualizing. The changes in Chapter 5, on *Bordertown* (1935) and the Chicano social problem films, for instance, will be found mainly in the footnotes. Chapter 6, on the representation of Latinos and other ethnics in the films of John Ford, has not been changed at all. I debated how much to alter Chapter 7, an essay based on the notion that aliens in science fiction films could be regarded as figures for real-life Latin American immigrants to the United States. In the end I pretty much left it alone. I know that since it was published, in the fall of 1989, there have been many more science fiction films released that could be added to the list. But any critical piece eventually falls behind the flow of film releases. And, in addition, I felt that the ideas in the essay are still sound. Moreover, it allows readers to apply those ideas to the newer films, as I do when I teach that essay in my classes. So I hope that readers will feel free to use the approach I delineate when they analyze more-recent science fiction films about aliens, such as *The Arrival* (1996), *Independence Day* (1996), and *Men in Black* (1997).

In Part 3, the Latino counterimages part of the study, Chapter 8, on Chicano border documentaries, has been improved by the addition of footnotes directing the reader to other criticism of the films of Lourdes Portillo. In my mind, the updating of Chapter 9, on Robert Rodríguez's early career, is Chapter 10, the interview with Rodríguez.

One clarification that I want to make about this counterimagery section concerns my focus. Though I center on *Latino* stereotypes in Hollywood film in the book's first seven chapters, in the last section I emphasize the *Mexican American* response. I do so for several reasons. One is that as a Mexican American I feel more qualified to analyze Mexican American films than I would if I were speaking of, say, the Puerto Rican cinematic response. A second reason is that I know Mexican American cinema better than other Latino cinemas (Puerto Rican or Cuban American, for example), having studied and taught it for nearly a decade and a half. A third reason is that Chicano film is a branch of Latino cinema that has a prolific and sustained thirty-year history. Moreover, it began specifically *in opposition to* the Hollywood paradigm, so my concentration on its history seems not only reasonable but called for. Finally, there is the interesting fact that so much of Chicano cinema originated in the cradle of mainstream studio cinema, Southern California. Viewed in that context, one might consider Chicano cinema of the past thirty years to have been mainstream American film's "shadow cinema," maybe even serving as Hollywood's "ethnic conscience." But whatever the case, I wish to make clear that by centering my attention on Mexican American films, I do not mean to diminish the role of other Latino filmmaking traditions or filmmakers.

Latino Images in Film, then, is a hybrid—part new, part old. It generally focuses on fiction film, though one chapter is devoted to documentary movies. It is about stereotyping in film, about Hollywood's representaton of Latinos, and the Latino cinematic reaction. It is not a comprehensive book about Latinos in film, nor is it meant to be. To paraphrase Robert Rodríguez in the interview in Chapter 10, one book can't do everything. Obviously there are gaps—many other films, actors, and filmmakers that need to be studied. But for now, take this book as one voice in a growing conversation about Latinos in film, one that indicates some critical and historical directions that future researchers may want to explore. My modest hope is that it adds positively to that discourse. For me, this is the book I was looking for back in 1987.

PART ONE

THEORY

ONE

CATEGORIZING THE OTHER
Stereotypes and Stereotyping

Before we can appreciate cinema's century-long pattern of stereotypical representation, we need to have a more precise understanding of what stereotypes and stereotyping are—in general and as they appear in the media. I address these fundamental issues in this chapter by focusing first on social scientific theory (surveying mainly psychological and sociological perspectives) in order to clarify some of stereotyping's more prominent features and develop a working definition of it. In the process, I gradually introduce notions of the representation of Otherness in the media from cultural studies. In this way, I synthesize a theoretical framework for my critical investigation of Latino stereotypes in cinema.

The first thing to note is that for all the worthwhile research done on stereotypes and stereotyping, stretching back over decades, social scientists have yet to agree on a definitive meaning for either term. The research and theorizing reflect different approaches and interests, and consequently, as one recent surveyor of the stereotyping literature commented, "A single and unified concept of stereotype cannot be found." [1] Even so, there is much to be gained by reviewing the ideas of various researchers. For one thing, examining many perspectives presents an opportunity to gain a deeper understanding of the process of stereotyping. For another, the lack of a consensus on a single definition allows us the freedom to forge one of our own.

COGNITIVE PERSPECTIVES:
PROCESSING THE INFLUX OF INFORMATION

For some cognitive psychologists, stereotyping describes a value-neutral psychological mechanism that creates categories and enables people to manage the swirl of data presented to them from their environment. This categorizing function was recognized in 1922 by Walter Lippmann, who first coined the term "stereotyping." For him, this was a necessary, useful, and efficient process, since "the attempt to see all things freshly and in detail, rather than as types and generalities, is exhausting, and among busy affairs practically out of the question."[2]

With this cognitive conception of stereotyping we can pause to consider some critical implications. The first is that in the sense that stereotyping means simply the creation of categories based on the recognition of gross difference(s), we all stereotype. Furthermore, this sort of stereotyping is not "wrong," nor is it something that only bad people, or prejudiced, ignorant, or racist people, do. We all do it, and—if cognitive psychologists are right about how the human brain perceives, processes, stores, and recalls information—we need to. It is important to accumulate experiences and be able to distinguish a door from a window, a male from a female, a snake from a twig.[3] And if we all create categories, then we are all, potentially at least, in a position to take the next step and imbue those categories with value-laden—that is, positive or negative—connotations.

This sort of negative generalizing is in fact what we usually mean when we think of stereotyping—not simply value-neutral category-making. For most of us, stereotyping is the act of making judgments and assigning negative qualities to other individuals or groups.[4] The question then becomes, How does stereotyping evolve from being a value-free process to being a value-laden one?

For this kind of "bad" stereotyping to develop, I believe two crucial elements need to be added to plain category-making. One is *ethnocentrism*, classically defined as the "view of things in which one's own group is the center of everything, and all others are scaled or rated with reference to it."[5] Adhering to the circular logic of stereotyping, the out-group ("Them") is compared to the standard defined by the in-group ("Us"). By this measure, and not surprisingly, "They" are always incomplete and imperfect.

The second necessary ingredient that transforms neutral categorization into a discriminatory practice is *prejudice*: judging Others as innately inferior based on ethnocentrically determined difference. Prejudice holds that They are *inherently* not as good (not as clean, civilized, righteous, religious, intelligent, trustworthy, respectful of life, decent, hardworking, honorable, etc.) as We are because They are different from Us (in the foods they eat, their religion, skin color, language, nationality, etc.). Judging the Other as *inherently* inferior is a key feature of prejudicial thinking, and its most troubling one in that it indicates the intransigent view that They cannot change. Later we will see what disastrous results can result from such extremely biased and rigid judgments about the out-group.

To sum up, stereotyping in the negative and derogatory way the term is usually applied can be represented thus:

category making + ethnocentrism + prejudice = stereotyping

A *stereotype* is the result of this process and can be defined as *a negative generalization used by an in-group (Us) about an out-group (Them).* Lippmann called these mental constructs "pictures in our heads." [6]

ELEVEN THESES ABOUT STEREOTYPES

Before we continue with sociological, psychological, and psychoanalytical approaches to stereotyping, there are a number of important characteristics common to all stereotypes—individual or collective, mediated or not—that merit our attention, if only briefly.

Stereotypes Are Applied with Rigid Logic

According to one view, stereotyping is triggered by a reductive, all-or-nothing logic, by which stereotypers place anyone identified as an out-group member into the stereotyped category, then assign the stereotypical traits to that individual. "If you are _____ (*fill in name of group*)," the thinking goes, "then you must _____ (*fill in predictable traits, characteristics, behavior, etc.*).[7] As Homi K. Bhabha says, fixity is a key component "in the ideological construction of otherness." [8]

There is a degree of psychic comfort in fixing the Other—and the world—in this way, as if once named and defined they could be contained once and for all. This attempt to control the world beyond the self by taxonomy is what Edward Said shows is at the heart of the scientific aspects of Orientalism.

Of course, the flaw in such thinking is that the world, the self, and the Other are organic, dynamic, and ever-changing, and attempts to freeze them can only lead to frustration. Indeed, stereotypes exist partly to cope with this confounding inconstancy. A primary function of stereotypes, says Richard Dyer, is "to make fast, firm and separate what is in reality fluid." [9]

Stereotypes May Have a Basis in Fact

There may be some correlation between the stereotype and lived experience, the "kernel of truth" aspect addressed by psychologist Joshua Fishman. For Fishman it was the "kernel of truth" that explained why large numbers of people agreed on many stereotypes; he posited that changes in stereotypes occurred in response to changes in political, social, and economic conditions. [10] But "kernel" is an unfortunate choice of terms, since it means the core or best part of the grain. In the case of the stereotype, any real-life correspondence between a group member's behavior and a quality said to be characteristic of the entire group is only an isolated part of a much larger story, and usually far from the whole truth. Yes, there indeed were and are Mexican bandits, lazy African Americans, and Italian American gangsters. But banditry, laziness, and criminality are not culture specific, nor do those qualities represent the group's complete experience.

Stereotypes Are Simplified Generalizations that Assume Out-group Homogeneity

A stereotype is the part that stands for the whole. But since any group's history is vast, complex, and variegated, stereotyping grossly simplifies that out-group experience by selecting a few traits of the Other that pointedly accentuate differences. [11] These traits are then applied to all members of the group, an operation that assumes out-group homogeneity. Ultimately, however, although similar in some aspects, individuals in groups (both out-group and in-group) are just that—individuals—and therefore exhibit heterogeneity, not homogeneity. Stereotypes flatten, homogenize, and generalize individuals within a group, emphasizing sameness and ignoring individual agency and variety. [12]

Stereotypes Work at Far Too General a Level to Be Worthwhile Predictors

A simple category has some value as a forecasting tool. However, stereotypical categorization based on ethnocentrism and prejudice is not only an unfair generalization but a very poor predictor. Knowledge of actual out-group experience, their history, culture, traditions—to say nothing of knowing actual out-group members—forces one to recognize the group's overall heterogeneity. Knowledge furthermore belies easy, homogenized generalities and forces exceptions to stereotypes and, all other things being equal, to their eventual breakdown. Unless, that is, stereotypers refuse to let go of their prejudice. In that case, they will likely remain attached to their stereotypical beliefs, completely disregarding contradictory information about the Other.

Stereotypes Are Uncontextualized and Ahistorical

Being gross generalizations, stereotypes are conveniently ahistorical, selectively omitting the out-group's social, political, and economic group history.[13] An excellent example is the stereotype of the Mexican *bandido*. As I pointed out at the beginning of this book, the power of stereotyping is demonstrated by our ability to summon up a fairly specific mental picture in our heads of the *bandido* stereotype. Indeed, after my experience with the Fulbright scholars I have found *el bandido* to be such a common mental image that when lecturing I routinely let students describe the main characteristics of the *bandido* image rather than doing it for them. And they routinely bring up the same details I listed in the introduction almost by reflex: the unkempt appearance, the weaponry and *bandoleras,* the funny-looking sombrero, the sneering look.

Together these elements form the cinematic sign of *el bandido,* one that is instantaneously read and comprehended by experienced film viewers. He is quickly and economically set apart from the Anglo cowboy hero and looks, in comparison, slightly ridiculous—recognition, differentiation, and devaluation being key functions of the cinematic stereotype. Beneath the stereotype does lie a kernel of truth—some Mexicanos did in fact look like this once upon a time, and violence was part of their life. The stereotype fails to convey, however, a number of crucial facts about them.

For instance, most of the men who dressed like this were not bandits—they were rebel soldiers who fought in Mexico's Revolutionary

War of 1910–1920. For starters, then, Hollywood's usual placement of these figures in the American West of the 1880s is historically inaccurate and anachronistic. Furthermore, in the Mexican experience, these men were the "good guys" who fought against the despotic dictator Porfirio Díaz under leaders like Pancho Villa (who once was a mountain bandit) and Emiliano Zapata (who was declared one by Díaz). Moreover, under the command of Villa and Zapata, who had no formal military training, these soldiers redefined modern warfare. By horseback and train, they covered great distances quickly, maintained the element of surprise over Díaz's larger and better-equipped but slower forces, struck without warning, and ultimately defeated them. The rebel horse soldiers' mobility was enhanced in no small measure by the fact that they carried their ammunition with them in the form of *bandoleras* across their chests. Even their sombreros have a positive signification, in that they were ingenious adaptations to a harsh environment allowing the wearer to "carry" his shade with him. All of these important historical details are either omitted or completely recast in the stereotype.

As a sort of shorthand, stereotypes necessarily preclude such background information. Instead, stereotyping creates facile abbreviations that, by virtue of their regular repetition, create their own history. Two dangers arise when in-group members have little exposure to out-group members or knowledge of out-group history. The first is that the virtual (stereotypical) history can replace the actual (lived) one. The second is that the stereotypical images can become familiar to the point that they eventually seem normal, even "natural."

Repetition Tends to Normalize Stereotypes

This book is part of a fairly new critical approach, representational studies. But it could be argued that Hollywood rarely claims that the characters in its films are meant to be taken literally (and therefore seriously), or ever meant to be representative of entire social groups. Rather, this line of argument goes, Hollywood is simply telling stories, and the characters within its films serve a narrational function, not a representational one. According to this logic, in the film story called *Clear and Present Danger* (1994) it just so happens that the villain (Joaquim de Almeida) is a Colombian drug lord and the hero (Harrison Ford) an Anglo male. If that were the only or a rare instance of a Latino being the bad guy in a U.S. movie, there might be some validity to this argument. But de Almeida's character is a descendant of a long line of Latino movie antagonists, stretching back to silent-era "greaser" bandits. Seen in that

18

Joaquim de Almeida, as the Colombian drug kingpin Felix Cortez in Clear and Present Danger *(1994), an all-too-familiar reincarnation of a convenient Hollywood villain:* el bandido. *(Photo courtesy of Luis Reyes Archives)*

light, the Colombian drug runner is an updated version of *el bandido. With repetition, therefore, narration becomes representation.*

A "vicious cycle" aspect to repeated stereotyping arises because expressing learned stereotypes reinforces and to that extent validates and perpetuates them. Stereotypes are false to history, but conform to another historical tradition—namely, the history of movies and movie stereotyping. They begin, over time, to become part of the narrative form itself—anticipated, typical, and well nigh "invisible." Ironically, then, *representation becomes narration:* we expect *el bandido* to appear in a Western set in the Southwest—he's part of the landscape—and when he does, we expect him to be villainous and to act in predictably despicable, criminal, and inhumane ways. Far from being surprised by this, we are instead more likely to be surprised when it *doesn't* occur.

Stereotypes Are Believed

There is a body of research literature that holds that stereotypes are not simply frames of mind, but actual beliefs.[14] Gordon Allport, for instance, theorized that an attitude toward a group is usually bonded to a belief about the group. Of the two elements, the attitude is the most important, most lasting, and the most resistant to change. It is the attitude that fixes the belief, and not the other way around. "Beliefs," Allport writes,

> have the slippery propensity of accommodating themselves somehow to the negative attitude which is much harder to change. . . . Thus the belief system has a way of slithering around to justify the more permanent attitude. The process is one of rationalization—of the accommodation of beliefs to attitudes.[15]

To the extent that they are believed, stereotypes have a psychological power that affects both in-group and out-group members. For the in-group individual, the belief associated with stereotyping colors encounters with the out-group. "Once formed," Allport writes, stereotypes "cause their possessor to view future evidence in terms of the available categories."[16] One series of experiments may indicate how early those attitudes are formed. In order to determine young children's racial attitudes, researchers presented youngsters with a black doll and a white doll and asked them questions about which were "nice" and which were "bad." Most of the young white children picked the white doll as looking nice and the black doll as looking bad.[17]

Stereotyping has an effect on out-group members as well. Black children presented with the dolls also labeled the black doll as not nice but bad, though not to the degree that the white children did. "The most common interpretation of the findings from the numerous doll studies," one team of researchers has noted, "is that whites reject and negatively evaluate blacks, and that blacks reject and negatively evaluate themselves,"[18] While this interpretation has not gone undisputed, my points here are that (1) stereotypes affect both in-group and out-group members, and (2) the resulting effect may well be linked to beliefs.

And beliefs can lead to actions. As one researcher put it, "When members of one group think about members of another as intrinsically different—as categorically bad, unworthy, despicable—they are capable of inflicting great harm upon them." Stereotypes, in this view, can become programs for action or "sanctions for evil" and "may induce or justify acts that would be unthinkable to commit against members of one's own group."[19] This is the kind of thinking that precedes racial violence and lynchings,[20] the kind of mind-set that led to the reprehensible genocide perpetrated against Jews by the Germans during World

War II.[21] Indeed, Daniel Jonah Goldhagen's extensive study of the Holocaust, *Hitler's Willing Executioners*, concludes that anti-Semitic stereotypical beliefs held by the German people as a whole were the prime cause of that nightmare:

> Germans' antisemitic beliefs about Jews were the central causal agent not only of Hitler's decision to annihilate European Jewry (which is accepted by many) but also of the perpetrators' willingness to kill and brutalize Jews. . . . Antisemitism moved many thousands of "ordinary" Germans—and would have moved millions more, had they been appropriately positioned—to slaughter Jews. Not economic hardship, not the coercive means of a totalitarian state, not social psychological pressure, not invariable psychological propensities, but ideas about Jews that were pervasive in Germany, and had been for decades, induced ordinary Germans to kill unarmed, defenseless Jewish men, women, and children by the thousands, systematically and without pity.[22]

Stereotypes can be believed and can lead to actions—sometimes of the most savage and reprehensible kind.

Stereotyping Goes Both Ways

The kind of stereotyping we have been discussing assumes a dominant in-group that creates the stereotype of a subordinate out-group. But even in this unbalanced situation, stereotypes can go the other way, from the subordinate minority to the dominant majority. However, concerning mediated stereotyping, clearly the mass media is the dominant's media and routinely reflects dominant attitudes. Furthermore, mass media reaches the widest audience. Where mass media is concerned, therefore, one can say that stereotypes generally go one way: from the dominant to the disenfranchised in the margins.

Stereotypes Are Ideological

Stereotypes don't just derogatorily depict the Other—they also indicate a preferred power relation. One way of thinking about the ideological component of stereotyping is to consider stereotypes as vestiges of the colonial system. Within that regime, once the native is "known" (i.e., set and defined by the colonizer in stereotypical terms), "discriminatory and authoritarian forms of political control are considered appropriate."[23] It is one way the dominant in-group continually convinces itself and the Other that it is morally superior, more civilized, and in all ways finer than the Other, and therefore ought "naturally" to be in control. And stereotypes illustrate why They, the subordinate out-group, based on their obvious inferiority, ought not, indeed could not, control anything. As Richard Dyer puts it, through stereotyping ruling groups attempt "to fashion the whole of society according to their own worldview, value-system, sensibility and ideology."[24] Inasmuch as it operates to identify, justify, and support mainstream (Anglo) beliefs, then, ideologically stereotyping is hegemony, the subtle, naturalizing way the ruling class maintains its dominance over subordinate groups.[25] The normalization of stereotypical images through repetition that I mentioned earlier can now be seen to have an important ideological function: to demonstrate why the in-group is in power, why the out-group is not, and why things need to stay just as they are.

The creation and circulation of stereotypes in the media function to maintain the status quo in yet another way: by defining the Other. Media stereotyping establishes the terms by which the Other can be known and situates the Other within dominant discourse. Consider the implications of a term in general usage today, "*illegal* alien," which offers a baseline understanding of Latino immigrants as criminals (rather than as people who have migrated here for a complex set of historical, political, and economic reasons, some of which involve U.S. business interests). In the cinema, the fact that Hispanics are depicted as variations of bandits and buffoons, whores, Latin lovers, and dark ladies defines them first and foremost as outside the mainstream. The stereotypical definition of Others, therefore, has powerful ideological consequences, simultaneously marginalizing Them and establishing and maintaining an explicit Us-Them boundary. "The most important function of the stereotype," writes Richard Dyer, is "to maintain sharp boundary definitions, to define clearly where the pale ends and thus who is clearly within and who is clearly beyond it."[26]

The In-group Stereotypes Itself

A curious feature of stereotyping is that it is applied *within the dominant* by in-group members to other in-group members. Examples of what the dominant finds unacceptable within its own ranks include dumb blondes, Neanderthal jocks, socially inept nerds, hayseed rednecks, and rich snobs, to say nothing of the stereotypes of children, the aged, the poor, the infirm, obese, disabled, or mentally ill. There exists, then, a different class of stereotype, the kind the dominant in-group makes of itself. These stereotypes delimit the boundary from inside the fence, so to speak, ostracizing "flawed" in-group members who, for one reason or another, fall short of dominant ideals. These are whites who do not possess the requisite amount of the in-group's superior characteristics, those WASPs who, in Richard Dyer's phrase, have failed "to attain whiteness"[27] and are consequently excommunicated.

The Antidote to Stereotyping Is Knowledge

So as not to end this section on too disparaging a note, I mention what I believe to be a way out of the stereotyping morass: knowledge, both about the Other and about the stereotyping process. If, as Chicano historian Michael R. Ornelas has said, "stereotypes fill the void created by ignorance,"[28] then more information about the Other makes the stereotype's simplified generalities less and less applicable. In the best-case scenario, stereotyping breaks down as a useful category. "Experience, contact and maturity usually erase [stereotypical] images among reasonable people," concludes Ornelas. The first beneficial result of learning about the process of stereotyping is that this knowledge makes it easy to detect stereotypes. The second is that once a stereotype is spotted, it becomes easier to see beneath its surface and understand how and why it works. Learning not only to see the stereotypical surface but also to understand what lies beneath stereotyping is the aim of this book.

SOCIOLOGICAL PERSPECTIVES: STEREOTYPES AS RESULTS OF ACCULTURATION AND GROUP INTERACTION

Moving to sociological views of stereotyping allows us to shift from the individual instance to the case of stereotyping as a shared group phenomenon. As psychologist Arthur G. Miller points out, the concern about stereotypes is one of social consensus—if only isolated individuals stereotyped, stereotyping would be a far different sort of issue. "Stereotyping is a complex psychological problem," Miller points out, that "is inextricably bound to a much broader social matrix. There are, in short, large numbers of people involved in stereotyping—both on the observer side and on the target side."[29]

One popular theory about how in-group members acquire stereotypes is that they do so through socialization. Ideas, including values and attitudes—and, hence, stereotypes—are conveyed to people by their culture as preexisting categories. These ideas are internalized as part of the process of socialization.[30] Once again, Lippmann was far-sighted. "In the great blooming, buzzing confusion of the outer world," he wrote, "we pick out what our culture has already defined for us, and we tend to perceive that which we have picked out in the form stereotyped for us by our culture."[31]

What the culture has already defined for us, however, is not neutral facts, objective rules of language, and cultural customs. The dark underside of socialization is that these come encrusted with attitudes and biases, which sometimes have dire consequences. Once again, Daniel Jonah Goldhagen's study of German attitudes toward the Jews before World War II provides a horrific example. Goldhagen uses the socialization model to explain how Germans learned to regard Jews as pariahs; indeed, he locates the root cause of the Holocaust in what he calls the people's "cognitive models," prevalent beliefs and values acquired via socialization, which were

> derivative of and borne by the societal conversation, linguistically and symbolically. When beliefs and images are uncontested or are even just dominant within a given society, individuals typically come to accept them as self-evident truths. . . . An individual learns the cognitive models of his culture, like grammar, surely and effortlessly.[32]

The attitudes about what constitutes the norms of the society go more or less unquestioned (because those who question them risk being ostracized) and mark a boundary between what the society considers normal and socially acceptable and what it does not. Among the cognitive models that are learned are the placement of Others outside of the norm, a process assisted by stereotyping.

The sociological approach also addresses group interaction and stereotype formation. This gives us a way to establish a link between real-world social relationships and stereotyping. Just as social scientists have traditionally examined and interpreted the terms used by one group to describe and define another, I am analyzing the ways a dominant group, the American social mainstream, portrays and depicts an ethnic minority, Latinos, via the mass medium of the Hollywood cinema.

My analysis is based on the following foundational assumptions:

1. The socially, culturally, and ideologically dominant group exists in the American popular consciousness and is represented in the mass media as a more or less homogeneous monolith, despite the actual variability and heterogeneity of any group. Furthermore, the mainstream defines itself by its core values, its domi-

nant ideological norms, namely, as "monogamous heterosexual bourgeois patriarchal capitalists," to use film critic Robin Wood's succinct phrase.[33] I would add the following as additional characteristics of the social dominant: nonethnic white, Christian (vaguely Protestant, though not Catholic), middle-aged, intelligent (excellent at problem solving, though not intellectual), healthy, and so forth. In short, the dominant ideal looks and acts like protagonists in Hollywood movies, like characters played by the likes of Harrison Ford, Kevin Costner, and Tom Cruise.

2. Hollywood studio films are the dominant's cinema. In the main they positively represent—and through their narratives and resolutions they typically endorse—the prevailing or dominant ideology.

3. This is not to say that the system is not conflicted. There are constant countercurrents to the dominant ideology's mainstream flow, caused mainly by the fact that very few, if any, can possibly be all the mainstream norm would have them be—monogamous, heterosexual, bourgeois, patriarchal, Protestant, white, nonethnic, healthy, bright, middle-aged capitalists who look like Tom Cruise. Friction within the dominant ideology starts where compliance fails—or is simply impossible to achieve.

4. Hollywood cinema is similarly conflicted and expresses various degrees of challenges to these dominant norms. A film like *High Noon* (1952), about the failure of a righteous frontier community to support its recently retired marshal (Gary Cooper), critiques the cowardly all-white majority. Similarly, the hero of *Blade Runner* (1982) ultimately turns his back on the corrupt white male power structure.

5. The overall process of stereotyping of out-group by in-group is roughly the same whether it takes the form of words used to describe the out-group (the focus of much social scientific research) or out-group images on a screen (the focus of critical analyses of representation). There are, of course, important distinctions between the two, as will be discussed in Chapter 2.

Intergroup Relations

To return to the matter of group interactions and stereotypes, sociologists have found that stereotyping is dynamic. It fluctuates based on the social and power relationship between the in-group and the out-group. Depending on the power relationship between these groups, one of three different stereotyping scenarios can arise: cooperative, stratified, or oppositional.[34]

First, groups may coexist peacefully in a mutually beneficial relationship. Such groups see themselves as working toward the same goals, and because they have to rely on one another, each group describes the other using terms such as "strong," "hardworking," and "friendly." In the American instance, when the dominant group and another group have about equal power, they eventually cease being two distinct groups. The out-group assimilates into the mainstream, becoming virtually indistinguishable from it—the "melting pot effect." When such social equilibrium is reached, the stereotypes diminish or evaporate altogether as a by-product of assimilation.

In the last hundred years, a good example of such a case of out-group entering the in-group and the corresponding elimination of their stereotypes is the Irish. In that time, they have evolved from being a thoroughly denigrated immigrant group to becoming so mainstreamed that there have been two presidents of Irish descent. In silent and early sound cinema, the Irish were commonly stereotyped as irresponsible and pugilistic, and represented as the dumb cop or the drunken, good-for-nothing, unemployed father. By and large, those stereotypes have ceased to exist in popular American media. A telling example is Tom Cruise starring in the title role of Jerry Maguire, a character who is nothing if not "strong, hardworking, and friendly." Jerry Maguire also exhibits the requisite qualities of the Hollywood hero—male, heterosexual, white, middle-aged, upper-middle class, possessing rugged good looks, and subscribing to American ideals and, by the film's end, Christian morals. Nothing is made, one way or the other, of his ethnicity, presumably because it does not stand in the way of his espousal of mainstream values. In U.S. society and in the movies, the Irish, one of the most despised and stereotyped groups in U.S. history, have assimilated, subscribing to and endorsing dominant values and ideology. Stereotypes evolve as relations between groups change. "Far from being rigid and unaccommodating," write three researchers who have focused on the connection between stereotypes and social reality, "stereotypes appear to be fluid and variable and to change with the social context."[35]

The bright side of stereotype evolution is that human consciousness can change and stereotyping can sometimes diminish and even be eradicated. The dark side is that time alone cannot be counted on to automatically end stereotyping. For example, consider the case of marginalized groups who, unlike the Irish, do not have fair skin, do not share the dominant's Christianity, and do not speak English. It has been considerably more difficult for Asians, Africans, natives, and dark-skinned Latin Americans to assimilate into the mainstream. Their experience falls under the two other group relationship categories.

Moreover, stereotype evolution is not always progressive, but can regress. Goldhagen's argument posits that the treatment of Jews in prewar Germany was built on preexisting, if relatively dormant, anti-Semitism. In the years following World War I, as life for most Germans became increasingly difficult, this slumbering prejudice was awakened, and more and more dehumanizing stereotypes of Jews appeared. In this case, stereotyping increased in ferocity and became *more* hateful, vicious, and, ultimately, lethal.

Before assimilation, groups are stratified and hold unequal power. In these cases, the dominant group will likely create stereotypes of the subdominant, clustering around two sets of characteristics: harmless (with out-group members portrayed as childlike, irrational, and emotional) when they pose no threat, or dangerous (treacherous, deceitful, cunning) when they do. Many film stereotypes and the Hispanic stereotypes I will delineate in Chapter 3 are clearly products of such a stratified case.

When the dominant group is threatened by the subordinate one, because it perceives itself to be competing for the same resources, the dominant's descriptive terminology about the subordinate becomes more severely derogatory: "aggressive," "brutal," "corrupt." The change is thought to be a convenient way for members of the group to rationalize "their own violent or ungenerous impulses."[36]

If these extremely virulent attitudes toward the subordinate group persist, there is a danger that the fear and hatred directed toward the Other will erupt into violence. Riots and lynchings are social explosions often ignited by such feelings, and the history of the U.S. Southwest includes numerous examples of violence directed at Mexicans and Mexican Americans.[37] Just so, argues Goldhagen, was the Holocaust the logical outcome of a systematic and prolonged stereotypical demonization of Jewry in Germany. The economic and political chaos in Germany following its defeat in World War I led to the search for scapegoats. And the preexisting anti-Semitic discourse conveniently provided one. Jews were cast in increasingly dehumanizing terms, and the anti-Semitic rhetoric gradually shifted from intolerance to exclusion to elimination.

Similarly in the movies, there are times when vehemence against the Other results in their portrayal as irrational, maniacal monsters. The casual bloodlust exhibited by Native Americans in scores of Hollywood Westerns is but one example. Others are the violent Mexican "greaser," the cannibalistic African native, and the twisted Middle Eastern terrorist. In its extreme form, as Robin Wood has argued, in science fiction and horror films, this sort of stereotyping transforms the Other into an actual monster. The threat to the dominant by the Other is so fearful that the nightmarish stereotypes are produced,[38] as I discuss further in Chapter 7.

DEVELOPMENTAL PSYCHOLOGY: WHY WE STEREOTYPE

The short answer as to why anybody or any group stereotypes is that they get something important out of it. What vital functions might stereotyping fulfill? Henri Tajfel lists five functions of stereotyping. The first two are at the individual level:

1. the *cognitive* function of systematizing and simplifying the environment

2. the *motivational* function of representing and preserving important social values

The remaining three are at the group level, where stereotypes contribute to the creation and maintenance of group beliefs, which are then used to:

3. *explain* large-scale social events

4. *justify* various forms of collective action, and

5. preserve *positive intergroup distinctiveness,* the tendency to differentiate the in-group positively from the out-group.[39]

These last three especially touch on a deeper and profound utilitarian function involving identity formation, namely, the notion that the self is partly defined via the Other. In this sense, stereotyping serves, says Lippmann, as "the guarantee of our self-respect . . . the projection upon the world of our own sense of value, our own position and our own rights."[40] Mikhail Bakhtin, as transcribed by Tzvetan Todorov, makes the same point in elaborating his aesthetic theory of literature. "The *other,*" says Bakhtin, "is necessary to accomplish . . . a perception of the self that the individual can achieve only partially with respect to himself." The self, he continues, realizes, "I cannot do without the other; I cannot become myself without the other; I must find myself in the other, finding the other in me (in mutual reflection and perception)." [41]

To begin our consideration of this complex process of comparative identity, let us review Sander Gilman's theory of the psychological roots of stereotyping. He begins by positing that the core function of stereotypes is to act "as our buffer against those hidden fears which lie deep within us." We need to separate and distance these fears from us, "for once they are separate from us we can act as if their source is beyond our control." Gilman traces stereotyping to a process that "all human beings undergo in becoming individuals." [42] It begins in early development (from six weeks to six months), when the child first makes the distinction between self and the world. The child's realization is accompanied by the dawning awareness of loss of control over his or her environment. In order to cope with this dwindling control, the developing child divides its psychological self into two parts: good (able to be controlled) and bad (unable to be controlled). Moreover, the child projects the qualities of the bad self onto the Other (bad world) in order to help preserve the illusion of maintaining power. [43]

All the world is correspondingly divided into "good" and "bad" objects. What is repressed within the self is thus projected onto the Other, and "the deep structure of our own sense of self and the world is built upon the illusionary image of the world divided into two camps, 'us' and 'them.'" Gilman identifies two kinds of stereotyping, a normal, or *benign,* form and a *pathological* one. The benign case is a momentary coping mechanism that preserves "our illusion of control over the self and the world." Benign stereotypers override an initial, generalized perception of an Other with a more sophisticated one. As a result, benign stereotypers are able to distinguish a specific individual from the crude category into which he or she might be automatically placed. In contrast, the pathological stereotyper "does not develop this [corrective] ability and sees the entire world in terms of the rigid line of difference" between self and Other. The pathological stereotyper's sense of self-integration is threatened by the encounter with the Other, which triggers the adherence of the stereotypical category and the relegation of the Other to it.

Gilman goes on to link his developmental psychological theory to the analysis of texts. He argues that texts—structured systems of representation—are ideal sites to study the continually varying patterns of stereotyping. For Gilman, "texts function as structured expressions of the inner world in our mental representation," and thus stereotypical structures "exist within all texts, since the creation of the text is an attempt to provide an image of control." Such systems of representation—whether in words or images—are constructed projections of our anxiety and are necessarily reductive, resulting in the creation of stereotypes.[44]

Using this projection process as a model for the social construction of cultural Others, as Robin Wood has done,[45] allows us to think of stereotyping as society's denial of its own negative tendencies by assigning them to an Other.[46] From this perspective, it can be seen that stereotypes reveal nothing about the stereotyped and everything about the stereotyper. To paraphrase Gilman: from our social, ideological, racial, aesthetic desire we generate who we are. What the cultural critic interested in the textual analysis of stereotypes should be alert to, according to Gilman, is "not what actually went on in the culture, but what the culture wanted (or was unable to repress) in representing itself."[47]

Robin Wood takes the discussion of the interpretation of texts—specifically popular horror movies—one step further by invoking the familiar analogy between dreams and films. In Freudian psychoanalytical theory, dreams are the embodiment of repressed desires, wishes, tensions, and fears that the conscious mind rejects. This raw material is transformed into a series of images—the dream—only when the censor that guards our subconscious relaxes in sleep. Even then, the desires emerge only in disguise as apparently random images and meaningless fantasies.

These ideas, Wood maintains, can be applied to films inasmuch as they are forms of popular entertainment: "One of the functions of the concept of 'entertainment'—by definition, that which we don't take seriously, or think about much ('It's only entertainment')—is to act as a kind of partial sleep of consciousness." To the extent that popular films may be thought of in this way, they can be approached analytically as simultaneously "the personal dreams of their makers and the collective dreams of their audiences—the fusion made possible by the shared structures of a common ideology."[48]

Like a dream, then, a critic using the psychoanalytical approach can read the text on a number of levels: (1) the level of manifest content—the images that appear on the screen; (2) the level of latent content—what this manifest content is concealing; (3) the dominant ideology—the "dreamer" that structured the images. The sort of criticism I mean to practice in this book is one that interprets the images presented by this mediated "dream" by looking at all three levels of meaning. In the case of stereotypical analysis, I submit that the classic Latino stereotypes are radical transformations of real-life Latinos, mainly Mexican Americans in the American Southwest, Mexicans along the border, and Latin Americans from South America, with the occasional depiction of the Puerto Rican in New York. The collective subconscious (the dominant ideology) produced these images of the Latino Other in order to symbolically mask what they represented—namely, threats to that ideology on a number of levels: social, political, economical, psychosexual, racial.

FEMINIST APPROACHES:
FEAR, AMBIVALENCE, AND GUILT

The individual's projection of the bad and absorption of the good is never fully successful. The very attempt is an acknowledgment that good and evil coexist within the individual. Melanie Klein theorized that in fact individuals oscillate back and forth between two positions.[49] The first, the "paranoid-schizoid" phase, is the one Gilman describes in which the individual fears the bad and idealizes the good. Klein's second position is the "depressive" phase, filled with guilt and regret.

We can generalize from this theory and extend that oscillation to group stereotyping and Hollywood filmmaking. This may help explain Hollywood's "stereotypical ambivalances," the fact that Hollywood films have historically demonstrated a repeated vacillation between the denigration of the Other and guilt over having done that. Generally, Hollywood films fall into three clusters along this denigration-guilt spectrum:

1. Those films that denigrate Latinos and present the stereotype in its "pure," degenerate state. Many Westerns did this with their "greaser" or *bandido* villains and Chicana prostitute stereotypes. More recently, these villains have been updated into urban *bandidos*, either East L.A. homeboys (*Falling Down*, 1993) or Puerto Rican toughs in New York City (*Badge 373*, 1973).

2. Those films that denigrate, but whose stereotypes are subverted in some way. One classic subversion is watching a crafty Latina performer like Lupe Vélez find ways to transcend the stereotype she found herself trapped in (see Chapter 3).

3. It needs to be recognized that there are films that are obviously trying to "do the right thing" vis-à-vis Latino representation. Some of these films do succeed in breaking with typical Hollywood stereotyping, but others—despite their good inten-

tions—fail and end up being condescending instead. Many examples could be found during World War II when Hollywood participated in the U.S.'s self-serving Good Neighbor Policy promoting hemispheric harmony against common Axis enemies. Disney's *The Three Caballeros* (1944) is perhaps the prime example of this effort, a travelogue that primarily patronized Latinos. On the other hand, a postwar film like *The Treasure of the Sierra Madre* (1948) might be seen as a more fair depiction of Mexico as well as a fable examining the U.S.'s imperialistic plundering of Third World resources.

Laura Mulvey's appropriation of the psychoanalysis of Jacques Lacan in her landmark piece of feminist criticism, "Visual Pleasure and Narrative Cinema," presents another way to think of these "stereotypical ambivalances." In her article, Mulvey investigates the gendered nature of roles in cinema narratives. Males are active and powerful bearers of the controlling gaze. Within the film narrative, male protagonists structure what is seen by the spectator. Females are passive and impotent objects of the gaze. This results in women being made erotic objects both for characters "within the screen story . . . and for the spectator within the auditorium." [50]

But in Mulvey's psychoanalytical schema, the female figure poses a fundamental problem to the dominant male. "She connotes something that the look continually circles around but disavows: her lack of a penis, implying a threat of castration and hence unpleasure." [51] The male unconscious has two ways of dealing with this castration anxiety, both of them strategic uses of the male gaze. The first is voyeurism, watching and investigating her so as to demystify her mystery. Here the male's pleasure lies in devaluation, punishment, and the assertion of control. The other avenue is fetishistic scopophobia, placing the female on a pedestal, building up her beauty and transforming her into something wholly satisfying, thus containing her threat by making her "safe."

By extrapolation, we can apply these ideas to stereotyping in film. "Ultimately," Mulvey writes, "the meaning of woman is sexual difference" and women pose a threat to male power structures by their very presence. [52] Similarly, the meaning of Latinos is cultural—and to some, racial—difference, and their very existence creates anxiety for the Anglo power establishment. Much of Hollywood cinema's treatment of Latinos reveals the same two responses that Mulvey suggests. As will be discussed in more detail in Chapter 3, Hollywood's stereotyping of Latinos ranges from devaluation (in the case of *el bandido,* the harlot, the male buffoon, and the female clown) to fetishization and overvaluation (the Latin lover and the dark lady). And, as we will see, there is a range of nonstereotypical American filmmaking as well that needs to be discussed.

LATINO CRITICS ON STEREOTYPING

Let me conclude with a brief review of critical approaches to Latino stereotypes in film. It might be helpful to relate this history of criticism by noting its various stages, much as I do with the brief history of Chicano cinema that I present at the beginning of Part 3. And as I do in that survey, I will focus primarily, though not exclusively, on Chicano criticism because of the way that the early critical agenda on Latinos in cinema was set by Chicano filmmakers.

The beginning of Chicano film theory and criticism was closely tied to the development of Chicano filmmaking, and evolved in relation to it. Initially, Chicano criticism developed on the same track; later it split off and took a separate but parallel path. Phase I (1969–1982) was the period of radical criticism in which the filmmakers themselves were the principal theoreticians and critics. In a sense, this criticism was all about Latino stereotypes in Hollywood film, and the criticism presented a polemical argument for reacting against them. The militant manifestos authored by Cine-Aztlán, Francisco X. Camplis, Sylvia Morales, and Jason C. Johansen exemplify this stage, in which Third Cinema in the Third World, specifically Cuban documentaries, were cited as exemplars for a burgeoning Chicano film aesthetic.[53] The audience for this initial criticism and theory building was *nosotros,* and its goals were to: (1) reveal the pattern of stereotyping of Chicanos and other marginalized groups in the dominant media, (2) sustain *el movimiento* (the Chicano Movement) and clarify Chicano cinema's relationship to it, (3) define a separatist Chicano filmmaking aesthetic resistant to assimilation into mainstream practice, (4) support and endorse Chicano filmmakers, and (5) aid in the development of a Chicano film culture. The political film theory and criticism that resulted provided the impetus for an impressive alternative cinema.

Phase II, the academic validation stage, began in the 1970s and early 1980s. José Limón's piece "Stereotyping and Chicano Resistance: An Historical Dimension" (1973), was the prototype for a systematic, scholarly investigation of issues surrounding Chicanos and film.[54] The Chicano film scholarship that followed was pioneered by Chicano academics such as Cordelia Candelaria, Carlos Cortés, Rolando Hinojosa-Smith, David Maciel, and Alex M. Saragosa.[55] Together with a number of other, similar, works produced around the same time by Allen L. Woll, Randall M. Miller, and Arthur G. Pettit,[56] Chicano and now Latino film criticism—the analysis of Chicano- and Latino-related issues in media—began gathering an interpretive critical mass.

Here, the audience was conceived of in broader terms, and the criticism reached out to anyone interested in cinema. Just as important as diversifying its readership, however, was phase II's need to legitimize itself as a valid scholarly enterprise. On this front, the main theater of operations was the academy. If phase I was agit-prop criticism, providing the philosophical and political rationale for a contestational Chicano filmmaking aesthetic, phase II consisted of intellectual guerrilla actions, fought on a broad academic front, one course offering, one journal article, and one conference paper at a time. The goal of phase II criticism was to create a space in scholarly discourse for the examination and criticism of Chicano cinema. This required everything from challenging and reshaping the curriculum (petitioning for courses that could and should be taught) to demanding a forum in journals, a voice on conference panels, and representation in professional organizations. It also involved the overhauling of the academic system so that tenure and promotion review committees might recognize and properly credit research on Chicano and Latino culture. By endorsing Chicano cinema as a valid form of cultural production and recounting the otherwise ignored history of Chicano filmmaking, phase II criticism sought to counteract the American academy's Eurocentric bias as well as the stultified tradition of film scholarship that together had marginalized Mexican American culture and trivialized its analysis. These initial efforts were largely undertaken by scholars in noncommunication fields like history, anthropology, art, literature, and Latin American studies, and because of them Chicano film and its criticism were placed on the academic map.

Of these phase II pioneers, one, Carlos Cortés, deserves to be singled out. Cortés began working on Latino and ethnic representation in media before it was fashionable, and those of us working in the field today are the fortunate beneficiaries of his pioneering research. Cortés's work helped set the agenda in several ways. First, by example: His thoughtful and thorough methodology illustrated the kind of careful work that needed to be done around the core issue of the representation of Latinos in the media. It wasn't griping, it was analysis, and to do it, one needed to engage with the history of media representation, and to observe and reflect upon a large body of texts. And it wasn't political grandstanding either, it was grappling with the complexities of media. Second, his work confronted key research questions, obvious ones that needed to be answered in order to lay the foundation for any future work. For example, how should we go about the analysis of ethnic images?[57] And, how does a viewer even know the ethnicity of film characters?[58]

Third, far from being an ivory tower scholar, Cortés sought to find practical ways to connect his ideas on media representation with actual media users, in particular students, teachers, and parents. In fact, in his role as a public intellectual, consulting with government agencies, running countless workshops for educators, writing on ways to incorporate media into school curricula, Cortés has probably affected more viewers than any other Latino media scholar. The culmination of his work blending media, multiculturalism, and education is his most recent book, *The Children Are Watching: How the Media Teach about Diversity*.[59] In it he offers succinct, precise, and helpful discussions of many of the concepts covered in this chapter. In a chapter entitled "Struggling with Stereotypes: Uses and Abuses of a Critical Concept," for example, Cortés makes critical distinctions between stereotypes and generalizations, which is close to the difference I stressed earlier between "benign" stereotyping, stereotyping as a value-neutral category-making process, and "malign" stereotyping, derogatory and rigid group generalizations.

In phase III, the poststructuralist stage (1985–2000), contemporary cultural and film theory is being employed by Chicano and Latino critics. This was foreshadowed in some of the pieces of Gary Keller's *Chicano Cinema: Research, Reviews, and Resources* (1985)[60] and was developed shortly thereafter in the published articles by Yolanda Broyles-González, Rosa Linda Fregoso, Kathleen Newman, Chon Noriega, Lillian Jiménez, Ana López, Angharad Valdivia, myself, and others.[61] It came to its fullest fruition in the anthology edited by Noriega in 1992, *Chicanos and Film: Representation and Resistance*.[62] These essays went far beyond the "images of" analysis of Latinos in films and began looking at how Latino images functioned within cinematic structures of narrative and genre.

While phase III criticism aimed to continue phase I's validation of Chicano filmmaking and phase II's validation of Chicano criticism, it also sought to demonstrate that Chicano/Latino critics could "do" cultural theory. By applying structuralist and poststructuralist approaches to ethnic issues in cinema or to Chicano cinema itself, Chicano critics could partake of the rarefied—but intellectually sanctioned and academically certified—discourse of film criticism and theory. As part of a process of gaining credibility for ourselves as critics as well as for the

Latino/Chicano films we analyze, we became, if you will, card-carrying members of the cultural studies club—precisely what was needed if we and the object of our research were to be taken seriously in the academy. A subset of this critical tradition is work that continues to deal with Latino stereotypes. Besides myself, there have been a handful of critics who have focused specifically on Latino stereotypes: Carlos Cortés, as I mentioned above, Gary D. Keller, Christine List, and Chon Noriega, and their contributions need to be highlighted. (Angharad Valdivia has also dealt with stereotypes in her analysis of the qualities of Rosie Pérez's characters in film, as I discuss in Chapter 4.) Keller approached the problem historically and empirically. In his *Hispanics and United States Film: An Overview and Handbook,*[63] he surveyed films from the first decades of U.S. twentieth-century filmmaking to create a list of eleven Latino types, and then charted their evolution across time. It is akin to the shorter list of six Latino stereotypes that I first delineated in 1988[64] and have revised and incorporated into Chapter 3, and which was itself indebted to Arthur G. Pettit's typology in *Images of the Mexican American in Fiction and Film.* The point, it seems to me, is not to quibble about which author's list of stereotypes is best or most complete. Rather it is to note the dramatic similarities among our findings. When you boil it all down, what the three of us discovered in our individual studies of American film was a steady repetition of the same basic traits assigned to Latino characters in the form of recognizable stereotypes.

For Christine List, Latino stereotypes provide an important context for the analysis of Chicano self-representation in feature filmmaking. As she has written,

> As Chicano and Chicana filmmakers embark on the difficult task of con-
> structing their own cinematic identity they necessarily inherit the baggage
> of Hollywood stereotypes. Some directors confront the Hollywood legacy
> by creating positive Chicano hero figures. Other Chicano directors have
> opted to construct complex characters using techniques of psychological
> realism. Cheech Marin has taken the unusual route of using the very same
> Chicano stereotypes entrenched in Hollywood and turning them on their
> head through subversive comic techniques.[65]

List helps us see that Hollywood's Latino stereotypes are one pole of a filmmaking dialectic for Chicanos. Hollywood stereotyping was the Thesis, if you will, and Chicano filmmakers, from their ideological short films and documentaries of the late 1960s and 1970s to their more recent forays into mainstream studio cinema, are busily creating the Antithesis.

And it is the initial counterhegemonic reaction by Chicano filmmakers in the late 1960s that is the subject of Chon Noriega's impressively comprehensive study, *Shot in America: Television, the State, and the Rise of Chicano Cinema*.[66] In it, Noriega marshals a mountain of evidence to make clear that Chicano activists' protests against demeaning stereotypes were a central motivating factor in the birth of Chicano cinema. In 1968 Chicano groups in Los Angeles, Washington, D.C., and San Antonio protested against advertisers, television networks, and film studios that disseminated "derogatory stereotypes against Mexican Americans, Mexicans, and other Latino groups." They were particularly incensed at depictions of "Mexicans as 'stupid, shiftless, dirty, immoral, and lackey-bandido types.'"[67] By 1970 the protests had spread to the Academy Awards, industry guilds, and television stations, and, as two activists, Armando Rendon and Domingo Nick Reyes, put it, "Chicanos no longer will stand to be stereotyped—the days of the 'bandido' and the sleepy Mexican caricature are gone. We are making demands of every institution of society and every agency of government."[68]

As Noriega so convincingly shows, stereotypes became a major site of struggle for the Chicano Movement, and the Chicano activism on Latino representation took dead aim at the structure and practices of the commercial broadcasting and film industries. The assumption was that the racist discourse within the larger society, and the resulting social relations, were to a great extent shaped by media stereotypes. According to Rendon and Reyes, the mainstream media were "destructive forces" in the Chicano community.[69] By the early 1970s, Chicano cinema had become an integral component of the broader Chicano social movement.[70] This counter-stereotyping rationale, then, formed the roots of Chicano filmmaking and of Chicano film theory and criticism, and this activist legacy continues to influence filmmakers and critics to this day.

Therefore, in order to better understand Chicano cinema and criticism, it is worthwhile to look at the actual stereotypes in Hollywood film that caused the initial furor. But before describing and analyzing the basic Latino stereotypes (in Chapter 3), I will discuss how stereotyping operates in films and how the stereotyping process is embedded within Hollywood film language and the norms of "good filmmaking."

STEREOTYPES IN FILM

PICTURES IN OUR HEADS AND ON OUR SCREENS: MENTAL IMAGES VS. MEDIATED STEREOTYPES

It should be stressed that there are significant differences between stereotypes as mental constructs, the topic that began the last chapter, and the stereotypes found in image-based mass media and in particular, the movies, which are the subject of the rest of this book. To begin with, "the picture in our heads" kind of stereotype exists in the individual mind, whereas the mediated stereotype exists on the screen as a public commodity. The individual's stereotypical mental construct may or may not remain a private image; it may or may not travel far beyond the individual or in-group circles; it may or may not be the basis for a racist tract. In contrast, the mediated stereotype is always public and, in the case of Hollywood cinema, has a global reach, as I discovered with those foreign Fulbright students who described *el bandido* so precisely. Media broadcast the in-group image of the Other indiscriminately, to in-group and out-group members alike—whoever sees the film sees the stereotype.

While there is usually some general agreement among in-group members about the rough contours of their stereotypical constructs, it could be claimed that each individual's mental stereotype is a personal one. But the mediated stereotype is definite—an agreed-upon vision and a shared sign of the Other in precise and material form. As Roland Barthes said about social signs, "We are no longer dealing here with a theoretical mode of representation: we are dealing here with *this* particular image, which is given for *this* particular signification."[1] In contrast, mental-construct stereotypes tend to focus more on generalized traits that are then applied to actual members of the out-group.[2] Indeed, a stereotype is often referred to as one of these general traits, as if the trait—laziness, let's say—is the stereotype. And the way the mental image stereotype works, it is.

But the mediated stereotype is a concrete depiction of the Other. In the "pictures in our heads" kind of stereotype, Mexicans and Mexican Americans may be stereotypically believed to be lazy, dirty, dishonest, immoral, and with a low regard toward life. These traits are then applied to actual Mexicans encountered in lived experience. In the movies, however, el bandido is a particular instance of the mexicano and embodies a specific array of negative traits (dirtiness, ugliness, sneakiness, ignorance, and a proclivity toward criminality and violence), and we speak of the entire mediated image as it appears on the screen as the stereotype, not merely one or another of its traits.

A mediated stereotype, then, operates by gathering a specific set of negative traits and assembling them into a particular image. But the list of negative traits ascribed to the Other by an in-group is usually much longer than a single mediated stereotype can bear. Interestingly, because they take concrete human form, mediated stereotypes have their stereotypical limits—seldom can one stereotype be assigned all of the negative traits attributed to the out-group at large. To handle this, these traits are parceled out among a handful of mediated stereotypes who together are meant to represent the Other. For example, Donald Bogle recognized five African American movie stereotypes, which he used to title his study: toms, coons, mulattoes, mammies, and bucks.[3] Similarly, in the next chapter I will identify six basic Latino stereotypes, which I arrange in three sets of male-female pairs: el bandido and the harlot, the male buffoon and the female clown, the Latin lover and the dark lady.

THE SEMIOTICS OF STEREOTYPING

Because the mediated stereotypical image is a message, a meaningful sign, it is important to understand all the layers of meaning that it conveys. From a semiotic perspective, we can say that the cinematic image of el bandido is the signifier, the recognizable part of the sign. At its most basic, most ideologically innocent, denotative level, what it signifies is simply a dark-skinned male with bullet belts adorning his chest and a sombrero on his head.

But at the connotative level much more is signified. There are a host of meanings that the image has accrued over nearly a century of repeated representation, and it is here that the movie stereotype carries most of its informational—and ideological—freight. Let me list, by function, all the kinds of connotative data the stereotype conveys.

Racial

The *bandido*'s darker skin immediately marks him as an individual outside the white Anglo norm. At best, as an Other he is different and perhaps suspect because of that; at worst, he presents a threat to the dominant society's purported racial purity.

National

He is obviously not a (North) American as such a person has been defined in the popular consciousness by movies and history books (i.e., someone of Western European stock). His nationality, therefore, is yet another way he is marked as an Other.

Narrative

According to time-honored Hollywood convention, hewn over decades of movie storytelling, this image is the sign for the Mexican bandit, one of American movies' favorite villains. As such, he is a threat that needs to be eliminated in order to return the diegetic world to its tranquil, prethreat status quo.

Behavioral

This character will act in predictably despicable, antisocial, sneaky, violent, criminal ways.

Psychological

Actions reveal psychology in the Hollywood narrative; accordingly, *el bandido*'s behavior unveils a warped worldview squarely at odds with what is considered normal human behavior. Based on his actions, *el bandido* is at the very least a simpleminded sociopath, though from decades of experience with his various screen incarnations, we gather that he is also maladjusted and unstable, alcoholic and sadistic, and a sexual psychopath.

Moral

Moral beliefs are the ultimate motivation in Hollywood films. Protagonists believe so fervently in the values of a society's moral norms that they are willing to risk everything in order to preserve and protect them; in so doing, they embody them. Villains oppose those values and work to overthrow them. Since we are seldom given convincing reasons for why he acts as he does, we are left with two possible explanations about the moral makeup of a villain like el bandido: he is immoral (he knows the difference between right and wrong but chooses to ignore it) or amoral (for him there is no dividing line between right and wrong). Either one places him far outside mainstream morality.

Ideological

The organizing principle of el bandido as an ideological force is his fundamental antiestablishmentarianism. Because his entire being stands against the nation's values and ideals, his very existence threatens dominant American ideology.

I compile this list to show what a potent and concentrated sign a single stereotypical image can be. Beyond this, however, I can also use the denotative/connotative split to refine the idea of stereotypical evolution that I discussed in the last chapter. In one superficial type of evolution, what I call a "stereotypical shift," stereotypes do not so much evolve as simply alter their guise at the denotative surface, while keeping all of the stereotype's connotations intact. For example, the Latino juvenile delinquent, a staple antagonist in Hollywood since the rise of the teen problem films of the 1950s (*Blackboard Jungle* [1955]), and a denizen of either the slums of New York City (*The Young Savages* [1961]) or East L.A. (*Colors* [1988]), can be understood as not an altogether new stereotype but in many ways a continuation of the old one: a contemporary, urban *bandido*. To be sure, it is not exactly the same stereotype; there are differences in the characters' ages and social environments to take into account. However, the differences between the two are almost exclusively at the denotative level; the same connotative traits that I just listed to describe el bandido apply to Hollywood's Latino homeboy.

Let me examine a scene from a recent American film containing this updated urban bandit, in order to address my next topic: how the

Hollywood filmmaking paradigm—understood as the norm of good, professional filmmaking practice—is implicated in the process of movie stereotyping.

THE POETICS OF HOLLYWOOD STEREOTYPING

The stereotypical image, the human stereotype, is the most obvious and prominent part of the stereotype, but it does not act alone. It is presented to the viewer along with a full array of stereotypical devices deployed at every cinematic register, everything from mise-en-scène to framing, from camera angles to shot duration, from set decoration to music and sound effects. These devices complement the image in crucial but nearly imperceptible ways and together help to create the complete stereotypical statement.

This poetics of stereotyping is derived from and embedded in the classical Hollywood cinema's narrative paradigm, the system of film conventions devised by early filmmakers to tell their visual stories clearly and efficiently. As I mentioned above, stereotypes are an important part of this paradigm, inasmuch as they facilitate narration. As a purely industrial practice, then, stereotypes are maintained because of their valued narrative economy, which is related to their financial economy as well. Because they require little or no introduction or explanation, and because they are so quickly and completely comprehended as signs, stereotypes are an extremely cheap and cost-effective means of telling a movie story.

Falling Down *and the Poetics of Stereotyping*

In order to demonstrate Hollywood's stereotyping poetics of Latinos working at peak efficiency at numerous cinematic levels, let me analyze a four-minute scene from *Falling Down* (1993, directed by Joel Schumacher). The film, a contemporary drama set in Los Angeles, follows a divorced, unemployed defense industry engineer (Michael Douglas) who snaps one morning in bumper-to-bumper freeway traffic, abandons his car, and sets off on foot to see his daughter. The movie uses his trek across Los Angeles to make its befuddled critique of the vacuity and absurdity of modern urban life. When D-FENS (the police refer to Douglas's character using the name on his personalized license plate) stops in East L.A. to rest and repair a hole in his shoe, he encounters two Mexican American homeboys (Agustín Rodríguez and Eddie Frias). They pull a knife on him and try to steal his briefcase, but D-FENS beats them off with a baseball bat.

Falling Down is unusual for a Hollywood film in that its protagonist is not a typical hero. Instead, D-FENS is a nerd, complete with over-grown crew cut, hard-shell briefcase, black-framed eyeglasses, plastic pocket protector wedged into the pocket of his ill-fitting white short-sleeved shirt, and drab polyester necktie. That the film's protagonist is himself an in-group stereotype is its most progressive element, and might lead one to believe that the film will be a sustained critique of the maddening way the Anglo dominant abuses its own. But the film is so entrenched in typical Hollywood clichés, conventions, and stereotypes that any possibility of a real critique is seriously undermined. There are plenty of film narrative cues, which I will discuss below, to signal to the viewer that D-FENS is indeed our hero and that the film is a lot more conventional than it may appear at first glance. One major one, for example, is the star casting: the fact that D-FENS is played by Michael Douglas, an Academy Award–winning actor-producer who is a certified box-office superstar commanding top salary and billing.[4]

A second way the film's ostensible criticism of the system is compromised is the unthinking way it uses standard movie stereotypes of Latinos, Asians, and even white males to score its thematic points. But beyond these there are a host of cinematic elements that contribute to the film's stereotypical depiction of these two East L.A. *bandidos* that deserve to be discussed in some detail.

Framing

As David Bordwell has shown, typical compositions in Hollywood films are centered. According to Bordwell, most shots in classical Hollywood films "work with a privileged zone of screen space resembling a T: the upper one-third and the central vertical third of the screen constitute the 'center' of the shot." Furthermore, "the human body is made the center of narrative and graphic interest." [5] Balance within the frame is maintained by the positioning of figures. The most important figure, usually the protagonist, or figures (the protagonist and the leading lady and/or sidekick) take the center of the frame, and the less important ones (the minor characters) are relegated to the edges. The usually Anglo male protagonist, as the center of interest, will therefore assume the center one-third of the frame. The composition will be balanced with minor characters who will fill out the sides of the frame.

These principles are clearly in evidence in the scene under discussion

D-FENS (Michael Douglas) stops for a rest in East L.A. in Falling Down
*(1993). An analysis of this scene illustrates how the basic elements of
Hollywood filmmaking practice contribute to stereotyping. Initially, the
mise-en-scène and set design establish two contrasting landscapes. Sitting
atop the graffiti-covered rubble in a vacant lot, D-FENS has obviously entered
a danger zone. Behind him, the distant skyline of the metropolis indicates
how far he has strayed from "civilization."*

in *Falling Down* (and Hollywood films in general). D-FENS is centered
within most frames in which he appears and the two Chicano hoods
(listed in the credits as Gang Members 1 and 2) are placed on either side
of him. From this and many other examples of stereotyping in Hollywood cinema we can draw a stereotyping corollary to Bordwell's obser-
vations: the center one-third of the frame is the realm of the dominant
hero, who is usually male, Anglo, Christian, etc., and the two-thirds on
either side are the realm of minor characters and stereotypes. Moreover,
applying this corollary, the narrative can be read in purely pictorial
terms. In fact, it is not too much to say that compositionally, the narrative of nearly every Hollywood film usually boils down to a struggle between the Anglo male hero and a villain (most often some form of class,
gender, race, nationality, or ethnic Other) to control and maintain the
center of the frame.

Mise-en-scène

The staging of the scene is yet another way stereotyping is enhanced. To
begin with, downtown Los Angeles can be seen in the distance behind
D-FENS, demonstrating in spatial terms just how far he has wandered
from "civilization." Second, as discussed above, the blocking of the ac-

Surrounded by the two circling Chicano toughs (Eddie Frias and Agustín Rodríguez), D-FENS remains calm at the center of the brewing confrontational storm. In addition, camera angles serve to indicate power. From the level of the homeboys, the camera looks up at D-FENS, giving him dominance.

tion places D-FENS at the center. So when the two gang members first encounter him alone on a deserted hill—they circle round him like animals circling their prey—he is the focus of their (and the film's and the audience's) attention.

Third and fourth, D-FENS is surrounded and stationary. In the movies, when a First World hero enters the Third World and confronts the native, two things are virtually guaranteed: he (or, if he is accompanied by the standard small band of explorers, they) will be surrounded by a larger band of natives, and his (their) immobility will contrast with their usually frenetic activity. This centered stillness connotes power, even majesty. (So it is no surprise when the natives sometimes mistake the white man for a god.) It also connotes intelligence (conserving energy for the violent confrontation that will inevitably occur), cunning (sizing up the situation; making mental preparations for the upcoming fight), and moral reserve (he will not resort to violence until provoked; after all, he's not savage—they are). The most familiar example of this in the movies is, of course, the settlers' circling the wagons or preparing the fort for the siege by the bloodthirsty Native Americans. D-FENS's cool jocularity while the two hoods buzz around him is consistent with a long history of Hollywood heroes' typically unruffled, smart-ass responses to danger when surrounded by natives in the Third World wilderness.

*The reverse angle, seen from D-FENS's point of view. Even though it is a
closer shot of the two hoods, and even though they are menacing, the camera
looks down on them, diminishing their power in the shot.*

Camera Movement

The camera's movement gives two perspectives on D-FENS. In most of
the shots in this sequence, the camera regards D-FENS not from a character's perspective, but from an omniscient point of view. In these shots,
the camera is stationary, mirroring the stillness of his commanding Anglo presence. In two shots that present D-FENS from the thugs' perspective, the camera is in motion, circling around D-FENS (in one shot
making a complete 360-degree move). Rather than allowing a viewer to
sympathize with the two Chicanos, whose point of view those shots are
aligned with, these low-angle shots show D-FENS as the calm at the center of a brewing storm. The reverse shots from D-FENS's point of view
are stationary, emanating from his centered and still power position. His
is the controlling gaze here. Furthermore, as I will discuss below, from
his elevated point of view, we look down on the two thugs, thereby diminishing their power and their threat.

Camera Angles

In the cinematic "language" of the classical Hollywood paradigm, low-
angle shots looking up at characters tend to give them importance,
power, and control, just as high-angle shots generally reduce their importance, making them less dominant and more vulnerable. In the be-

46

*When he descends to talk to them, framing, costuming, and staging combine
to convey the superiority of the white male protagonist. D-FENS is centered
in the frame, the position of greatest graphic importance, is the brightest
area because of his white shirt, and is the tallest figure.*

ginning of this scene, D-FENS is sitting atop the rubble of a demolished
building and the gang members are below. Since the camera usually
records action from the protagonist's point of view, the camera shoots
down on the Mexican American youths, quickly proclaiming the Anglo
character's importance, power, and dominance—as well as the Chicanos' lack of it. And when the camera shoots from their point of view,
it is a low-angle shot looking up, giving him power.

The shots after D-FENS comes down to meet them at ground level are
not angled, but straight-on. But these shots also emphasize him and
stress his dominance. First, he is centered in the frame. Second, he is just
slightly taller than they are. Third, to assist viewer identification with the
hero, "normal" (nonangled) shots are typically set at the protagonist's
eye level (actually, in practice, just above his shoulder level). Therefore
D-FENS's face-to-face confrontation with the two Chicanos is recorded
from his subtly higher eye-line. In every shot, then, the Chicanos are at
a pictorial power disadvantage.

Editing: Shot Selection and Duration

Except for an opening close-up of D-FENS, the scene generally follows
the standard Hollywood progression of establishing long shots (LS), followed by contextualizing medium shots (MS), and emphatic close-ups

47

In tighter close-ups, D-FENS is again centered and seen in full face, while the Mexican Americans are at the margins and in profile.

(CU) for meaningful details and dramatic emphasis. But as the main character, D-FENS has more close-ups than the other two characters, and his are tighter and last longer. So by the framing and editing rules of proximity (the tighter the close-up in Hollywood films, the more important the character) and duration (the longer a shot lingers on a subject, the more important the character), the film indicates who is the most significant character and where viewers' sympathy and ultimately their identification ought to lie.

Music

The music in the scene is a combination of eerie electronic sounds and more conventional Hollywood movie soundtrack melodies. The ominous technomusic used early in the scene underscores the growing unease between D-FENS and the gang members. When the fight starts and D-FENS beats them into retreat with the bat, it gives way to the sort of Hollywood-style "tribal" music often heard in films with African or Third World jungle settings: conga drums providing the reverberating bass backbeat while bongo drums ripple across the track providing more nervous staccato rhythms. Thus the musical soundtrack adds a subtle layer of stereotypical meaning, based on decades of Hollywood's conventionalized and imperialistic portrayals of Others. The drums say that the natives of the barrio jungle are restless, even if they have—for the moment at least—retreated. And sure enough, the hoods appear later in the film, trying to get their revenge on D-FENS.

Sound Effects

Besides the sound of children playing in the distance, the main sc fects, which fade in and out of this scene, particularly in its first hall, are animal sounds (a crowing bird, other birdsongs, a dog barking), the sound of an unseen helicopter, and a song in Spanish. The soundtrack effectively reiterates what the visuals suggest, that D-FENS has wandered into a Third-World-within-the-First-World war zone. Moreover, there is tension on the sound effects track. More often than not, birdsong simply connotes the serenity of nature. But here this is offset with contrasting sounds of the crowing bird, the dog's barking, and the helicopter propeller noise, which combine to jar the initial pastoral tranquility, especially when juxtaposed with the disquieting layer of electronic music. The cackling bird sound (in the movies, a familiar sound effect often denoting an uncharted jungle world) also betokens a wild (rather than domesticated) animal presence, further accentuating the dangerousness of "darkest" East L.A.

The helicopter sound, especially after its exquisite use in Francis Ford Coppola's *Apocalypse Now* (1979), has since come to indicate in American films a military presence in a battle zone and, connotatively, the futile attempt to find a rational explanation for the irrationality of war. In *Falling Down,* the chopper's sound links D-FENS's quest for sense in a senseless world with Lieutenant Willard's (Martin Sheen) similar journey in *Apocalypse Now.* But the helicopter with its signature sound are also common in urban crime dramas, in everything from *Blue Thunder* (1983) to *Boyz N the Hood* (1991) to *Heat* (1995). In these cases, it depicts the out-of-control criminal element that has forced the police to resort to military hardware and tactics. Thus from recent movie conventions, the chopper sound suggests that East L.A. is an out-of-control urban no-man's-land where (presumably, though we never actually see the helicopter in the scene) hovering police surveillance helicopters are the only way to maintain any semblance of law and order.

The song in Spanish places the protagonist outside the Empire of English, which in Hollywood movies means beyond the pale of rational discourse. Spanish (as opposed to other Western European languages like French, German, or Italian) spoken outside of Spain in American films signifies that (a) the narrative has moved to a Third World country (or the barrio, or a Puerto Rican ghetto in New York, or the Southwestern border, which for Hollywood are all the same thing) where the rules of "civilization" no longer apply; (2) because English cannot be relied on in this place, words and reasoning will be of little use (since rationality exists only in English); therefore, violent action is a very likely outcome.

Costuming

Costume provides another common narrative cue. The most familiar example of this is the well-known Western genre convention whereby good guys wear white hats and villains dress in black. This elementary color coding is part of long-standing Western cultural traditions (white being the color associated with purity and goodness, black the color of darkness and evil). Pictorially, white creates a bright area in the frame that attracts viewers' attention, so it is no surprise that it is the color most often associated with the protagonist. This costuming practice is carefully observed here, with D-FENS wearing a nerdy white shirt, but a white shirt nonetheless, and the barrio gangstas wearing darker, more muted colors. Gang Member #1 wears a dark blue shirt and Gang Member #2 wears a sleeveless red plaid shirt over a T-shirt. As is often the case in Hollywood cinema, costume design is narrative.

Makeup

Skin color follows the same pattern as costuming: protagonists are usually white, antagonists often dark. In its history, Hollywood has gone to extremes to preserve this system of representation, such as putting white actors in brown face to portray "greasers" or other Latino villains or in black face to play African American villains. More recently, however, conventions of realism have changed, and for the sake of verisimilitude it has become less and less acceptable for a white actor to play a character of color. Here, with Latinos playing the parts of the homeboys, casting did what makeup historically did in the past.

But there are other, carefully placed signs of Otherness the makeup artist has employed. Gang Member #1's ponytail is one such indicator, long hair being a counterculture signifier. In addition, Hollywood uses visible skin marks, usually scars, and other bodily handicaps or imperfections (the gold or missing tooth, the eyepatch, the limp, the wheezing cough) as an external indicator of the deformed psychology of the villain. In *Falling Down*, the Chicano characters' tattoos serve this purpose. This contrasts with the physical perfection of the hero, attesting to his good psychological health and moral righteousness. (Hidden scars, however, are a different matter. They are given to the hero to denote some heroic rite of passage that shaped and strengthened his character—physical medals of valor. He and his beloved will talk about them during their lovemaking.)[6]

Set Design and Art Direction

The action takes place on a deserted hill, amid the graffiti-laden rubble of the decaying ghetto. D-FENS sits on the stoop of a destroyed building, and contorted rebar protrudes from exposed edges of crumbling concrete. This is the stereotypical habitat of American Others—the dilapidated inner-city war zone. Outsiders, like D-FENS, clearly enter at their own risk. Here the stereotypical point is not whether places like this actually exist in our cities—of course they do—but rather the repetitive frequency with which Hollywood visits them. It does so because such settings fulfill its dramatic and narrative needs so well. Extreme locales—the jungle (South American or African), the ghetto (East L.A., East St. Louis, or the South Bronx), the desert (the U.S. Southwest or the Middle East)—are, in the movies, inherently hazardous. The terrain is a crucible that the Anglo protagonist enters to test his mettle. And the inhabitants are as treacherous as the locale. Audiences have become conditioned to know that the very location supplies conflict, with danger (what perils await our hero in such a place?) and suspense (how will he survive?) framing viewers' expectations.

Scripting

The unspoken conventions of screenwriting are yet another aspect of Hollywood's stereotyping poetics that informs the audience as to the superiority of the hero and the inferiority of the Others. Naturally, the best and most entertaining lines go to the protagonist, and so does any dialogue that illustrates intelligence, rationality, or wit. The Others' dialogue reveals them to be literal-minded and humorless (they exhibit only a gruesome, sadistic kind of humor, laughing, for example, at the violent end about to befall the white interloper). In addition, their speech typically exposes slow, unimaginative, and shortsighted thought processes.

Most of these characteristics are illustrated in the following exchange, which comes early in the scene when D-FENS, seated on a concrete ruin covered with graffiti, is surrounded by the two Chicanos, who accuse him of trespassing and loitering:

51

D-FENS: I didn't see any signs.

GANG MEMBER #1: (*pointing to a red graffiti skull*) What you call that?

D-FENS: Graffiti?

GANG MEMBER #1: No, man, that's not fuckin' graffiti, that's a sign.

GANG MEMBER #2: He can't read it, man.

GANG MEMBER #1: I'll read it for you. It says this is fuckin' private property. No fuckin' trespassing. This means fuckin' you. (*He points at D-FENS menacingly.*)

D-FENS: It says all that?

GANG MEMBER #1: Yeah.

D-FENS: Well, maybe if you wrote it in fuckin' English, I could fuckin' understand it.

GANG MEMBER #2: He thinks he's being funny.

GANG MEMBER #1: I'm not laughing.

GANG MEMBER #2: I'm not either.

They are serious and literal-minded, and he is funny and ironic.

Consistent with the fact that the Anglo protagonist gets the most screen time is the rule that he gets the longer speeches. In D-FENS's speech that immediately follows he demonstrates his quick analysis of the situation, his grace under pressure, and his ability to opt first for reason over violence—all demonstrating his underlying moral and intellectual superiority:

D-FENS: Wait a minute. Hold it, fellas. We're gettin' off on the wrong foot here, OK? This is a gangland thing, isn't it? We're having a territorial dispute, hmm? I mean, I've wandered into your pissin' ground or whatever the damn thing is, and you've taken offense at my presence. And I can understand that. I mean, I wouldn't want you people in my backyard either. This is your home, and your home is your home and I respect that. So if you would just back up a step or two, I'll take my problems elsewhere. OK? Fair enough?

Of course it isn't OK. The two stereotypical homeboys are incapable of heeding the Anglo voice of reason and demand his briefcase as a trespassing "toll." "Listen, fellas, I've had a really rare morning," he pleads,

D-FENS's measured, rational, and witty pleas for a peaceful resolution fall on deaf ears. The two threaten him at knifepoint and demand that he give them his briefcase.

but they insist. When he refuses, Gang Member #1 pulls a knife on him. D-FENS then goes into a slow burn and delivers another speech in which he tells them how unreasonable their demand is. And since Hollywood heroes use violence only when all other options have been tried and have failed, the speech also explains, mainly for the audience's benefit, why he will now have to resort to the use of force:

D-FENS: *(Close-up; at knife-point)* OK. OK. I was willing to mind my own business, I was willing to respect your territory and treat you like a man, but you couldn't leave it alone, could you? You couldn't let a man sit here for five minutes and take a rest on your precious, piece-a-shit hill. OK, you want my briefcase? I'll get it for you, all right? You can have my briefcase.

Crossing to his briefcase, he pulls out the baseball bat concealed beneath it and attacks them, sending them fleeing.

The hero is patient and reasonable; he must be goaded into violence. The Other is pure aggression whose only mode of expression is violence.

Acting Conventions

A crucial element of a character's psychology is revealed in the classical Hollywood cinema via gesture. Acting conventions are based on the fact that heroes and villains behave in certain circumscribed ways. Here, Agustín Rodríguez and Eddie Frias play their parts in the standard tough homeboy mode, which is a variation of Hollywood villains in general. The facial scowl, the aggressive attitude, the simmering hostility are its basic features. Similarly, Michael Douglas plays his part in typical heroic fashion. If they are hot and agitated, he is cool and collected. They taunt and point, he looks and listens serenely. He is the hero because he can control his feelings and, in the face of danger, can channel his violence against evil, exhibiting heroic qualities. They, on the other hand, are unalloyed danger—unstable, irrational, combustible.

Lighting

If this were an interior shot, the lighting scheme would light the set and highlight the Anglo hero, drawing the viewer's eye to the important character. In daytime exterior shots, however, the action is mostly lit naturally, by sunlight. Additional illumination is most often provided by reflectors, which bounce the sunlight onto the actors' faces. "Normal" Hollywood lighting, though, is based on a white skin standard, on getting the proper exposure for the faces of white actors.[7]

One result of this system is that in a scene like this one, in broad daylight and in an uncovered area, fair-skinned actors reflect more light into the camera lens and thus require less supplemental illumination (fill light) than darker-skinned ones. Since actors of color require more lighting in order for the film emulsion to record their facial details, this means that—all other things being equal—actors of color have more light bearing down on them. Therefore they are made hotter than their white counterparts and presumably perspire more. Within the poetics of stereotyping, that is fine, because it conforms with the understood coolness of the Anglo protagonist and the heated impetuousness of the dark and sweaty Other. Here, especially in the close-up shots of the two gang members, beads of perspiration can be noted on their faces, sometimes even revealing a hot or shiny spot (a cardinal sin of Hollywood lighting—at least for a white actor playing the protagonist). In contrast, Michael Douglas's composed D-FENS never breaks a sweat, even after he sends them fleeing in pain.

STEREOTYPES, MINOR CHARACTERS, AND THE ARCHETYPE

What I have endeavored to show above is how the classical Hollywood paradigm—the accepted conventions of "good, professional" filmmaking—contributes to stereotyping in the movies. If the typical Hollywood film story follows the pattern of equilibrium-disequilibrium-equilibrium, then from our perspective it is often the tale of a valiant Anglo male overcoming the threat posed by some Other. Eliminating the Other eliminates the threat, restores equilibrium, and leads to closure. Minor characters of color and villains are typically Others (of one kind or an-Other—race, class, ethnicity, gender, etc.) and usually stereotypes. The protagonist and his love interest are handsome Anglos. As defenders of the dominant and representative of the dominant ideal, they are the two Beautiful People in the story—let's call them the archetypes.

But if, as we have said, with repetition the stereotype comes to represent the Other group, whom do the archetypes represent? And what about the many other Anglos in the story? How should we classify them, and whom do they represent?

To begin with the archetypes, as representatives of the dominant ideal they possess the full complement of dominant virtues. They have it all, and, as we have seen, as the focus of the narrative the classical cinema does all it can to enhance viewer identification with them. But audience identification is clearly an asymptotic affair. As viewers, we may to a greater or lesser extent approach the archetypal ideal, but most of us do not have—and will never have—the perfection of the male protagonist or his beloved. After all, how many of us look like Tom Cruise or Demi Moore? How many of us have the degree of heroic characteristics that the characters such actors play exhibit in film after film?

Rather, most viewers have more in common with the minor characters, who are "minor" precisely because they lack qualities possessed by the archetypes. Because the classical Hollywood narrative must be absolutely clear about who the protagonist is, it is populated with secondary characters who cannot be confused with primary ones. This is achieved in two main ways. First, by the cinematic techniques I just enumerated above, the Hollywood paradigm focuses the narrative on one and only one subject. To make doubly sure there is no confusion, the protagonist couple are surrounded by in-group characters who physically could not possibly be mistaken for the leads: parents and relatives, rival love interests, best friends, and sidekicks who are conveniently too old, too young, too heavy, too plain, too ethnic. For in-group characters in Hollywood cinema, "too ethnic" generally means not completely assimilated, not American enough, and thus "too Jewish" or "too Swedish," "too Irish," or "too Italian," and so forth. They are also marked emotionally and/or morally as unfit for leading-role status—they are weak, dumb, overly excitable, and impulsive, or they operate out of a skewed value system. They might place, for example, self or career above the greater moral good, which is just the opposite of the hero's altruism. The hero does the morally right thing, defeats the forces of evil, garners acclaim, and gets a beautiful woman as his reward.

Out-group characters, when they appear at all, are by definition already marked as unsuitable candidates for the pivotal role of the protagonist and are therefore relegated to the farthest reaches of the narrative margins. At best they are the minor-minor characters such as extras in crowds, or the token minority member (the Latino policeman at the murder scene, the Asian jury member, the silent Black at the boardroom table). At worst, they are the stereotypical antagonists.

To ensure that secondary in-group characters are not mistaken for the protagonist, that they remain minor characters, they are assigned some characteristics viewed unfavorably by the in-group; that is, they are stereotyped. Like the Latino out-group stereotypes we have been discussing, they too are "decentered" and marginalized by standard Hollywood filmmaking practice. In-group stereotypes expose a representational hierarchy. What this reveals is that, in terms of representation at least, the Anglo dominant is not quite so monolithic after all, made up as it is of "imperfect" and therefore stereotyped subgroups (the insensitive rich, the lazy poor, the obese, the young, obnoxious Jews, loud New Yorkers, etc.). Following this line of reasoning, at the pinnacle of this representational pyramid is the smallest minority of all: the male archetype. Indiana Jones is only one character (though of course he is the one invested with the ideals of the dominant), and no one else in the Jones trilogy is even remotely like him. The bourgeois hero's inherent contradiction is that he displays and promotes the dominant ideal, and at the same time demonstrates that only one person in the world can actually achieve that ideal.

TOWARD A THEORY OF STEREOTYPING RECEPTION: STEREOTYPING AS TRIANGLING

The Paramount Studios logo—a white mountain in a field of sky blue—dissolves into an actual mountain. Then the subtitle: "South America, 1936." Four men make their way through a dense rain forest: two Peruvian wranglers, a Quechua Indian porter, and an Anglo adventurer. This is the familiar beginning of one of the most popular movies ever made, *Raiders of the Lost Ark* (1981), and one of the cleverest cinematic openings of any Hollywood film of the 1980s. By the time this introductory sequence is over, the film's hero, archaeologist Indiana Jones (Harrison Ford), will be betrayed by Hispanic males four different times. To begin with, the Quechua native makes a cowardly, screaming exit when he uncovers a huge stone head of what the script calls a demon. (Why doesn't he warn the others?) Moments later one of the Peruvians tries—unsuccessfully—to shoot Indy in the back. The other leaves him for dead inside the temple after tricking him out of the golden idol ("Adios, señor"). Finally, Indiana runs for his life being chased by barbaric Hovito "warriors."[8] The Hovitos just miss capturing him, and Indy flies off, leaving the stereotypical view of South America and its inhabitants behind.

In this brief prologue the film ethnocentrically sets in place Hollywood's colonial worldview, which includes such tenets as the intellectual, physical, and moral superiority of North American Anglos (Belloq, the bad Anglo, is a French Nazi sympathizer); the treacherousness of the Third World and the cowardice, duplicity, and ignorance of its citizens; and the First World's unquestioned right to exploit the Third's cultural, human, and natural resources. Much of the narrative work done to convey so much information so efficiently is done by stereotypes and stereotyping poetics.

One reason I refer to *Raiders of the Lost Ark* is because it illustrates so well how naturalized the process of stereotyping truly is. When I show this clip to students and ask how many noticed the way it denigrated Hispanics *the first time they saw it,* few can truthfully say they did. To be honest, neither did I. Like everyone else in the theater around me when I saw it in 1981, I was too busy rooting for Indiana Jones. I am seeking to understand why I did so, and I want to conclude this chapter by proposing a theory to explain how this happened.

The operation of stereotyping I have described thus far emanates from the Anglo dominant, stereotypes Others and less desirable ingroup Anglos, and promotes an archetypal ideal so exclusive that scarcely anyone can meet it. What I seek to know is a variation of an issue many others have investigated: how does identification work in American cinema? My inquiry will be based on the stereotyping model I have outlined thus far, and can be expressed as follows. If, as I argued in the last section, so few—if any—of us in the audience completely match up with the ideal bourgeois hero and his ideal bourgeois love mate, how is it that we viewers end up identifying with them and broadly subscribing to what they stand for, even overcoming differences in cultural identities?

How it is that I, a Mexican American, sided with Indiana Jones at the beginning of *Raiders of the Lost Ark*? Or with Gary Cooper's marshal Will Kane the first time I saw *High Noon* (1952) as a child, rather than with the character of Helen Ramírez, played by Mexican actress Katy Jurado? To cite another example, how is it that a colleague of mine, who is Puerto Rican and grew up in New York, after seeing *West Side Story* as a young boy, identified with the Jets (the Anglo gang), not the Sharks (the Puerto Rican gang)? Broadening the inquiry further, we might well ask why Hollywood films that so blatantly denigrate Third World peoples are often such big box office hits in the Third World.

As we have seen, this happens in part because Hollywood deploys the techniques of the dominant narrative paradigm so expertly. But those cinematic strategies operate at the production end and are part of the encoding that takes place on the sender's side of media transmission. What I will now theorize is how receivers decode the film and thereby complete the stereotyping process. To discuss how movie viewers read the archetype and the in-group and out-group stereotypes presented to them, I will employ a theory advanced by psychotherapist Murray Bowen, who has developed it to explain the interaction of the nuclear family. I have chosen this non-Freudian approach because it is commonsensical, corresponds to lived experience, and has significant explanatory power.

Bowen's family systems theory is a new conceptualization of human emotional functioning that, unlike the Freudian paradigm, views "the family as an emotional unity and the individual as part of that unit rather than as an autonomous psychological entity."[9] Building upon psychoanalysis, family systems theory does not forsake the individual but situates it within a more complex family dynamic. Bowen's essential interactive family unit is the triangle: a three-person relationship that is, for Bowen, "a natural way of being for people."[10] There are as many triangles in a family as required to include all the members in all possible triad combinations. In a small family, for example, of two parents and two children there are four triangles; a family of five has ten. The triangles are interconnected and interactive, creating a familial emotional web; each triangle and its members affect the other triangles and their individual members in a number of ways.

The major factor affecting a triangle is anxiety. When the anxiety level is high enough, two powerful family members, in order to reduce their anxiety and insecurity, pick a defect in a third person and position the third as deficient.[11] Forming such a triangle with two positive sides against a negative one, where two parties have reached an agreement about another, describes the process of triangling:

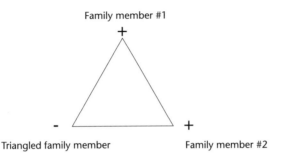

Family member #1

Triangled family member

Family member #2

Bowen extends his theory beyond the nuclear family to consider the same process at work among individuals and groups. Since the essential elements of triangling are three people and anxiety, it can occur in any social situation. "Two people," he says, "get together and enhance their functioning at the expense of the third, the 'scapegoated' one." [12] For instance, Bowen describes a case of triangling taking the form of workplace gossip wherein two workers talked about an absent third:

> This mechanism conveys, "We understand each other perfectly (the togetherness side of the triangle). We are in agreement about that pathological third person." At social gatherings people would clump in small groups, each talking about someone outside that clump, and each apparently unaware that all the clumps were doing the same "triangling" gossip about them. [13]

On a broader scale, Bowen hypothesizes that societal scapegoats are vulnerable minority groups, particularly Blacks, though he does not elaborate on this point. [14] Even so, a fuller articulation of how scapegoating might operate as social triangling might be explained in the following way.

Scapegoating and the Ideology of Social Triangling

Based on Bowen's theory, we can begin sketching in the elements of social triangling, whereby two groups become allies against a targeted third:

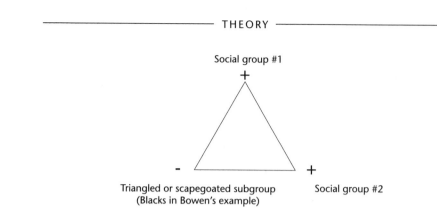

Social group #1

Triangled or scapegoated subgroup   Social group #2
(Blacks in Bowen's example)

Using the terminology I have employed, Bowen's social triangle consists of the dominant in-group at the top, positive point and the targeted out-group subgroup (Blacks in this case) at the negative point. At the second positive point are the remaining out-group subgroups (the other minorities), who for the moment are not being scapegoated:

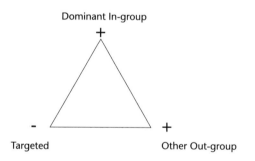

Dominant In-group

Targeted   Other Out-group

In Bowen's view, the Anglo dominant in-group pitted itself against the scapegoated Black subgroup. The most comfortable choice for the remaining minorities (immigrants, ethnics, poor whites, and so on) was to position themselves at the remaining positive corner, siding with the Anglo dominant against the Blacks. Through this process of stigmatizing and consequently stereotyping Blacks, the Anglo dominant and the "positive" minority groups said to one another, "We are in agreement about that pathological Other (Black) group." Using this model, then, stereotyping is an ideological game of odd man out: the dominant builds a coalition with out-group subgroups against the stigmatized Other.

Let me refine this model in two important ways. First, as we saw in the previous chapter, stereotyping is a social process in continuous flux. Many groups are stereotyped, both over time (diachronically) and contemporaneously (synchronically). Because of that, it is probably more accurate to say that specific Other groups rotate in and out of targeted stereotyping, depending on social, economic, and political conditions. What this suggests, however, is that when a group is not being actively scapegoated, its members are presented with an exacting Hobson's choice: align themselves with the dominant against the current scapegoat or remain stigmatized at the negative end of the social pyramid. Thus the stereotyped role passes among out-group Others. One after another the various subgroups are temporarily aligned with the dominant against the targeted subgroup, until they themselves take their turn as the object of social stigmatization.

The second point is based on the fact that, as we discussed in Chapter 1, very few can completely adhere to all the tenets of the dominant ideology or to the dominant's idealized definition of itself. Thus various in-group subgroups are marginalized, finding themselves outside the dominant, relegated to the second positive point of the triangle, along with Others from the out-group. What this recognizes is a hierarchy of Otherness, with in-group Others higher in the pecking order and out-group Others lower. A more accurate triangle of social stigmatization would look like this:

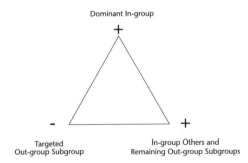

The dominant class maintains its position of power by social cooptation: it instigates a series of allegiances with disenfranchised out-groups and imperfect members of the in-group. All those not conforming with the dominant ideal oscillate back and forth between positions where their difference is targeted then temporarily ignored while another's is focused on. Thus Others (both in-group and out-group) are sometimes stigmatized and estranged from the dominant, but sometimes allied with the dominant in a placating arrangement.

The Triangled Viewer

Let us now see how this triangling process might operate in the case of stereotyping in Hollywood cinema, and particularly how it applies to individual movie viewers. My hypothesis is that a viewer watching a Hollywood film is invited to enter and complete a triangle and asked to take sides. From Bowen's perspective, the classical Hollywood film sets up a stereotyping triangle with the dominant ideal—the archetype protagonist—at its positive apex, the stereotype in the negative corner, and the viewer as the third—and ostensibly neutral—point of the triangle:

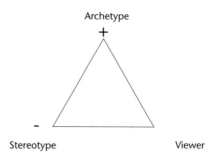

At the movies, the viewer in effect enters a force field and is prompted to take sides—either the hero's or the other character's (it may be a stereotyped Other or, in fact, any character). The viewer thus chooses a point of the triangle to identify with, one with which she has the most in common, one with which she can feel the most comfortable, the one about which she can say, "We understand each other perfectly." Because Hollywood does such a superb job of cinematically stacking the deck in favor of the dominant's hero, it is usually difficult for the viewer to identify—to align oneself emotionally—with anyone Other than the archetype. Usually, the easiest way for the viewer to enter and complete the movie-watching triangle is by becoming the second positive point:

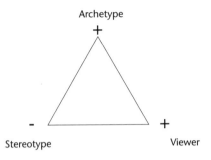

In any given film, a choice between hero and stereotype is offered the viewer, and the viewer makes a decision each time the archetype is confronted or juxtaposed with any character. This is very clearly seen in the opening from *Raiders of the Lost Ark*. Each time the film sets up a relationship between Indiana Jones and a Hispanic man, we can see why most audience members would dutifully, "naturally"—and well-nigh effortlessly—complete the triangle by taking the positive point against the Hispanic stereotype. This triangled identification with the hero is also likely to occur when Indy confronts Belloq the villain. It even happens with Jock, the bewildered seaplane pilot, who is an in-group stereotype: the slow-witted assistant. This triangling of the viewer happens throughout *Raiders of the Lost Ark,* and throughout, I suggest, most Hollywood films. Siding with the archetype is not the only option open to viewers, and not every viewer takes it every time it presents itself, but Hollywood narratives are constructed to draw viewers into the stereotyping triangle in a way that aligns them with the Anglo dominant via its bourgeois hero.

We can further hypothesize the reasons that viewers identify with the hero. First of all, it is because of the efficient workings of the Hollywood paradigm, which deploys a host of cinematic effects to ensure that they do. Second, identification is facilitated because of the archetype's attractive heroic qualities (bravery, daring, composure, intelligence, experience—for example, the knowledge that allows Indy to enter the throne room unarmed and exit unharmed) and physical skills (in Indy's case his dexterity, his expertise with a whip), valued attributes that define heroes in many cultures. And finally, identification is facilitated when view-

ers feel some kinship with him. Initially, as with the very beginning of
Raiders of the Lost Ark, an affiliation between viewer and archetype will
probably be based on gross phenotypical and cultural similarities—skin
color, language, nationality, temperament. Later, as we get to know Indiana Jones better, we may find deeper shared qualities, such as morals
and values. And the more of these that are shared, the easier viewer identification becomes.

Conversely, when a viewer shares few similarities with the hero,
identification can be problematic or rejected altogether. African Americans, for example, might have difficulty identifying with a white hero.
Japanese could have trouble identifying with an American. Chinese
communists could refuse to side with a fair-skinned, English-speaking,
American capitalist hero. To some extent, these difficulties might be
overridden by the genius of Hollywood's stereotyping system, which
seamlessly combines a disdainful view of the Other with the language
of film.

The other factor that works on such potentially contrarian viewers,
and might enable them still to identify with the hero and enjoy the pleasures of the Hollywood narrative, is the process of triangling. Triangling
helps ensure that the maximum number of viewers are fused (Bowen's
term for entering a triangle) into the narrative in the "right" way—*pro*
the Anglo dominant and *contra* the Other. This is the most comfortable
choice to take. In fact, by narrowing the viewer's options to only two—
hero or villain—triangling forces the issue. The viewer's choices boil
then down to the following:

1. Choose to side with the archetype, suspending other differences between self and hero, and partake in the formidable pleasures the narrative has to offer (riding to the rescue with Indiana
Jones—and on a white horse yet!—and saving the world from
Nazism).

2. Choose to side with the minor characters, in-group and out-
group stereotypes, which, as presented in most Hollywood films,
is an unpleasant prospect at best. And, in narrative terms, a difficult choice to select and sustain. One can imagine the tension
the triangling decision presents to Other viewers, with their root
culture pulling them in one direction and the mainstream culture,
the sweep of the narrative, and Hollywood's stereotyping poetics
all pulling in another. But one can understand why they make it
(who wants to root against the hero?).

3. Reject the proffered pleasures of the narrative. This could be something as simple as leaving the theater (after asking for your money back, of course). But it might also include what I hope readers of this book will be spurred to do, namely opt for "Other" pleasures such as analyzing the dominant ideology's demands for social conformity as filtered through Hollywood stereotyping.

THREE

A CRASH COURSE
ON HOLLYWOOD'S
LATINO IMAGERY

The history of Latino images in U.S. cinema is in large measure a pageant of six basic stereotypes: *el bandido,* the harlot, the male buffoon, the female clown, the Latin lover, and the dark lady. Sometimes the stereotypes were combined, sometimes they were altered superficially, but their core defining—and demeaning—characteristics have remained consistent for more than a century and are still evident today. But there have also been exceptions to this rule: studio-made films that went against the stereotyping grain, stars who managed to portray Latinos with integrity despite a filmmaking system heavily reliant on stereotyping, and, more recently, a growing number of Latino filmmakers who began consciously breaking with the stereotyping paradigm of classical Hollywood.

This chapter provides a broad overview of Latino images in mainstream Hollywood film, delineating the main currents of representation, beginning with Hollywood's sadly routine stereotyping. I then discuss instances of resistance within the Hollywood paradigm, by non-Latino filmmakers to show that the history of Latino representation has not been entirely one-sided, something I will pick up on later in the book, in the chapter on John Ford's Westerns.

Our starting point is an introduction to the narrative and cultural logic of Hollywood's filmmaking and storytelling paradigm, the narrative context necessary to fully appreciate Hollywood's Latino imagery, in both its predominantly denigrating and occasionally more positive aspects.

THE CULTURAL AND NARRATIVE DYNAMICS
OF HOLLYWOOD CINEMA

The stereotyping of U.S. Latinos and Latin Americans, and the defamatory stereotyping of many other socially marginalized groups (gays, Native Americans, African Americans, Asians and Asian Americans, the working class, the poor, immigrants, women, and so forth), is largely a result of entrenched Hollywood storytelling conventions. If one of the distinguishing features of the Hollywood cinema is its goal-oriented protagonist, we can say with a high degree of certainty that, sociologically speaking, that goal-driven hero will be a white, handsome, middle-aged, upper-middle-class, heterosexual, Protestant, Anglo-Saxon male.

This great white hero is the sun around which the film narrative revolves, and the rationale of a typical Hollywood story is to illustrate how moral, resourceful, brave, intelligent—in a word, *superior*—he is. It follows that the rest of the characters must necessarily be shown to be *inferior* in various ways and to varying degrees. In order to prop the protagonist up, characters of cultural/ethnic/racial/class backgrounds different from the hero's are therefore generally assigned sundry minor roles: villains, sidekicks, temptresses, the "other man." Their main function is to provide opportunities for the protagonist to display his absolute moral, physical, and intellectual preeminence.

The standard Hollywood story featuring this WASP male hero is, as I've said earlier, a formulaic narrative that proceeds from equilibrium (a tranquil status quo) to disruption (a threat to the status quo) to the ultimate restoration of the status quo (the Hollywood happy ending). Looking at this narrative framework culturally, however, one sees it in a slightly different light. The status quo posited in the movies as the best of all worlds is one that is safe, peaceful, and prosperous. But it is also one that is white, upper-middle-class, Protestant, English-speaking, one that conforms to Anglo norms of beauty, health, intelligence, and so forth. This WASP way of life is asserted as a norm worth fighting for, as what must be regained if the film is to deliver its happy ending. In such a scheme, not just Latinos but all people of color represent an inherent threat to the status quo simply because they are markedly different from the established WASP norm.

THE SIX LATINO STEREOTYPES

The following Latino stereotypes exist within this moviemaking paradigm, and are part of its storytelling conventions;[1] they are the most commonly seen Latino stereotypes that have appeared in the first century of Hollywood cinema.

\ El Bandido

This stereotypical character is, most familiarly, the Mexican bandit in countless Westerns and adventure films. His roots go back to the villains of the silent "greaser" films (for example, *Broncho Billy and the Greaser*, 1914) but his appearance continues in a long list of Westerns and adventure films (for instance, the two guides who betray Indiana Jones at the beginning of *Raiders of the Lost Ark* [1979], and the demented antagonist [Manuel Ojeda] who pursues Joan Wilder [Kathleen Turner] in *Romancing the Stone* [1984]). *El bandido* is dirty and unkempt, usually displaying an unshaven face, missing teeth, and disheveled, oily hair. Scars and scowls complete the easily recognizable image. Behaviorally, he is vicious, cruel, treacherous, shifty, and dishonest; psychologically, he is irrational, overly emotional, and quick to resort to violence. His inability to speak English or his speaking English with a heavy Spanish accent is Hollywood's way of signaling his feeble intellect, a lack of brainpower that makes it impossible for him to plan or strategize successfully.

Though the Western genre is far past its heyday, *el bandido* lives on in contemporary Hollywood films in two incarnations. The first is the Latin American gangster/drug runner, such as Andy Garcia's sadistic Cuban-American gangster in *Eight Million Ways to Die* (1986), Al Pacino's mobster in *Scarface* (1983), and Joaquim de Almeida in both *Clear and Present Danger* (1994) and *Desperado* (1995). He is slicker, of course, and he has traded in his black hat for a white suit, his tired horse for a glitzy car, but he still ruthlessly pursues his vulgar cravings—for money, power, and sexual pleasure—and routinely employs vicious and illegal means to obtain them.

A second *bandido* variant, as discussed in the preceding chapter, is the inner-city gang member seen in numerous urban thrillers and crime dramas. If the story takes place in New York, he is the volatile Puerto Rican (the toughs in *The Young Savages* [1961] and *Badge 373* [1973]); if in Southern California, he is the East L.A. homeboy (the gang mem-

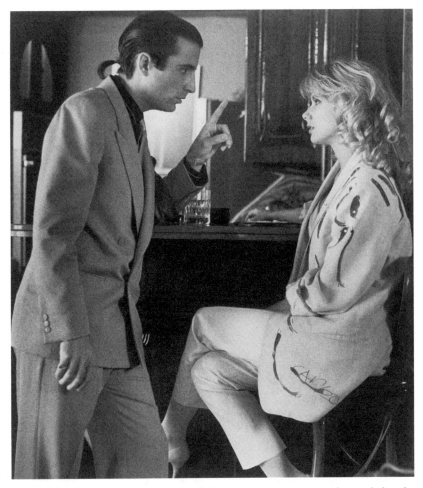

Angel (Andy Garcia) warning Sarah (Rosanna Arquette) that being disloyal to him can be lethal in 8 Million Ways to Die *(1986). Though the external details have changed—he is well groomed and impeccably dressed— behaviorally Angel remains essentially the same familiar vicious, violent, criminal* bandido. *(Photo courtesy of Luis Reyes Archives)*

bers in *Colors* [1988], the two hoods who taunt D-FENS [Michael Douglas] in *Falling Down* [1993]). As I've argued in Chapter 2, both the drug runner and the East L.A. gangsta make only superficial changes to the external details of the stereotype; at their core these characters are the same inarticulate, violent, and pathologically dangerous *bandidos*.

Chihuahua (Linda Darnell), the classic Latina harlot stereotype, in John Ford's
My Darling Clementine *(1946). (Photo courtesy of Luis Reyes Archives)*

The Harlot

The female stereotype corresponding to *el bandido* is a stock figure in
the American cinema, particularly in Westerns. Like the bandit, she is a
secondary character, lusty and hot-tempered. Doc Holliday's woman,
Chihuahua (Linda Darnell), in John Ford's *My Darling Clementine*
(1946) is an archetypal example of this type. Without a man she is a
leaf in the wind, so when Doc (Victor Mature) is out of town, she fixes
her amorous attentions on Wyatt Earp (Henry Fonda). When Earp, decent WASP hero that he is, ignores her flirtations, she responds the only
way she can: by helping a cardsharp cheat Earp during a poker game to
get even.

Angelica (Jacqueline Obradors) in Six Days, Seven Nights *(1998), an interesting combination of the harlot and female clown stereotypes. Here she performs a seductive, erotic dance.*

Since the harlot is a slave to her passions, her conduct is simplistically attributed to her inherent nymphomania. In true stereotypical fashion we are never provided with any deeper motivation for her actions—she is basically a sex machine innately lusting for a white male. A notable recent example is the character of Angelica (Jacqueline Obradors) in *Six Days, Seven Nights* (1998). She is the traveling companion of a small-time airplane pilot, Quinn Harris (Harrison Ford), and obviously romantically involved with him. But as soon as he leaves her at an island resort on some business, she has no qualms about sleeping with the nearest available Anglo, Frank Martin (David Schwimmer). Angelica is an interesting example of a stereotyping blend, exhibiting characteristics of the harlot and the female buffoon, and I will discuss her and the film in more detail below.

3 The Male Buffoon

Serving as second-banana comic relief, classic male buffoons from television include Pancho (Leo Carrillo) in "The Cisco Kid," Sergeant Garcia in Walt Disney's "Zorro" series, Ricky Ricardo (Desi Arnaz) in "I Love Lucy." In films, the classic example is Chris-Pin Martin's sidekick character, Gordito, in the Cisco Kid series (*The Cisco Kid* [1931], *Return of the Cisco Kid* [1939], *Viva Cisco Kid* [1940], *Lucky Cisco Kid* [1940], *The Gay Caballero* [1940], *Cisco Kid and the Lady* [1940], *Romance of the Rio Grande* [1941], *Ride on Vaquero* [1941]). What is funny about this character, what audiences are given to laugh at, are the

The Latino male buffoon stereotype: Alfonso Arau as the Colombian drug smuggler in Romancing the Stone *(1984), with Kathleen Turner and Michael Douglas. (Photo courtesy of Luis Reyes Archives)*

very characteristics that separate him from Hollywood's vision of the WASP American mainstream. For example, he is simpleminded (the bumbling antics of Gordito or Sergeant Garcia), he cannot master standard English (Gordito's trademark phrase, "I tink," ["I think"], in the film versions of the Cisco Kid; Leo Carillo's "Let's went, Cisco!" in the television series; and Ricky's "Lucy, you got some 'splainin' to do!"), and he childishly regresses into emotionality (Ricky's explosions into Spanish).

In the 1980s the Mexican comic actor and director Alfonso Arau (*Like Water for Chocolate* [1992]; *A Walk in the Clouds* [1995]) played two roles based on this type: the romance novel–reading Colombian gangster in *Romancing the Stone* (1983) and the bandit leader El Guapo in *The Three Amigos!* (1986). Are these male buffoon stereotypes? One thing in their favor as nonstereotypes is that at the very least, a Latino is playing a Latin character. Another is that Arau is obviously throwing himself into these roles with great gusto. It could be argued that these are parodies of the stereotype, and healthy in breaking down stereotypical representations. But another view might question whether *any* use of such an oft-repeated and well-known comic stereotype—given the history of Latino images in Hollywood film—can exist without in some ways serving to reinforce it.

One way to check for stereotypes in a case like this is to perform what I call the "stereotype commutation test."[2] Try to substitute another ethnicity into the role being analyzed. If the part can be played just as well as another ethnic, national, or, for that matter, gender group, then it is probably not a stereotype, but rather a stock comic or dramatic type (the jealous husband, the flirtatious wife, the deceptive best friend, and so forth). If no other ethnicity can be readily substituted for the role, then chances are that it relies on specific stereotypical traits of a particular cultural group to make its comedic or dramatic impact. In these roles played by Arau, the former is specifically a Colombian drug runner, the latter a Mexican bandit, and it is impossible to replace those parts with any other ethnicity. Arau's drug kingpin in *Romancing the Stone* plays on the typical Colombian drug lord, a modern variant of the *bandido* stereotype, and the joke is that he reads romance novels. Similarly in *The Three Amigos!* the joke is that a familiar stereotype of countless Westerns—(stereo)typically crude and ignorant—knows the word "plethora" and can use it in a sentence. Both cases, it seems to me, rely on recognition of the stereotype to get their laughs. In essence, it's simply Hollywood making an old stereotype fresh again by making him a comic version of classic screen *bandidos*.

The Female Clown

The female clown is the comic counterpart of the Latino male buffoon and, like the harlot, exemplifies a common device that the Hollywood narrative employs to neutralize the screen Latina's sexuality. This is a necessary requirement because the hero must have a reason to reject the Latina in favor of the Anglo woman, thereby maintaining the WASP status quo. For that to occur, the Latina's sexual allure must somehow be negated. Generally, her character is sullied (she is made promiscuous and criminal, as is the case with the harlot stereotype) or ridiculed (portrayed as sexually "easy" or simply silly and comical, as with the female buffoon).

This is exactly what happens in *Six Days, Seven Nights*. The romance that Quinn, Harrison Ford's scruffy and ultimately noble and heroic pilot, has with the WASP leading lady, Robin Monroe (Anne Heche), perfectly conforms with Hollywood's storytelling logic. It also illustrates how Hollywood narratives, through the romances they depict, often en-

The romantic dynamics in Six Days, Seven Nights *illustrate well the narrative uses of stereotyping. Stranded on a desert island, the Anglo leads, Robin (Anne Heche) and Quinn (Harrison Ford), gradually fall in love, though they each have a romantic partner back at the resort. They can do so without tarnishing their morality for two reasons. First, because they never consummate their relationship . . .*

dorse a subtle kind of racial purity, saying, in effect, that Anglos should mate only with their own kind. The film's narrative does this by demonstrating to the audience that Angelica, Quinn's Latin bombshell of a girlfriend, is promiscuous. Making things even worse is the fact that the man she seduces, on her first night without Quinn, is Robin's fiancé, Frank (David Schwimmer). Quinn, however, is unaware of this, since he and Robin are stranded on a deserted island and their radio is broken. But because he has been betrayed, viewers are able to perceive him a free romantic agent. He may not know what Angelica has done, but the movie goes to pains to make sure the audience knows. This allows Quinn to pursue Robin and still adhere to the moral norms required of Hollywood's protagonists. According to the logic of Hollywood, then, he is not really unfaithful since Angelica was unfaithful *first*.

In contrast, Angelica's sleeping with Frank, the secondary Anglo male character, is framed as casual sex and paints her as sexually frivolous. Furthermore, Frank's infidelity with a Latina provides the reason why he is no longer worthy of Robin. Quinn's falling for the WASP woman, Robin, however, is "more serious," developing into "the real thing," that is, "true love"—as opposed to the fling he was obviously having with Angelica. It's one more illustration of Latino stereotypes being used to demonstrate the moral rectitude of Hollywood's WASP film heroes. Though Anglo heroes are tempted by and may have sexual di-

. . . and second, because back at the tropical resort, Quinn's partner, the clownish temptress Angelica, seduces Robin's weak-willed fiancé, Frank (David Schwimmer), thereby economically but stereotypically demonstrating their moral inferiority and unworthiness as suitable mates.

versions with Latinas, they can still "redeem" themselves from this moral and racial transgression if in the end they (1) reject the Latina and (2) are faithful in their "important," i.e., Anglo, relationship.[3]

The antecedents of Angelica's female buffoon stretch back to the golden age of the studio system. One might say that the striking Mexican actress Lupe Vélez, a comic star working in Hollywood from the late 1920s to the early 1940s, is a classic female clown. Vélez is best known for her role as the ditzy "Mexican Spitfire" in a series of eight films, though she also starred in a number of other comedies and melodramas. While she is seemingly caught in the stereotype, especially in the "Mexican Spitfire" films, I will later show that Vélez found ways to subvert it.

A better example is another well-known female clown, Carmen Miranda, who provided colorful portrayals of Latin American women in numerous films in the 1940s. What is operative in Miranda's case is exaggeration to the point of caricature, another way to elicit derisive laughter and belittle the Latina Other. Miranda's multicolored costumes and fruit-covered hats donned to perform splashy "Latin" musical numbers (most notoriously "The Lady in the Tutti-Frutti Hat" number from Busby Berkeley's *The Gang's All Here* [1943]) instantly mocked the folkloric costumes—and customs—of Brazil and Latin America in general. This tradition of the exotic, comical, and oversexed Latina showbiz performer lives on with Angelica in *Six Days, Seven Nights*, a dancer whose Latin exoticism and eroticism are once again played for laughs.

 The Latin Lover

The origin of this male stereotype can be traced to one star: Rudolph Valentino. An Italian immigrant, by 1921 he had worked his way up from minor movie parts to a starring role as the protagonist in *The Four Horsemen of the Apocalypse,* a story of the effect of World War I on young Argentinean men. In a famous scene, Valentino dances seductively with a cantina woman (again, the barroom harlot) and finishes by almost kissing her but suddenly flinging her to the ground instead. With this and other of his film roles as the dashing and magnetic male Other (in *The Sheik* [1921], *Son of the Sheik* [1926], and as the rising bull-fighter in *Blood and Sand* [1922]), he defined a new kind of screen lover. Valentino's smoldering presence in these films created the basis for the Latin lover as the possessor of a primal sexuality that made him capable of making a sensuous but dangerous—and clearly non-WASP—brand of love.

Since then, the Latin lover has been a continual screen character, played by a number of Latin actors, for example, Ricardo Montalbán (most notoriously in a film called *Latin Lovers* [1953]) and occasionally Gilbert Roland (as an Italian Latin Lover in *The Racers* [1955]) to Antonio Banderas in films like *Never Talk to Strangers* (1995). In these roles, the actors haplessly reiterate the erotic combination of characteristics instituted by Valentino: eroticism, exoticism, tenderness tinged with violence and danger, all adding up to the romantic promise that, sexually, things could very well get out of control.

The Dark Lady

The female Latin lover is virginal, inscrutable, aristocratic—and erotically appealing precisely because of these characteristics. Her cool distance is what makes her fascinating to Anglo males. In comparison with the Anglo woman, she is circumspect and aloof where her Anglo sister is direct and forthright, reserved where the Anglo female is boisterous, opaque where the Anglo woman is transparent. The characters Mexican actress Dolores Del Río played in a number of Hollywood films in the 1930s and early 1940s exemplified this stereotype well. In both *Flying Down to Río* (1933) and *In Caliente* (1935), for example, she played fascinating Latin women who aroused the American leading men's amorous appetites the way no Anglo woman could.

A contemporary incarnation of the dark lady is María Conchita Alonso's character in *Colors* (1988), another stereotype blend. She is the

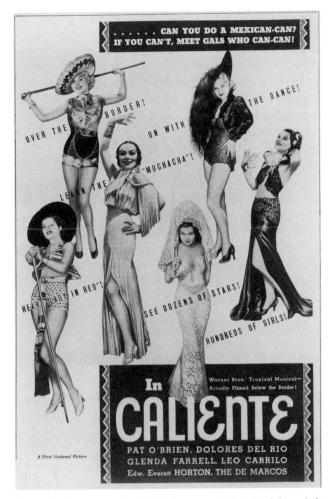

An ad for In Caliente *(1935) with Dolores Del Río (third from left) as the dark lady. In contrast with the Anglo women surrounding her in the ad (and in the film), who often wear more revealing clothes and are more blatantly sexual, the dark lady combines sex appeal with reserve. (Photo courtesy of Luis Reyes Archives)*

dark lady for the first half of the film (where she is the love interest for Sean Penn's Anglo cop), then suddenly reverts to the harlot (when she becomes the mistress of one of the gang leaders to spite the cop and to demonstrate how little he understands the realities of the barrio). According to Hollywood, then, beneath every Latino is a savage, a Latin lover, or both, and at heart every Latina is a Jezebel.

BUCKING THE PARADIGM AND COUNTERING IMAGES

Although the vast majority of Hollywood films have utilized these stereotypes when Latinos were portrayed, Hollywood cinema is not as simple, static, or ideologically one-sided as *that*. To begin with, as I mentioned in Chapter 1, many films were ideologically conflicted when it came to their Latino images, vacillating between negative portrayals and stereotypical idealization. And some films did at times arrive at more enlightened imagery. Then there were filmmakers who contested the simplifications of Hollywood's filmmaking conventions, for either aesthetic or ideological reasons. And there were also Latino actors who subverted or resisted stereotyping in their performances. It is important to acknowledge the progressive imagery of the conflicted films, as it is to remember the contestational films. First, out of historical fairness and critical evenhandedness, and second, to counter the claim that it is impossible for Hollywood filmmaking to break with stereotypes or avoid them altogether.

This more comprehensive view of Hollywood cinema history reveals that, besides the familiar Latino stereotypes, there are five categories of films that feature Latino counter-stereotypes:

1. those that were conflicted, partly stereotypical and partly progressive;

2. those that departed from the dominant filmmaking paradigm, sometimes simply by casting Latino actors to play Latinos;

3. those that were ideologically oppositional;

4. those in which Latino actors subverted the stereotypes; and, finally and most recently,

5. those made by Latino filmmakers whose project was overtly, or, in the case of filmmakers like Cheech Marin and Robert Rodríguez in *El Mariachi*, covertly, to counter Hollywood pattern of Latino imagery.

I will discuss the first three in the remainder of this chapter, and the fourth, acting subversions, in Chapter 4. The final category, those films made by Latinos, I introduce and discuss in Part 3.

Progressive Images from Conflicted Ideology

Much film criticism of the last two decades has been based on the notion of the incoherent text, positing the contradictory nature of dominant cinema that resulted in many Hollywood films' running the ideological gamut from conservative to progressive. Consequently, it should not be surprising that this conflicted pattern holds true when it comes to stereotyping. A good example is a film like *Flying Down to Rio*, which, although producing the prototypical dark lady stereotype and stereotyping Latinos (and people of color) in other ways, still exhibits a number of impressively progressive elements.

Among the more obvious stereotypical images is the already mentioned dark lady, Belinha de Rezende (Dolores Del Río) who is fetishized as a highly charged, sexually mysterious feminine ideal—and thereby marked as Other. An American blonde sitting at Belinha's nightclub table in an early scene in the film utters a double entendre that expresses the stereotypical thinking about the dark lady (and the Latin lover, for that matter) perfectly. When the rich, handsome, and available band leader, Roger Bond (Gene Raymond), only has eyes for Belinha and eventually temporarily abandons the conducting of his orchestra so that he can dance with her, the blonde wonders aloud: "What have these South Americans got below the equator that we ain't got?" Furthermore, in later scenes Belinha reveals a sexual passion smoldering beneath her surface reserve, Hollywood again resorting to the stereotypical pattern that every Latina is at heart a vixen. When she's stranded on a deserted beach with Roger, the film displays her two sides, the restrained woman and the libertine, arguing about her true desires. "After all," her good side says, "I must keep my reserve." To which her "dark" side replies, "You and your reserve. If people knew you as I do, they would be shocked."

In order for the dark lady to be a suitable object of Roger's desire, she is propped up while the other major female character, Honey Hale (Ginger Rogers), is put down, stereotyped as the easy blonde. Honey is the sassy singer for Roger's band, the Yankee Clippers, and is the North American female contrast to Belinha's Latin American dark lady. Honey is casual and uninhibited, and Belinha is formal and restrained. One indicator of Honey's character is her costume. The dress she wears when she sings her solo musical number, "Music Makes Me," early in the film, is dark and sheer, revealing her arms and legs. It contrasts with Belinha's white dress in the same scene, which is white and buttoned up at the neck, where it too is diaphanous and reveals her shoulders.

Further evidence of Honey's promiscuity can be found in the lyrics of the song she sings, which proclaim her cheery nymphomania, specifically that she is unable to control herself sexually at the sound of music:

> I like music old and new
> But music makes me do
> The things I never should do.
> I like music sweet and blue,
> But music makes me do
> The things I never should do.
>
> My self-control was something to brag about,
> Now it's a gag about town.
> The things I do are never forgiven,
> And just when I'm livin' 'em down,
> I hear music, then I'm through,
> 'Cause music makes me do
> The things I never should do.

Clearly a sexual free spirit, and therefore morally unsuitable for Roger, the WASP lady-killer of a leading man, Honey is thus relegated to the narrative's second-string romance, with Roger's assistant, Fred (Fred Astaire). This is formalized in the narrative when they team up for the next dance number, "The Carioca" (the musical number that marked the beginning of the legendary Astaire-Rogers partnership).

Another Latino stereotype in the film is the male buffoon, in the person of the Brazilian nightclub manager who mispronounces "Schenectady" and "Syracuse," and calls Roger's band "the Yankee Clippings." But beyond the presentation of standard Latino stereotypes, the film exhibits another kind of stereotyping by illustrating a sort of cultural sexuality gradient in the ten-minute-long "Carioca" production number. As the number develops, a series of groups perform the mildly suggestive dance, in which partners dance provocatively while touching foreheads. The dancing becomes more sensuous and erotic as the performers' skin color darkens. The first wave of well-heeled, fair-skinned patrons gives way to Brazilian dancers in their folk costumes, and then, finally, to black dancers, who are the most overtly sexual of all, thrusting their pelvises to the music's rhythms. Interspersed are a couple of sophisticated Astaire-Rogers renditions, executed with the grace and fluidity that came to characterize the duo's routines.

In sum, the "Carioca" provides a graphic, skin-color-coded demonstration of the allowable standards and practices of sexual expression in pre-Code Hollywood cinema. The Astaire-Rogers WASP version is the most inhibited and reserved, sexually abstract in its smooth elegance. The Brazilian elites are more sensual, the folk dancers more primitive, and the blacks the most erotically explicit. This American-white-to-Third-World-black sexual spectrum stereotypically marks people of color as different in sexual norms. And, because Hollywood films generally equate variances from American sexual mores as signs of moral turpitude, the dance number also comments negatively on the Latin Americans' moral values.

On the progressive side of the ledger, however, there are a number of noteworthy elements in *Flying Down to Rio*. The first is the use of an effective anti-stereotyping technique I call "stereotypical reversal," invalidating a known stereotype in an interesting and unexpected way. For example, when Roger and Belinha are stranded on the island, they are confronted by a bare-chested black man. Roger and Belinha (and we viewers too) read this movie situation as Hollywood has prepared us to, that is, stereotypically. As I said in Chapter 2, away from the Western metropolis, the male of color represents danger. So, given the conventions of American filmmaking, in this particular case it is not unlikely that the Black man might well belong to a tribe of African savages, headhunters, or cannibals. A moment later, however, when the man actually steps away from the bush, he's wearing slacks and golf shoes, is carrying a golf bag, and speaks with a British accent. It turns out that Roger and Belinha have landed in Haiti, right next to a country club. The Black man is playing a round of golf and is looking for his lost ball.

Another example of stereotypical reversal occurs at the beginning of the Carioca. The native Brazilian band at first consists of a handful of sleeping musicians—the stereotypical lazy Latinos. Sizing up their musical competition, Roger's Yankee Clippers figure they'll be a cinch to succeed in Rio de Janeiro. When the Brazilians are asked to play, though, they suddenly come to life, are joined by a number of other musicians, and in the blink of an eye a full orchestra is playing and the joint is jumpin'. In this and in the previous example, we can see that stereotypical reversal works so well because it is based on the shared knowledge of the stereotype (by the filmmakers, the characters in the film, and the film viewers). Once the reversal occurs, characters (and, more important, viewers) are brought up short, and the stereotype is effectively deconstructed. It is a powerful counter-stereotyping technique because it teaches characters and viewers that easy, stereotypical assessments are unreliable. That lesson may be something that viewers take with them when they leave the theater.

The eventual outcome of the narrative is another interesting progressive component. As I have discussed, the romantic subplot in most Hollywood movies concludes with the WASP hero and the virtuous Anglo woman united in love. So just the fact that *Flying Down to Rio* ends with a bicultural romance (Roger and Belinha about to be married) is notable in itself. But how the narrative arrives at that point is even more fascinating and counter-hegemonic.

As we saw in the case of *Six Days, Seven Nights,* the compulsory pairing of Hollywood's "ultimate couple" requires the elimination of other suitors. In *Flying Down to Rio,* we have seen how Honey was devalued and shunted off to Fred, a supporting male character. Belinha's romantic choices thus boiled down to Roger, the wealthy Anglo bandleader, and a Latino male, her Brazilian fiancé, Julio Ribeiro (Raul Roulien). Typically, Hollywood films either stereotype such a character, in the process making it clear that he and the leading lady are somehow incompatible, or give him a personality flaw (selfishness, for example), a physical impairment (a limp, say), or both. Interestingly, though, Julio is not a Latin lover stereotype, is not portrayed as a bad match, and displays neither psychological nor physical defects. Rather, he is a noble gentleman. He gallantly steps aside and allows Roger to marry Belinha. With the marriage ceremony about to occur onboard an airborne plane, he makes his exit by suddenly parachuting out of the cabin, the action that ends the film.

What's so remarkable about Julio's actions is that in the classical Hollywood cinema, nobility and sacrifice are almost exclusively the WASP hero's attributes. Take the ending of *Casablanca* as an example. Though the conclusion of the film was said to be in doubt throughout the filming, with several endings proposed and considered, in fact the film's now-familiar ending was inevitable given the dynamics of Hollywood's narrative paradigm. Why? Because only the ending that we know, Rick (Humphrey Bogart) sending Ilse (Ingrid Bergman) and her resistance-leader husband (Paul Henreid) off to defeat the Nazis, allowed Rick to be the most complete hero. By striking a blow against the Nazis and sacrificing his love for Ilse in favor of the greater good, Rick becomes Our Hero: more courageous, altruistic and noble than anyone else in the film.

Similarly, in *Flying Down to Rio*'s final scene, Julio is shown to be more noble (and more decisive) than Roger. So rather than presenting a convincing case, as most films do, of how perfectly suited the male and female main characters are for one another, *Flying Down to Rio* instead raises an intriguing question at the end: Did Belinha wind up with the right man?

Another more recent case of an ideologically conflicted film that makes a progressive statement in its casting is *Anaconda* (1997). The film relies on a familiar movie trope dating back at least to the silent adventure film *The Lost World* (1925), which presents Latin America as a treacherous wilderness filled with unimaginable danger. In *The Lost World* it is prehistoric dinosaurs, in *Anaconda*, a giant snake. But Jennifer Lopez's casting in the role of documentary filmmaker Terri Flores does for Latinas in action adventure films what Sigourney Weaver's Ripley did for women in science fiction in *Alien* (1980). Just as Weaver took command of a male genre and thereby forced viewers to reconceptualize it, so too Lopez is a modern-day Latina adventure heroine (following in the footsteps of Lupe Vélez's fearless mountain woman in *The Gaucho* [1927]). With grit and perseverance Terri ultimately triumphs over the gigantic snake, while the handsome, virile Anglo lead, Dr. Steven Cale (Eric Stoltz), who would normally be the take-charge hero of such a film, lies unconscious for half the film. Her heroics, therefore, seriously undermine the entire genre's raison d'être: the ritual commemoration of WASP male heroism in hostile territory (and, ideologically and symbolically, of U.S. imperialism in the Third World).

Latinos Playing Latinos

The second counter-stereotyping instance involves films that deviated from the Hollywood filmmaking paradigm outlined in the previous chapter. The simplest and often most progressive move was an obvious one, yet not a standard practice of classical Hollywood-era moviemaking: the casting of Latinos to play Latinos. I do not want to adopt the essentialist position that holds that only members of a group can play that group. Still, it is generally true that over a century of filmmaking, standard Hollywood casting norms most often called for Anglo actors to play Latinos, usually in brown face and, with the coming of sound, speaking English with a thick Spanish accent (from the silent era's "greaser" bandits to Eli Wallach's *bandido* in *The Magnificent Seven* [1959]). And, I would argue, the representation of Latinos suffered as a consequence. On the other hand, striving for ethnic authenticity in casting makes sense in terms of verisimilitude, and it often has a beneficial side effect on characterization too, allowing for cultural shadings that might not have occurred otherwise.

As I will discuss in Chapter 5, in John Ford's *Fort Apache* (1948) the respected Mexican character actor Miguel Inclán was cast as Cochise, and he speaks Spanish and his *indio* dialect, bringing to his depiction a cultural resonance and authenticity that an Anglo actor would have been hard-pressed to provide. The film also stars Pedro Armendáriz as Sergeant Beaufort, a Mexican American with a heterogeneous ethnic background. Once an officer in the Confederate army, he then acquits himself admirably as a capable frontier soldier, and, because he is Mexican American and speaks Spanish, he is chosen to interpret between the army officer and Cochise. It amounts to probably the most interesting, complex, and fully realized portrayal of a Mexican American in any studio-era film.

Other memorable portrayals due directly to casting decisions include Katy Jurado's Helen Ramírez in *High Noon* (1952) and Anthony Quinn's "Mex" in *The Ox-Bow Incident* (1943), two performances so rich in cultural texture that it's difficult to imagine any Anglo actors playing those roles. A lesser-known but still impressive example is *Crisis* (1950), the story of a couple, Dr. and Mrs. Ferguson (Cary Grant and Paula Raymond), who find themselves caught up in a South American civil war. Director Richard Brooks made what could have been a cardboard view of Latin America three-dimensional by his inspired casting of Latinos in key roles: Puerto Rican–born José Ferrer as the megalomaniacal dictator, Ramón Novarro as his chief military henchman, Antonio Moreno as the dictator's private physician, and Gilbert Roland as a rebel leader.

Its fidelity to casting Latinos as Latinos, in both speaking and bit parts, makes *Crisis* one of the most evenhanded treatments of Latin America in all of studio-era Hollywood cinema. Brooks created a more naturalistic Latin American world than is typically seen in Hollywood cinema by making a simple, commonsensical, but all-too-rare creative decision: to populate his fictional Latin American country with Latinos, rather than Anglo extras in garish costumes and brown face. (For contrast, compare *Crisis* with *Juarez* [1939], in which the title role was played by Paul Muni, Porfirio Díaz by John Garfield, and Anglo character actors played the majority of the other Mexican characters. An even more telling comparison can be made with a film made around the same time as *Crisis, Sombrero,* a 1953 MGM musical melodrama set in Mexico. It surrounded Ricardo Montalbán, who *was* Mexican, with a cast of players such as Cyd Charisse, Pier Angeli, Vittorio Gassman, and Yvonne De Carlo, non-Hispanics all, playing Mexicans.) The cast of *Crisis* is so overwhelmingly Latino that the film might give the impression of being shot on location; in fact, it was shot on the MGM studio back lot.

One reason that the setting in *Crisis* seems more like a foreign country, and less like Hollywood's stereotypical view of Latin America, stems from a fundamental decision that Brooks made when he was writing the script. Brooks's Latin America is one in which the natives speak Spanish fluently as their first language. Rather than appear ignorant or slow-witted because they speak broken English with a thick Spanish accent, these characters speak fluent Spanish to one another, and if their English is poor, they acknowledge that to Dr. Ferguson, just as he readily acknowledges that his Spanish is rudimentary at best. (Indeed, in an interesting linguistic reversal for a Hollywood film, we see—and hear—Dr. Ferguson butchering Spanish.) All of this is a result of casting actors who can speak Spanish fluently, namely Latinos.

One propitious side effect of this enlightened approach to filmmaking is its presentation of a wide range of character types. Typically, the evil Latino antagonist (in this case, Farrago, José Ferrer's nefarious dictator) is a *bandido* variant who is contrasted with the upright Anglo protagonist. Here, Farrago's villainy is offset by Dr. Ferguson (Cary Grant), but his potentially stereotypical traits are diluted by the presence of so many other Latino characters: a revolutionary leader (Gilbert Roland) and his brave band of rebels, a competent physician (Antonio Moreno), a pious priest (Pedro de Cordoba), and a professional musician (Vicente Gómez).

Ideological Opposition

Films in the third, ideologically oppositional, category need not necessarily be radical in content or form; it is enough that they question the status quo, rather than blindly accepting it as the best of all possible worlds. A case in point is John Huston's *The Treasure of the Sierra Madre* (1948), which at first glance may seem to be another Hollywood foray into stereotypical Mexico. After all, its lead bandit character, Gold Hat (Alfonso Bedoya), is the quintessential *bandido,* and he does deliver that classic *bandido* line "Badges, we don't need no stinkin' badges." But Huston's Mexico is more than simply a haven for bandits, and he depicts a fairly broad sampling of Mexican society, from village administrators to Mexican *indios,* most of them played by Mexicans who speak Spanish to one another (Robert Blake's shoeshine boy being the notable exception).

Yet the film's most convincing counter-stereotyping aspect by far is its critique of U.S. imperialism in Mexico, beginning with the American oil company's exploitation of its workers. In this light, the quest of the three prospectors for gold becomes a cautionary tale condemning North American greed for Mexico's natural resources. And in the character of Fred C. Dobbs (Humphrey Bogart), it posits madness as the end point of that greed. In more recent cinema, there are other exposés of U.S. covert Latin American operations in Oliver Stone's *Salvador* (1986) and Roger Spottiswoode's *Under Fire* (1983). Although these films do follow the "WASP adventurer in the Third World" formula, they nevertheless make some pointed critiques of U.S. interference in the internal affairs of Latin American nations.

There have been other forms of resistance to the dominant stereotypical imagery of Latinos. Some Latino actors, even those who worked in the classical studio era, found ways to subvert the system. These forms of subversion and reaction I turn to in Chapter 4. And later Chicano and Latino filmmakers used their anger at Hollywood's Latino stereotypes as the basis for their oppositional aesthetic. This cinematic response I discuss in Part 3.

FOUR

SUBVERSIVE ACTS
Latino Actor Case Studies

I maintain that there have been Latino actors whose performances have managed to resist stereotyping—resisted, that is, as much as they could while being caught in the grip of Hollywood's stereotypical filmmaking conventions. It's a claim that several critics of women actors and performers of color have made over the years.[1] But proving that actors have subverted stereotypes has always been difficult. To begin with, the actor tends to possess the least amount of authorship of any of the key creative artists on a film set. Actors have always been hired hands. In the Hollywood studio era, actors were contracted to studios and assigned to play whatever roles studio executives deemed appropriate. They were even loaned out to other studios like so much chattel. Even today, except for superstars who are able to initiate their own film projects, most actors are still hired by powerful producers, agents, or directors.

For performers of color this lack of power is exacerbated because Hollywood filmmaking has predominantly been a white enterprise. As Angharad Valdivia points out, "individual actors may be of a particular ethnic or racial background," but "they may not necessarily be powerful enough to demand a sensitive portrayal, whatever it may be." Beyond that, there is the crucial issue of casting practices, in which some actors of color may be regarded as not black or Latino enough "according to stereotypes that have become paradigmatic in producers' minds." Finally, "not all actors of a particular ethnic or racial background will necessarily want to deviate from stereotypes or to acknowledge that there are stereotypes!"[2]

Then there is the fact that, as Peter Krämer and Alan Lovell point out, "acting is an elusive art." An actor's performance, they say, consists of:

a large number of actions, gestures, facial and vocal expressions. It's made all the more elusive when the dominant acting convention is a naturalistic one. Viewing a naturalistic performance, it's easy to assume that the gestures, actions, and expressions are the only appropriate ones—anybody would have lit a cigarette at a moment like that! The decisions the actor has made are invisible. Given this, it becomes almost inevitable that the actor disappears into the character or, vice versa, the character disappears into the actor.[3]

Because of this "disappearing act," it is not surprising, as the authors point out, that many purported analyses of film acting are actually discussions of a fictional character, which is created by the screenwriter, rather than the way that character is embodied, which is the work of the actor.[4]

And even when the actor's work *is* focused upon, there is the vexing problem of how to isolate the actor's contribution. After all, the actor is dressed by costumers, coifed by hairstylists, made up by makeup artists, lit by the director of photography, and presumably guided in every shot by the director. In addition, actors speak words written by the screenwriter, and the editor shapes their performances into their ultimate form. Where, then, is one to locate the actor's creative participation?

These questions have understandably stymied critics and stunted the serious analysis of film acting. But there has been a steadily growing body of film criticism that has addressed these very issues in an attempt to define the ways that actors can claim a degree of authorship.[5] An extremely helpful starting point was Richard Dyer's *Stars,* in which Dyer sets about the important work of defining terms. He stipulates that performance "is what the performer does in addition to the actions/functions she or he performs in the plot and lines she or he is given to say. Performance is how the action/function is done, how the lines are said."[6] He then goes on to define, semiotically, the basic performative elements:

> The signs of performance are: facial expression; voice; gestures (principally of hands and arms, but also of any limb, e.g. neck, leg); body posture (how someone is standing or sitting); body movement (movement of the whole body, including how someone stands up or sits down, how they walk, run, etc.).[7]

James Naremore's *Acting in the Cinema* is another key work, and may be seen as a careful elaboration on Dyer's ideas of film performance.[8]

Naremore gives detailed attention to the history of the expressive form we call acting and to the evolution of film acting, and discusses some of its key components: gesture, costume, and makeup.

In the sections that follow, I want to expand on Dyer's and Naremore's ideas and, by applying them to Latino film actors, to argue that there were specific actors who subverted the stereotyping system *by their acting*. In analyzing the work of three well-known Latino actors— Lupe Vélez, Gilbert Roland, and José Ferrer—I intentionally focus on films in which the roles these stars were given to play were, as written, stereotypical, or at least potentially so, and would very possibly have been so in the hands of less skillful actors. Furthermore, it would have been extremely difficult to avoid the stereotype had non-Latinos played their roles, since, at least in the cases of Lupe Vélez and José Ferrer, their fluency in Spanish is crucial to their performances. I hope to show that the acting choices they made resulted in performances that succeeded in thwarting Hollywood's stereotyping poetics and transcending stereotypes.

The basis of my argument goes back to the claim I made in Chapter 1, that the antidote to stereotyping is knowledge, that is, information. In social stereotyping, the more the in-group knows about the Other, the less accurate they will find the maligning stereotype to be. A stereotype's usage declines as it becomes a less reliable category.

In film representation, as Richard Dyer has argued, white characters are depicted as individuals, and people of color as part of an undifferentiated mass. "White people in their whiteness . . . are imaged as individual and/or endlessly diverse, complex and changing."[9] Anything the filmmakers can do to enrich the flat, stereotypical image of an Other character is probably a progressive blow against stereotyping. The more the film contextualizes its Latino characters, the more background the screenwriters provide for them so that they appear as fleshed-out characters as opposed to cardboard types, the less stereotypical they will appear.

Following this line of argument, it stands to reason that one major way that Latino characters can appear less stereotypical is through the actor's performance. Stereotypes are built for economy. They are signs, designed to convey a bundle of simplified information about the Other as quickly as possible. The more textured the performance, the more facets the actor is able to provide for the character, the more, I'd even say, viewers are called on to simply notice the Latino character, the less that character exists as a stereotype. Anything actors can do to enrich their screen characters, to allow them to become individuals rather than remain types, undermines their existence as a mere stereotypical sign. In a way what I'm proposing here is a theory of "performative excess," the idea that these Latino actors are providing more than is strictly necessary for Hollywood's streamlined transmission of narrative.[10] These extra touches—Lupe Vélez's frenetic performance style, Gilbert Roland's erect posture and attention-getting costume choices, and José Ferrer's dulcet voice and lyrical line delivery—go beyond what is required by the film narrative. Inasmuch as these actors' choices give depth to what might otherwise have been flat stereotypes, their performative excesses are counterstereotypical.

One final caveat. I am not asserting that these performers necessarily broke with stereotypes intentionally. Of course, it would be nice if they did, but they may or may not have had that as a conscious goal. For my purposes here, however, it really doesn't matter. Just the fact that each one made acting decisions that succeeded in creating more complex characterizations in their roles suffices for me to qualify their performance as a break with the stereotype. Whether the actor's choice came from ethnic pride, ideological conviction, careerist ambition, or professional dedication, any resulting embellishment of the character as written confounds and counters Hollywood stereotyping.

Defying the Center's Gravity

Lupe Vélez was born Guadalupe Villabos Vélez in San Luis Potosí and for a brief time attended a U.S. convent school, Our Lady of the Lake, in San Antonio, Texas. When her father died, she began a career in show business in Mexico City, appearing in stage revues. She was discovered and brought to Hollywood, where her first major film role, at age nineteen, was starring opposite Douglas Fairbanks as the athletic mountain girl in *The Gaucho* (1927).[11] She then appeared in a handful of dramas, such as Cecil B. DeMille's remake of his silent melodrama *The Squaw Man* (1931) and *Kongo* (1932), but shifted to comedies such as *The Half-Naked Truth* (1932), *Hot Pepper* (1933), *Strictly Dynamite* (1934), and *Palooka* (1934), for which her irrepressible talents were better suited. Her tempestuous five-year marriage to Olympic star swimmer Johnny Weissmuller (star of the *Tarzan* films) ended in divorce in 1939, about the same time that she revived her flagging career by playing Carmelita, a hot-tempered Mexican, in the *Mexican Spitfire* films. From 1939 to 1944, she made eight of these popular B-movie comedies in

Lupe Vélez in an animated confrontation with costar Gary Cooper in
Wolf Song *(1929). (Photo courtesy of Luis Reyes Archives)*

which she received top billing. Evidently despondent because a disintegrating love affair with a French actor had left her pregnant, she committed suicide in 1944.

Vélez is mostly forgotten today, underresearched by both popular
and scholarly historians and critics.[12] This is an unfortunate historical
omission, because, as an early 1930s sex goddess, she possessed a screen
presence that, like Mae West's, pushed the limits of pre–Production
Code sexuality in Hollywood movies. But Vélez added ethnicity to her
sex appeal. As Ana López so correctly writes, "Vélez's beauty and sexual appeal were aggressive, flamboyant, and stridently ethnic."[13] Her
singing and dancing number in *Palooka,* for example, showcased her as
a provocative sex symbol, in a low-cut gown, doing a pelvic thrust to the
music's pulsating rhythms. And in *The Half-Naked Truth,* dressed in a
revealing Art Deco shorts-and-halter costume, she sings a song, "Oh,
Mister Carpenter," whose lyrics and saucy delivery are every bit as
risqué—and transgressive—as any of Mae West's:

Could you, would you
Do some work for me too?
Bring your tools up here and begin,
Turn the knob and walk in.

Oh, mister carpenter,
I wondered where you were.
Oh, mister carpenter,
I got a big job for you.
My cupboard doesn't swing,
My doorbell doesn't ring,
My bed has no more spring,
You ought to know what to do.

. . . my neighbor
Tells me you work for her.
You better say goodbye now, you're mine now—
You chiseling carpenter!
So . . . if you're satisfied,
Each day when you come by
I've got a big job for you!

As Sharon Smith has written, "research desperately needs to be done about [1930s] censorship and Mae West," [14] and I agree, but why stop with Mae West? What needs to be researched is the transgressive nature of early 1930s screen performances of stars like Mae West, who pushed sexual boundaries, and Lupe Vélez, who pushed sexual boundaries for women of color. If the Production Code is seen as a way to contain the sexual threat of unruly women like West, then was it not also a way to contain the sexual threat of an unrestrained ethnic female like Vélez? Who can say how much her career—not just Mae West's—prompted the adoption of the strict Production Code in 1934? Who can say how much her stardom was hurt by the Code's subsequent enforcement?

Sadly, if she is remembered at all today, it is because of her suicide. In fact, I'd wager that more people have heard of Lupe Vélez due to her extensive mention—as a protracted joke, based on the alleged gruesome circumstances of her death—in the inaugural episode of NBC's *Frasier* (1993) than have actually seen her films. [15]

I want to focus on the little-known *Mexican Spitfire* films and Vélez's participation in them to suggest how her frenzied comedic performances can be read not as female clown stereotypes but as landmarks of sound-era slapstick for a female comedian. Because these films were made after the institution and enforcement of the Production Code, most of the sexual charge evident in Vélez's earlier film roles is gone. Because of the Code's enforcement, she was unable to appear as an uninhibited sex goddess, as she did earlier in the 1930s. And, although Vélez's character, Carmelita, was an entertainer, most of the *Mexican Spitfire* films denied her the opportunity to sing or dance—these films were comedies, not musicals. Working within these constraints, however, Vélez in the *Mexican Spitfire* series is able to steal the show by exhibiting her considerable comic abilities. On the surface it may appear that all she does is resort to the female clown stereotype, and, to be sure, there are plenty of stereotypical elements. For example, many laughs come from Carmelita's mangling of the English language. "Don't jump over any conclusions," she says in *Mexican Spitfire's Baby* (1942), and, in *Mexican Spitfire Sees a Ghost* (1942), "Everything's going to be honkey-donkey," (combining "hunky-dory," "okey-dokey," and a farm animal), and "That was a pretty tight hug" (instead of "tight squeeze").

But, I would argue, it is not the strategy of the films to make Carmelita look stupid. Her constant partner in these films is her husband's Uncle Matt (Leon Errol), and the two, as Leonard Maltin writes, "have a great screen rapport." [16] Uncle Matt courteously corrects her language mistakes, never ridiculing her. There are other reasons I think the films do not stereotype Carmelita. First, the films are farces, comedies in which a group of characters find themselves in an isolated location (a resort lodge in *Mexican Spitfire's Blessed Event* [1943], a country estate in *Mexican Spitfire Sees a Ghost,* a ship at sea in *Mexican Spitfire at Sea* [1942]). The plots revolve around many mishaps caused by mistaken identity, characters disguised as other characters, characters appearing without others being aware, and so forth. In the farcical world of the *Mexican Spitfire* movies, *all* of the characters are silly and do silly things. Given the comic landscape, Carmelita's antics are not unusual or demeaning, only more animated, which, I will argue below, is a plus.

Second, it is Carmelita who often finds a way to resolve the narrative confusion. For example, in *Mexican Spitfire's Blessed Event,* it is she who finds a way to straighten out the complicated mess the characters have gotten into—and get her husband, Dennis (Walter Reed), an important business contract. Carmelita "saves the day" over and over in these films and is the "heroine" of the series.

Third, in the films, Carmelita is the wronged party. A repeated plot device is her being (justifiably) upset because her husband, Dennis (Donald Woods in the first three films, Buddy Rogers in the next three, and

Walter Reed for the two remaining films of the series), is paying more attention to his business affairs than he is to her. On top of that, Dennis's Aunt Della (Elizabeth Risdon) is a borderline racist. She dislikes Carmelita and shows it, repeatedly remarks on how she is hurting his career, and constantly questions why Dennis ever married her. Ana López, reading this differently than I do, sees Carmelita marginalized by the series. "As the series progressed," she writes, there were "specific references to Carmelita's mixed blood, lack of breeding and social unacceptability, her refusal to put the entertainment business behind her to become a proper wife, her inability to promote his [Dennis's] (floundering) advertising career, and her apparent lack of desire for offspring." [17]

I must admit that my first reaction to *the Mexican Spitfire* films was exactly the same, and in an earlier essay I used Vélez's Carmelita as an example of the female clown stereotype.[18] Upon closer examination of the films, however, I have changed my mind and come to appreciate the subversive nature of Vélez's performance in these films, and of her screen career as a whole. My present interpretation, which is arguably a too optimistic and hopeful one, now takes the opposite view, noting that because she is the top-billed star of the series, the Hollywood paradigm "centers" Carmelita. Because of that, Carmelita is the protagonist, Aunt Della is the series' mean-spirited and hard-hearted antagonist. Her constant jabs at Carmelita are quasi-villainous, and because of this dynamic, the films are subtly progressive.

Ideologically, then, the films are sly critiques of patriarchal capitalism's dehumanizing focus on business, money, and profits at the expense of human relationships. *Mexican Spitfire's Baby* (1942), for example, opens with an argument between Carmelita and Dennis at a nightclub. She's angry because they're supposed to be celebrating their first wedding anniversary, but Dennis keeps dancing with another woman. He explains that he is trying to get an important business contract with the woman's father, which would amount to $50,000 per year. Typically, his Aunt Della supports his behavior. Finally Carmelita explodes:

Ha! This is a fine wedding anniversary. *Me sacas a pasear . . . no bailas con migo, nomas bailando con esa mujer [con] cara de palo. Y despues de eso no mas habla de "business, business, business, business, business."* [You invite me out . . . you don't dance with me, just with that wooden-faced woman. And after that you only talk about "business, business, business, business, business."] Why don't you dance with me? Why do you have to dance with somebody else?

As Carmelita in the Mexican Spitfire series, eight films Lupe Vélez made from 1939 to 1943, she and Leon Errol made an effective comic team. She was a commanding presence by virtue of her effervescent personality, her stylish dress, and the fact that she was slightly taller than Errol. (Photo courtesy of Luis Reyes Archives)

Finally, as I've already mentioned, because she is the star of these films, the poetics of Hollywood filmmaking constantly favor her. As the top-billed performer, she is usually centered in the frame, or shares it with her second-billed costar Leon Errol. She was not tall (reportedly five foot even), but neither is Errol, so that in the frame she is slightly taller and therefore is not diminished in terms of stature. Furthermore, Carmelita does not wear stereotyped costuming. She wears none of the Latin markers that Hollywood typically uses to denote Latino Otherness. Rather, her costumes are contemporary and fashionable, arguably the most stylish of all the players.

But beyond this, there is the matter of her masterful comic performance. One minor attribute is the way Vélez cheats herself nearer to the camera, especially in the two-shots that she shares with Errol. Positioning herself closer to the camera (and to us), she thereby foregrounds herself in the frame, in effect making her image slightly larger than his.

Two more central aspects of her performance that define her screen-acting style are her animated movements and her Spanish ad-libs. She is an extremely expressive performer, using her entire body, the gesticulation of her face, hands, arms, and legs being a key feature of her performance style. Moreover, she moves all over the frame, and her appearances in the series are a succession of her swiftly walking, running, hopping, or jumping across the frame. In *Mexican Spitfire Sees a Ghost*, for example, she makes her first entrance by swinging through a window. These films were shot in the conventional classical Hollywood fashion, favoring rather static "proscenium" frames in which the characters gather together and position themselves in carefully arranged groupings to deliver their lines for the camera. Because none of the other actors in these films was nearly as animated as Vélez, and since, in general, the viewer's eye is drawn to movement in the frame, given the inert world of the *Mexican Spitfire* films, Vélez is that movement. In sum, her vivacious performance contrasts a lively and humane Mexican lifestyle that appreciates life beyond the monetary bottom line with a sedentary, humdrum Anglo one that is obsessively hungry for profit.

In terms of the history of performance in film, what Vélez was doing—and this is unique for a woman in American sound cinema—was continuing the slapstick tradition of silent comedies into sound films. Her whirligig comic style had its roots in Mexican vaudeville and was similar to the slapstick pioneered in film by Mack Sennett and developed into an art form by Charlie Chaplin, Buster Keaton, Harold Lloyd, and others. Slapstick died out as a viable comic convention with the coming of sound, and the careers of some silent comedy giants suffered. Chaplin made a difficult transition to sound. Keaton was asked by MGM to replace his brilliant physical routines with verbal comedy, and it ended his career. The sound cinema comedians who did thrive were those who found a way to marry silent-era slapstick with sound-era verbal play, but they were mainly male acts—the Marx Brothers, the Ritz Brothers, the Three Stooges. Thus in the late 1930s and early 1940s, female slapstick in film was almost exclusively Lupe Vélez's terrain. True, Lucille Ball had some ventures into physical comedy in films like *The Affairs of Annabel* and *Annabel Takes a Tour* (both 1938), but until television's *I Love Lucy*, Ball never lost herself in slapstick the way Vélez did. Ironically, after Vélez, there would not be another great physical female comic until Ball took the form to early television.

A crucial final element of her performance is her Spanish dialogue. Given the English-language dominance of Hollywood studio production, Hollywood's generally dismissive attitude toward non-English speech, and the fact that the scriptwriters were not Latinos (they do not have Spanish surnames, and in my researches I have discovered only a handful of Latino screenwriters who worked in Hollywood during the classical era),[19] we can assume she was allowed to ad-lib her Spanish outbursts as long as they were not offensive. As I demonstrated in the dialogue quote above, she takes these opportunities to wink at the Spanish speakers in the audience, underscoring for them the difference between stiff and cold Anglo values and human and warm Mexican ones.

Another good example of this from the series occurs in *Mexican Spitfire's Blessed Event,* in a scene where Dennis's securing the ubiquitous business contract is in jeopardy. Considering that Carmelita is already married to Dennis, she is harshly chastised by Aunt Della. "You ought to be ashamed of yourself," she tells Carmelita. "You've ruined Dennis' career. Why don't you get out of his life before you ruin it completely?"

As Aunt Della exits, Carmelita responds in Spanish:

¡Cayese la voca, vieja habladora! Nomás hable y hable, siempre. A mi me hecha la culpa de todo, y yo ¿que culpa tengo?

["Shut your mouth, you old chatterbox. Always talking and talking. Blaming me for everything. And why is it always my fault?"]

These may appear to be throwaway lines to non-Spanish speakers, but to those who understand, they are at least humorous cultural in-jokes and, at most, pointedly oppositional moments in which Carmelita takes the hard-hearted gravity of the Anglo dominant society to task. Looked at in this way, Vélez not only avoids the stereotype but also counters the excesses of American capitalism.

Gilbert Roland: Scene Stealing 101

Gilbert Roland, who evolved from a matinee idol in the late 1920s and early 1930s into a well-respected character actor, was another Mexican native. Born in Juárez, Chihuahua, he grew up in El Paso, Texas, and made his way to Hollywood in his teens. He began by playing bit parts in numerous films such as *Blood and Sand* (1922) and *The Phantom of the Opera* (1925), and his big break came when he was cast as the second lead in the Clara Bow vehicle *The Plastic Age* (1925). This was the start of an impressive screen career that lasted six decades, stretching into the 1980s (his last film role was as the Mexican patriarch in *Barbarosa* [1982]).[20]

His considerable screen presence avoided stereotypes in two ways: by his distinctive athletic posture and by his flashy apparel. First, Roland always presented himself in the frame with a straight (but, as we will see, not too straight) and graceful posture (he was said to have trained as a bullfighter). Whenever his trademark costume tricks were constrained, he still stood erect in the frame, never slouched or drooped at the shoulders. In graphic terms, the vertical line created by upright posture is a strong power line in the frame, and when standing, Roland always presented such a figure to the camera.

A good example of this is his playing of the Latin star "Gaucho" in Vincente Minnelli's *The Bad and the Beautiful* (1952). The film is part exposé, part celebration of an ambitious but manipulative David O. Selznick–Val Lewton-type film producer Jonathan Shields (Kirk Douglas). For one important project, he desperately needs the participation of the best Latino star in Hollywood, Victor "Gaucho" Ribera (Roland). To interest him in the film, Shields provides him with a beautiful blond escort and takes him out on the town. Shields drinks himself unconscious and Gaucho takes him home, carrying him over his shoulder and laying him down on the sofa. Standing above the drunken producer, Roland strikes his characteristic pose, in which he bows his body slightly forward from his knees to his head, thrusting his chest out just a bit. Roland's trademark stance helped him quite literally stand apart from the other, more relaxed Anglo actors with which he appeared and added to his commanding presence in the frame.

But Roland's main attention-grabbing technique was as old as performance itself—scene stealing. The way he usually did this was by adorning his costume. The first thing to notice about his wardrobe choices was that he avoided the stereotypical look. His outfits were not Hollywood films' stereotypical garb for Latinos. Typically Roland appeared with a wristband (wide and usually made of leather), a kerchief (preferably red) tied around his neck, his shirt (preferably white) unbuttoned to reveal his bare chest, and a thick chain with a large gold medal dangling from his neck. Even though Roland was usually playing a secondary character, these wardrobe accents constantly called attention to him, almost as if he had a flashing neon arrow pointing at him.

In this publicity photo, Gilbert Roland displays the key elements of his
scene-stealing style: the light-colored shirt open at the collar, the contrasting
brightly colored kerchief, the wristbands, and, in this case, an arresting white
hat. In addition, he would often sneak in a bit of eye-catching business—
here, it's the way he holds the cigarette near his face.
(Photo courtesy of Luis Reyes Archives)

But can we credit Roland with making these accessory choices? I
think we can, based on two pieces of evidence. First, it was a costuming
style that Roland repeated consistently in many films throughout his career. He seemed to have developed it in the late 1940s and early 1950s,
and he employed it when it was appropriate for the film and if, apparently, the director gave him the latitude to do it. (Two examples of his
costume being more carefully controlled are *Crisis* and *The Bad and the
Beautiful*.) When allowed, it was a consistent costuming style that
Roland maintained for decades, from the 1950s to his very last film,

Barbarosa. Second, this was how Roland dressed for publicity photos, so we can infer that this was the look he was comfortable with and the way he wished to promote himself.

Is the image Roland created for himself a variation on the Latin lover? Visually, he certainly accented his sexuality and virility. But this was generally offset by other characteristics in the parts he played. Indeed, except for *The Bad and the Beautiful,* where he was the Latin lover but, curiously, did not dress this way, the love-'em-and-leave-'em womanizing characteristic of the stereotype was *not* part of his character. In fact, a survey of Roland's filmography shows that in the vast majority of his roles he did appear in his recognizable getup but was not playing the Don Juan character.[21] This in itself might be seen as countering the stereotype.

By examining his work in several films we can discern how Roland used this attire to make himself the center of visual interest in the frame, or at least to vie with the Anglo leading man for the viewers' eyes, even when he was at the margins of the frame. One good example is Roland's role as the Mexican rebel leader Colonel Escobar in the Robert Mitchum Western *Bandido* (1956). Roland plays Escobar as a confident and decisive military leader, and he creates a visually interesting costume for him. To begin with, he wears a white shirt (which is flamboyantly tied around his waist rather than being tucked in) and a light-colored hat. (As I noted in Chapter 2, a center of graphic interest in a frame is the area that contains the lightest, brightest color.) Against this white backdrop, Roland ties a deep-red kerchief around his neck, creating an emphatic color highlight. Later in the film, the red kerchief is moved (the change of placement itself attracts attention) and is partially tucked into one of his shirt pockets, creating a visually arresting red flair against the shirt's white background.

Probably his most baroque scene stealing occurs in the film noir Western *The Furies* (1950), Anthony Mann's brooding variation on Shakespeare's *King Lear.* Roland plays Juan Herrera, the scion of a humble Mexican ranching family who falls in love with the headstrong daughter ("Vance," played by Barbara Stanwyck) of the region's powerful and despotic rancher, T. C. Jeffords (Walter Huston, in his final role). Roland appears in only six scenes, but he finds a way to upstage the other actors in every one.

To appreciate his scene stealing, and the way it helps break down any possibility of a stereotypical reading of his minor role, one needs to note how he varies his costume from scene to scene. In a textbook example of inventive upstaging, Roland manages to make his appearance conspicuous in each of his first three scenes, despite the fact that he is basically wearing the same thing. In his first appearance, when Juan and his brothers are riding the range and come across Vance, T.C., and some of his henchmen, Roland presents the complete scene-stealing package. He wears a light-colored cowboy hat cocked back to reveal a lock of hair on his forehead, his signature leather bracelet, and a white shirt with the top three buttons unfastened.

In his second scene, a meeting with Vance at a favorite hideaway, he appears in the same costume, only this time with his hat strings cinched up around his chin as he chews on a twig. The hat strings are very long, hanging nearly down to his waist, and they blow in the wind when he stands. Thus, in close-up two-shots of Stanwyck and Roland, the twig in Roland's mouth draws attention to him, as does the hat string fastened tightly at the rim of his chin. When this relatively static, talky scene cuts to medium shots, Roland maintains visual interest on his side of the frame with motion—in this case, his extra-long hat strings swaying in the wind. In his third appearance, again a rendezvous with Vance out in the countryside, they sit on a fallen log and discuss their relationship. This time the attention grabber is what Roland does with his hat. Instead of wearing it, he hangs it on the butt of his pistol, which is in his holster on his hip. It's a minor but unusual bit of costuming business, and graphically it forms a light-colored oval mass at Roland's midsection, drawing attention to him during this dimly lit nighttime scene.

In all, despite the fact that Roland was usually playing a minor character, and that he was usually relegated to the fringes of the frame, he demonstrated how it was possible to subvert such representational marginalization. By his costuming choices he drew viewers' eyes toward him and his characters. And maybe by drawing their interest he captured their sympathy as well. At the very least, he showed how to create memorable, distinctive, and consequently nonstereotypical characters.

José Ferrer and "The" Voice

Born in Puerto Rico in 1912, José Ferrer became a major talent in theater and film, not only as an actor but also as a writer, director, and producer. Among the many honors he garnered during his long career (Ferrer worked steadily until his death in 1992) are three New York Drama Critics Circle Awards, five Tony Awards, and two Oscar nominations. He was the first Latino to win a Best Actor Academy Award (for *Cyrano de Bergerac* in 1950).[22] He worked with some of the most renowned film directors, including Otto Preminger in *Whirlpool* (1949), John Huston for his starring role as Toulouse-Lautrec in *Moulin Rouge* (1952), Edward Dmytryk in *The Caine Mutiny* (1954), David Lean in *Lawrence of Arabia* (1962), Stanley Kramer in *Ship of Fools* (1965), Billy Wilder in *Fedora* (1978), Woody Allen in *A Midsummer Night's Sex Comedy* (1982), and David Lynch in *Dune* (1985). Known as an actor, not a *Latino* actor, Ferrer was never typecast in Latino roles, as other Hispanic performers have been. In fact, he rarely played Latinos. One of the most memorable times that he did, and one in which he deftly avoided an easy stereotype, was in the role of the dictator Raoul Farrago in *Crisis*. How did he do this? In large measure, with his voice.[23]

Ferrer was blessed with a wonderfully pleasant actor's voice— sonorous, euphonic, and low-pitched. Among screen actors, Ferrer's voice is one that has been noted for its power, authority, and richness, along with the likes of Orson Welles and James Earl Jones. One of the ways Ferrer avoids the stereotypical pitfall of his character falling into a tyrant caricature in *Crisis* is simply that his voice commands attention. It is also one of the ways that Ferrer, though very early in his career, cannot only share top billing with a star of the stature of Cary Grant, but hold his own with him on the screen.

Beyond commanding attention, his voice rewards attention. In the first place, his delivery achieves musical prosody. That is, his combination of stress, duration, and rhythm achieves a lyricism that is pleasing on its own, independent of the meaning of the words, in the same way that the lines in a Shakespeare play read by a gifted actor can be appreciated as melodious sound. His delivery is always fluid, never choppy; even when he speaks rapidly, Ferrer never runs out of breath or cuts off word endings. Because he never strains his voice and stays within his vocal range, he never sounds shrill, even when shouting. The ability to avoid piercing registers is invaluable for a performer because it means that audiences can "trust" his or her voice—not only because it is pleasant-sounding in general but also because they know it will not become unpleasant. His voice is a soothing one, a trustworthy sound viewers can select to listen to on the soundtrack. Quite literally, Ferrer's is a voice worth listening to.

Then there is the matter of his phrasing. As I've already noted in Chapter 3, director Richard Brooks himself wrote an intelligent script that gave Latin America and Latinos their due. Thus much of what is counter-stereotypical in *Crisis* can be traced back to the script. But in addition to the lines written for Farrago, there is the way that Ferrer delivers them. One of his talents as an actor is his ability to "versify" his lines, arranging them into regular, metrical rhythms that enhance their lyricism and improve comprehension.

There is an excellent example of this in *Crisis,* in a scene where Farrago explains to Dr. Ferguson the truth behind the charge that Farrago murdered a political opponent, a college professor. The man was not assassinated by him, he says, but was actually killed by a jealous husband. Farrago then remarks on the irony of the amorous professor's having become a martyr for the rebel cause. The line he is called upon to deliver is this:

> To think that because a little professor was indiscreet with another man's wife my entire regime is in danger!

It's an ungainly line of dialogue, a long, nineteen-word sentence containing thirty-one syllables. Furthermore, it scans awkwardly, changing its stress pattern two-thirds of the way through. It is iambic (repeating short–long, or unstressed–stressed, syllables) up to the word "wife":

> To thínk/ that becaúse/ a lít/tle profés/sor was ín/discreét/ with anothér/ man's wífe

It then shifts into an irregular pattern where trochee (long–short, stressed–unstressed) alternates with iambic:

> my´ en/tíre/ regíme/ ís in/ dánger.

Ferrer rephrases the line brilliantly and varies the tempo, thereby masking its inherent awkwardness and improving its communicativeness, its ability to transmit meaning. He breaks the line up into two units. The first consists of two lines of iambic tetrameter (four beats to the line), the second unit comes after a slight pause that occurs at the point where the iambic pattern becomes the trochee–iambic mix. In the verse form that Ferrer delivers the line, it looks and sounds like this:

> To think that because a little professor
> was indiscreet with another man's wife
> (brief pause)
> my entire regime is in danger!

Cary Grant (left) as the American surgeon, Antonio Moreno (center) as his Latin American counterpart, and José Ferrer as the ailing dictator Farrago in Richard Brooks's Crisis *(1950). (Photo courtesy of Luis Reyes Archives)*

He says the first unit quickly, producing a staccato rhythm. Then he slows down just a bit after the pause, giving the last words longer duration.

The effect of his rephrasing is twofold. It improves the line's scansion, emphasizing its rhythmical qualities and deemphasizing its irregular cadences. His slower ending allows listeners to grasp the line's two key pieces of important information, which, because of the way Ferrer delivers it, are easily boiled down to the following: (1) my regime is in trouble, (2) because of a professor's affair.

To sum up, Ferrer the actor breaks with the dictator-as-*bandido* stereotype by creating a character who is far from a one-dimensional caricature. He is a complex of contradictions, part visionary, part savage, and always intelligent (both because the part is so well written by Brooks and because it is so well spoken by Ferrer). Ferrer's voice imbues Farrago with wit and authority, with charm and grace. It's clear that he possesses an orator's gift for the memorable rendering of the apt phrase—and sometimes Ferrer makes Brooks's less than apt phrases *sound* apt.

There are shadings of character in Ferrer's performance that don't appear on the script page. Ferrer's Farrago purrs like a well-educated kitten, but roars like a ruthless despot. "I *am* the law!" he bellows at one point, in a voice that stresses the fact that in the case of this dictatorship this claim is not hyperbole but fact. Listening to his resonant voice, one can begin to see what a powerful orator he must have once been, how his speeches might have once inspired the nation's multitudes, and how he gained power. In short, Ferrer's performance insinuates a context for Farrago, sketching in the skills he possessed that led to his becoming the head of the country. Ferrer's Farrago is not another Hollywood banana republic dictator but a tragic figure who squandered his clearly considerable intellectual and political talents, compromised his ideals, and became an oppressor of his people.

Other Examples and the Case of Rosie Pérez

This is not an exhaustive list, nor is it meant to be. Obviously, there is plenty of work to be done in this area, and what I hoped to do was to suggest a starting place for evaluation of ethnics playing ethnics. There are certainly other Latino actors whose work deserves this sort of scrutiny and who did manage to subvert stereotypes. Dolores Del Río's ironic portrayal in *In Caliente* (1936), where she plays a combination of dark lady pin-up girl and savvy manipulator of an Anglo wise guy (Pat O'Brien) who has fallen for her, is but one example. Another is the career of Cesar Romero, whose height (he was said to have been 6′ 2″ tall, and he looked it in the frame) made him tower over most other actors who appeared with him, thus giving his characters graphic prominence.

More recently there was Raúl Julia, another tall actor, who never let himself be cornered into a type, even when it seemed there was no way out. In *Tequila Sunrise* (1988), for instance, he played the Mexican drug runner and deftly evaded the *bandido* stereotype and created the most interesting character in the film. His entertaining characterization is based on textures present in Robert Towne's script, which created a character who was sharp, witty, charming, and in possession of a healthy, self-deprecating sense of humor. Julia played it with such élan that his character, the drug dealer Carlos who disguises himself as a Mexican policeman named Escalante, was a fascinating rogue in the tradition of Orson Welles' Harry Lime in *The Third Man* (1949). Like Welles in that film, Julia, though a relatively minor character, steals the picture from the rest of the cast, in this case the superstars Mel Gibson, Michelle Pfeiffer, and Kurt Russell.

What about Rosie Pérez—stereotype or subversion? It has been ar-

Raúl Julia (left), as a Mexican drug lord in Tequila Sunrise *(1988), with Mel Gibson, an American smuggler. Performing his role with great gusto, Julia is easily the most captivating character in the film and subverts the stereotype in the bargain. (Photo courtesy of Luis Reyes Archives)*

gued both ways. In an extensive analysis, Angharad Valdivia wonders if her screen roles (in films like Spike Lee's *Do the Right Thing* [1989], Ron Shelton's *White Men Can't Jump* [1992], and Andrew Bergman's *It Could Happen to You* [1994]) can be viewed as contestational. She does allow that, for some viewers at least, Pérez "thickens, complicates, and deconstructs her own stereotypical representation."[24] One way to gauge Pérez's screen presence is to plot it against the performative grid I have just utilized to examine the acting of Vélez, Roland, and Ferrer. Since many of the key elements of Pérez's screen images are precisely the ones that I singled out above—animation, comedy, costume, and voice—it should prove to be an illuminating exercise. Like Vélez, Pérez is a hyperactive performer who combines sex with comedic skills. But whereas the three actors I analyzed found ways to blunt and undermine their roles' stereotypical possibilities, Pérez typically does not.

As Valdivia points out, in most of her roles, Pérez's "Latina/Puerto Rican ethnicity is collapsed with her working-class status in an inextricable manner. She is at once Latina because she is working class and working class because she is Latina."[25] Accordingly, her appearance

In films like White Men Can't Jump *(1992), Rosie Pérez (right) was confined to the stereotype of the shrill, lower-class Latina. Seen with Tyra Ferrell (left), Wesley Snipes, and Woody Harrelson. (Photo courtesy of Luis Reyes Archives)*

tends to be what could generally be described as Hollywood lower-class gauche: teased hair, big hoop earrings, gaudy clothes, too much eye makeup. As opposed to Roland's self-styled character, Pérez is typecast and dressed, made up, and coifed to fit her established screen type—the loud, brash, bewailing Latina.

Then there is her voice, which, like José Ferrer's, may be her most memorable—"notorious" might be a better word—characteristic. Whereas Ferrer's voice was always soothing, Pérez's characters have uniformly shrill, piercing, and grating voices. Whereas Ferrer's voice comforted viewers, Pérez's annoys them. Valdivia quotes one reviewer who characterized Pérez's voice as being "a whine like a high-speed drill" and concluded that she predictably "wears out her welcome." [26] Her voice coupled with the harpy she plays in *It Could Happen to You* only intensified rather than lessened the stereotypical aspects of the role. By the end of most of her films she becomes the irritating Other rather than an interesting one. In short, Pérez's performances and the characters she plays favor a stereotypical reading, not a subversive one. Which is a shame, because I know Pérez is capable of so much more.

I know because I have seen her in *The 24 Hour Woman* (1999), her most controlled and nuanced performance to date, and she is a joy to behold. If you didn't know Rosie Pérez from her previous screen incarnations, you might well think that this was a Latina actress worth watching. In it she plays Grace Santos, the director of a hit television morning program, and her character is competent and professional, accomplished and assured. She speaks in a normal voice, and even when angry, stressed, or upset, she never resorts to her clichéd, spine-tingling, high-pitched squeal. She dresses in fashionable clothes appropriate for a New York City working woman and wears reasonably sized earrings, and we at last get to see that she was not born with teased and dyed hair.

What happened? How did Pérez manage to so dramatically break the stereotype? First of all, a script (by the screenwriting team of Richard Guay and Nancy Savoca, who previously wrote the quirky *Household Saints* [1993]) was (finally) written that featured not only a Latina protagonist but one who existed outside the barrio and beyond the stereotype. Second, it was directed by Savoca, who has demonstrated a marked sensitivity to her women protagonists (besides *Household Saints*, Savoca has directed *Dogfight* [1991] and two segments of *If These Walls Could Talk* [1996] for Home Box Office). And third, Savoca cast Pérez against (stereo)type and gave Pérez the chance to reveal that she has the talent to be much more than just the Latina caricature she is routinely asked to play.

In Chapter 2 and at the beginning of the previous chapter, I analyzed the denigrating pattern of stereotypical representation of Latinos in Hollywood film. But at the end of Chapter 3 and in the entirety of this one I also highlighted the fact that stereotypes *can* be avoided. It takes work, talent, and desire, but it can be done. Now that I have laid out the general features of stereotyping and of Latino representation in mainstream American film, both the bad and the good, I will look at how that representation plays out in three popular genres.

PART TWO

THE HOLLYWOOD VERSION

Latino Representation in Mainstream Cinema

FIVE

BORDERTOWN, THE ASSIMILATION NARRATIVE, AND THE CHICANO SOCIAL PROBLEM FILM

One of the key tenets of genre criticism is that genre films embed social concerns within their repetition of familiar narrative patterns, stock characters, genre-specific locales, and iconography. But as authors Peter Roffman and Jim Purdy argue in their book-length study, *The Hollywood Social Problem Film*, the Hollywood social melodrama or "social problem" film is the exception. A genre that flourished from the 1930s to the early 1960s, the social melodrama's project was to expose topical issues rather than to conceal them. "The problem film," Roffman and Purdy say, combined "social analysis and dramatic conflict within a coherent narrative structure," the genre's distinguishing feature being its didacticism.[1]

Among the myriad issues these films addressed were prejudice (for example, anti-Semitism in *Crossfire* and *Gentleman's Agreement* [both 1947]; racial hatred in *Pinky, Intruder in the Dust, Home of the Brave* [all 1949], and *The Defiant Ones* [1958]; the neglect of the Native American in *Jim Thorpe—All American* [1951] and *The Outsider* [1961]); alcoholism (*The Lost Weekend* [1945]); drug addiction (*The Man with the Golden Arm* [1955]); the reintegration of World War II soldiers into peacetime society (*The Best Years of Our Lives* [1946]); problems of soldiers crippled in combat (*The Men* [1950]); corruption in politics (*All the King's Men* [1949]); labor unions (*On the Waterfront* [1954]); and the media (*A Face in the Crowd* [1957]).

Roffman and Purdy's book is without a doubt the most thorough study of these films. But its attention to movies that focus on the intolerance experienced by Hispanics is slight and incomplete. In a chapter titled "The Minorities," they devote only three and a half pages to Hispanics, who share space with Native Americans under the heading "Chi-

canos and Others." A couple of paragraphs in another chapter on postwar labor problems compare *On the Waterfront* with *Salt of the Earth*
(1954, d. Herbert Biberman). *Bordertown* (1935, d. Archie Mayo) is
mentioned briefly in a discussion of ethnic/racial films of the 1930s.[2]

In all, the authors look at five social melodramas that deal with Hispanics—all concerning Chicanos: *Bordertown, Salt of the Earth, Right
Cross* (1950, d. John Sturges), *My Man and I* (1952, d. William Wellman), and *The Lawless* (1954, d. Joseph Losey). Since there were more
social melodramas than these dealing with Hispanics in American society, a closer and more detailed analysis is called for. Fortunately, that
work has already begun with Richie Perez's discussion of some of the
social melodramas that focused on Puerto Ricans—a Hispanic group
completely ignored by Roffman and Purdy's study.[3]

In this essay I want to begin to fill the gap left by Roffman and Purdy
by examining as a group those social melodramas that dealt with the
problems of Mexican Americans in the United States. In my mind the
Chicano social problem film genre comprises nine such films. To the five
mentioned by Roffman and Purdy, I would add *A Medal for Benny*
(1945, d. Irving Pichel), *The Ring* (1952, d. Kurt Neumann), *Trial*
(1955, d. Mark Robson), and *Giant* (1956, d. George Stevens).[4] Although one or another of these has been dealt with on occasion, they
have generally been approached individually and from a different critical vantage point.[5]

Leaving aside for the moment the question of whether social problem
films as a whole truly constitute a genre, looking at them collectively allows us to note the overall trajectory of their approach to the issue of
Chicano assimilation. More often than not they endorse the very system
they set out to criticize. Their obligatory happy ending metaphorically
or actually sends the Chicano (the films' Mexican American lead characters, except for *Salt of the Earth,* are all male) back to the *barrio*
where he began, leaving him to cope with the negligible opportunity that
exists for him there. In an alternative ending, the Chicano overcomes the
barriers to assimilation and mainstream success only after he purges
himself of the (from the patriarchal WASP point of view) more "problematic" aspects of his character. Regardless of resolution, however,
these films clearly raise more questions about the station of Chicanos in
U.S. society—and about the cherished melting-pot myth—than they
answer.

I will frame my investigation by discussing the Chicano social problem film as part of a more encompassing narrative pattern: the pan-
generic group of films I will call the "assimilation narrative."[6] A close

analysis of the earliest of these films, *Bordertown,* will reveal its debt to the assimilation narrative as well as uncover the major ideological characteristics of the Chicano social melodrama. As I go I will refer, necessarily briefly, to the remaining films, postponing a more detailed reading of them for another time. For now I hope this introductory survey furnishes the reader with an overall sense of the ambivalent attitudes of these social melodramas toward Chicanos.

BORDERTOWN AND THE ASSIMILATION NARRATIVE

It's like the judge said: this is the land of opportunity. In America a man can lift himself up by his bootstraps. All he needs is strength—and a pair of boots. And I got 'em!

—JOHNNY RAMÍREZ (PAUL MUNI) AFTER
GRADUATING FROM LAW SCHOOL

Bordertown, the first Hollywood sound film to deal with a Mexican American's attempt to enter the mainstream and participate in the American Dream, is the prototypical Chicano social problem film. It foreshadows the Chicano social melodramas in the same way that *Little Caesar* (1930) forecasts the main themes of the gangster genre and *42nd St.* (1932) anticipates the backstage musical. *Bordertown* is (to use Robin Wood's words in a slightly different context) that "early major work in which all the tensions and contradictions that structure the later films are articulated, manifesting themselves as uncontainable within a coherent traditional value system or a 'satisfying' resolution." [7] Containing all the major elements of Chicano social melodramas, *Bordertown* also demonstrates Hollywood's contradictory attitudes about Chicano assimilation in particular and out-group assimilation to the patriarchal WASP mainstream in general.

Moreover, its story of Johnny Ramírez's quest for success and his subsequent realization of the vacuity of the American Dream constitutes the rough outline of the "assimilation narrative." This familiar formula dramatizes the trade-offs involved when first- or second-generation immigrant protagonists (or sometimes class, race, or gender Others) set out to better themselves in the American system. In this formula, success is defined in upwardly mobile, professional, and socioeconomic terms and goes hand in hand with mainstream assimilation. (There is no success outside the dominant.)

113

The general pattern that assimilation narrative movies follow is that the protagonists realize that American success is incompatible with "the best human values," namely, those espoused by their root culture. Since mainstream success in these films requires compromise and the loss of identity—giving up who you are for what you want to become—few protagonists from the margin ever really achieve success *and* assimilation. Trying to have it both ways exacts a high price, resulting in a tragedy of some kind, often involving the protagonist's death—as in the case of gangster movies, or Midge Kelly in *Champion* (1949)—or the death or misfortune of others. Jack Robin (born Jakie Rabinowitz), the cantor and music-hall performer played by Al Jolson in *The Jazz Singer* (1927), loses his father—first emotionally, then physically—on his rise to Broadway stardom. Johnny Ramírez's rise to wealth and power in *Bordertown* results in the death of two people and the madness of another.

This two-way split is the same predicament women characters face in the movies, and it is true, I think, for all Other characters seeking mainstream approbation. Just as women characters find themselves unable "to achieve a stable sexual identity, torn between the deep blue sea of passive femininity and the devil of regressive masculinity,"[8] so are Others from the margin caught between the socially constructed marginal roles they are assigned and the self-actuating ones they would like to adopt. In fact, Julia Kristeva has equated the marginality of women as defined under patriarchy with other fringe groups so positioned. "Call it 'woman,'" she writes, "or 'oppressed classes of society,' it is the same struggle, and never the one without the other."[9]

The best course of action is for ethnic/immigrant/class/gender Others to go home to their old ethnic neighborhood, the locus of all that is good and true. Abandoning their aspirations of mainstream integration and success, these characters can remain content in the knowledge that they have gained morality, a prize far greater than fame or fortune.

These films want to say that cultural pluralism—diverse peoples bringing the best human traits to the melting pot—renews national ideals and makes America great. They seemingly celebrate ethnic Americans by showing that their traditions, practices, and core beliefs contribute to—and in fact are identical with—established American values. But the assimilation narrative allows marginalized groups only some, not all, of the vaunted American traits. Among those sanctioned for minority group use are respect for truth and honesty, hard work, devotion to family, and loyalty to community (and, by extension, to the dominant ideology). It should be noted that these are passive, cooperative values that can be subscribed to by ethnic and minority citizens without their entering the mainstream and threatening the dominant. According to the assimilation narrative, these are most accessible to ethnic Americans who have succumbed to the de facto segregation that restricts them to the Other side of the tracks.

Paradoxically, then, those at the margin can best practice these "all-American" traits by remaining in the ghetto or the *barrio*. Others venturing into the Anglo mainstream looking for success betray both their cultural heritage and their national values. Accordingly, the best way for them to become good Americans is to stay where they are, the best way for them to assimilate is not to try, the best way for them to share in the American Dream is to select from the menu of passive values the dominant hands them.

At the same time these stories demonstrate that more active and aggressive traits—ambition, competitiveness, shrewdness, goal directedness coupled with delayed gratification, business acumen, thrift, organizational and managerial expertise, all qualities highly regarded by the dominant culture and characteristic of Anglo success in and out of the movies—are dangerous when practiced by ethnics/minorities. They are dangerous to the dominant, of course, but in these films the threat to the system is transformed into personal dissipation—adoption of these traits by the ethnic protagonist brings moral decay, not success. This being the case, the only recourse for ethnic protagonists is to save their souls: eschew such self-empowering characteristics, retreat from the corrosive mainstream, and return—geographically and socioeconomically—to the east side of town, where they can survive in moral bliss, if in material and creative poverty.

Attempting to portray the unlimited range of upscale opportunities available to ethnics in America, these films instead preach class and economic stasis. Bucking the system is perilous. Ethnics who do so lose cultural identity and moral purity, and become cultural criminals twice over: traitors to their ethnic heritage and traitors to the "American way of life." "The successful man is the outlaw," Robert Warshow wrote in his famous essay on the gangster genre, referring to Hollywood's—and America's—ambivalence about success.[10] As regards the master assimilation narrative (of which the gangster genre is a substantial subset), we can say, "The successful Other is the outlaw." The message—racial/ethnic/female/working-class protagonists "succeed" in the American system by staying on the fringe—may be confounding for marginal groups, yet it remains an ideologically consistent maintenance myth for the dominant.

The assimilation narrative takes many forms in many genres and, as

I've suggested, may apply to all sorts of Others. I will cite just a few examples to illustrate how prevalent the assimilation narrative has been in Hollywood sound cinema: the successful but guilt-ridden Jewish doctor in *Symphony for Six Million* (1932); the rise and fall of the ethnic gangster in any number of gangster movies; and the temptation and ensuing corruption of the working-class or ethnic/racial minority fighter in the boxing genre. In the female variation of the assimilation narrative, a woman's success demands her forsaking her femininity to become, in act and in fact, a male: from Ingrid Bergman's coolly rational psychiatrist in *Spellbound* (1948), who is subsequently "corrected" into a warm, "feeling" woman, to the twisted, cartoon villainy of Sigourney Weaver's gruff, butch business executive in *Working Girl* (1989).

All these cases describe a narrative process that Teresa L. Ebert calls "ideological recuperation." Speaking about the heroines of romance fiction, Ebert notes that the woman protagonist's main problem is that she "is not sufficiently a woman; she has not yet fully realized her sexuality, which in patriarchal ideology can only be her heterosexuality and which is synonymous with her gender." [11] Narrative closure occurs when her "lack" or "deficiency" is "remedied" and she becomes the "right" kind of woman. Similarly, in movie assimilation narratives subjects from the margin are also "deficient" (that is, outside the mainstream). What they are supposed to learn is not how to assimilate, but rather how to become the "right" kind of marginalized subjects. Johnny Ramírez, the Mexican American lawyer in *Bordertown*, learns his lesson well.

FROM ASSIMILATION NARRATIVE TO SOCIAL "PROBLEM": *BORDERTOWN* AS CONFLICTED PROTOTYPE

Not only is *Bordertown* an excellent illustration of the way the assimilation narrative overlaps with the Chicano social melodrama, it is also a paradigmatic example of the entire class of Chicano social problem films. Here, Robin Wood's delineation of the horror genre's normality–Monster conflict as symbolic of the tension between the dominant and the Other will prove useful. [12] Wood gives the formula for the basic horror film as "normality threatened by the Monster." [13] Similarly, the basic formula for the minority social melodrama is the mainstream threatened by the margin. Indeed, the "problem" of the ethnic/racial problem

Bordertown *(1935) may have been an earnest attempt to tell a progressive tale about a struggling Mexican American youth from East Los Angeles. The original lobby card, however, reverts to a familiar stereotype, reducing Paul Muni's struggling lawyer to a dark, ominous bandido. (Photo courtesy of Luis Reyes Archives)*

films is the perceived threat that the margin's very existence poses to the dominant. The dilemma ethnic/racial Others raise for the American mainstream is how to combine two essentially incompatible ideas: the dominant's desire to preserve and protect its identity as a superior, racially pure in-group by exclusionary practices, and the implementation of the democratic ideal that guarantees freedom, equality, and opportunity for all American citizens. *Bordertown* follows the standard rags-to-riches-to-rags assimilation narrative. Johnny Ramírez, a tough kid from East Los Angeles, matures into a responsible adult and acquires ambition and dedication when, as the judge who delivers his law school commencement address puts it, "he realized his opportunities and duties as an American citizen." Johnny dreams of being on the Supreme Court, but his first court appearance reveals him to be a miserable lawyer. He loses an easy case against rich socialite Dale Elwell (Margaret Lindsay), who is defended by an upper-crust lawyer friend. When he is called a "shyster" by the defense attorney, Johnny throws him to the ground, a violent outburst that results in his being disbarred.

Rejecting the entreaties of the parish padre to content himself with humble work in the Mexican Quarter, Johnny leaves Mamá and the *barrio* to obtain what he now understands to be the only things that matter in America: power and money. "A guy's entitled to anything he can grab," he tells his uncomprehending mother just before he goes. "I found that out. And I'm for grabbing from now on." Before long he is managing a casino for a bumbling but well-meaning Anglo proprietor, Charlie Roark (Eugene Pallette), in a Mexican bordertown. Though he rebuffs the amorous advances of Charlie's wife (Bette Davis), she falls so deeply in love with him that she secretly murders her husband to free herself for Johnny. When he still shows no interest in her, Marie frames him for Charlie's murder, jeopardizing his ongoing courtship of Dale. Marie's crack-up on the witness stand (in one of the most memorable scenes of Davis's career) frees Johnny to return to Dale. But on a deserted highway one night, she rejects his proposal. "Marriage isn't for us," she tells him. "You belong to a different tribe, Savage." Pulling free from his grasp, she accidentally runs into a passing car and is killed. Johnny sells the casino, uses the money to endow a law school in the *barrio*, and returns, in his words, "back where I belong . . . with my own people."

Let me now single out some of the narrative and ideological features of *Bordertown* that are common to the Chicano social problem films that followed.

Stereotypical Inversion

Hollywood films that try to boost ethnics often begin by denigrating Anglos (think, for example, what a band of oafish louts the Anglos in *Dances with Wolves* are). *Bordertown* is no exception, peopled as it is by frustrated, oversexed blondes (Marie); flighty, materialistic socialites (Dale and her "fast" crowd of idle-rich thrill-seekers); harsh and inflexible authority figures who operate from a strict brown-and-white moral code that justifies their intolerance of others ("If you knew any law," the judge tells Johnny after his fight in the courtroom, "you'd still be mentally unfit to practice"); crude simpletons (like Johnny's boss, Charlie Roark); and gangsters (the group that eventually buys the casino from Johnny). Naturally the Chicano protagonist makes the sound ethical choice when he recoils from such a thoroughly venal Anglo universe and retires to the moral haven of the *barrio*.

This pattern is the basis for the conflict in the Anglo-centered social problem narratives—the stories about an Anglo protagonist fighting for social justice. In these films the white hero mediates between an oppressed Chicano and a monolithically hostile Anglo citizenry: Leslie Benedict (Elizabeth Taylor) versus the intolerant Texans in *Giant;* the idealistic law professor (Glenn Ford) pitted against a politically ambitious lawyer and an angry mob in *Trial;* and the cynical-but-courageous newspaper editor (Macdonald Carey) opposed to the racist townsfolk in *The Lawless.* In a couple of Chicano-centered films (those with a Mexican American protagonist) the stereotypical inversion is even more pointed. Except for a sympathetic sheriff, the Anglos in *My Man and I* are a band of chiseling lowlifes, and those in *A Medal for Benny* a community of hypocrites.

The Undiminished Stereotyping of Other Marginal Groups

In Hollywood films dealing with a particular ethnic or racial group, the three key elements are the Anglo mainstream, the minority group, and the relationship between them. Busily building that specific ethnic group up and knocking the Anglo down, these films generally partake in a strange kind of Other tunnel vision, losing sight in the process of their insensitive stereotyping of any but the focused-upon ethnic or racial group. (An extreme recent example is the positive portrayal of the Sioux in *Dances with Wolves* existing alongside the film's vicious, cardboard depiction of the Pawnees.) In *Bordertown,* though Marie's Chinese servant appears in only a handful of scenes, he is the stereotypical hopping, misarticulating (substituting *l*'s for *r*'s) Chinese presence. Marie herself is a variation on the stereotypical "easy" blonde. Another example: Johnny may be a bad lawyer, but he is a lot better than his Mexican defense attorney. Johnny has to prompt him to move for a dismissal of charges after Marie's breakdown on the witness stand.

This practice in effect maps Others' relation to the mainstream. In *Bordertown,* for instance, Mexican Americans are marginal, Mexican nationals more so, and Chinese Americans even more so. Interestingly, both *Giant* and *My Man and I* place their poor white characters—Jett Rink (James Dean) in *Giant,* and Mr. and Mrs. Ames (Wendell Corey and Claire Trevor) in *My Man and I*—further from the center than Mexican Americans.

The Male Chicano Protagonist

Hollywood follows the path of least resistance in constructing its heroes. In the rare instance of a film hero being an ethnic character, Hollywood is careful to make him as palatable to mainstream audiences as possible. This is done mainly in three ways: (1) by making the protagonist male, (2) by casting Anglos in ethnic and racial roles (Douglas Fairbanks in *The Mark of Zorro* [1920] and Tyrone Power in the 1940 remake), and (3) by giving the Other protagonist upper-class status (Zorro is a member of the landed gentry; his rebellion is in essence the struggle of New World elites to wrest California from Spanish aristocrats). It should not be surprising, therefore, that only one of the protagonists of these social problem films (Esperanza in the progressive *Salt of the Earth*) is female. Since in Hollywood films an ethnic woman can be only an overprotective matriarch, the "other woman," or a harlot, this practice automatically relegates Chicanas to stereotypical roles.

The Overprotective Mamá

The naive, good-natured, long-suffering mother, like Johnny's, is the norm in these films and is the typical way ethnic mothers are portrayed in Hollywood movies in general, from *The Jazz Singer* to *I Remember Mama* (1948), from *Scarface* (1932) to *The Godfather* (1972). In the assimilation narrative, the mother figure serves as the font of genuine ethnic values and is the protagonist's (and the narrative's) cultural conscience. When the hero listens to the voice of "his people" he is listening to his mother. (In *A Medal for Benny,* the one case where this is reversed and the father is present but the mother is absent, Benny's simple, ineffectual father simply takes the mother's place as the resigned but authentic voice of goodness.) The Chicano protagonist's coming home to mamá in the end (having failed to establish a relationship with any other woman) confirms her castrating power. From the patriarchal point of view, she makes him a weak hero with an unresolved Oedipal complex, incapable of straying far from her apron strings.

Usually she stunts his growth by her smothering solicitude. But Johnny Monterez's mother in *Right Cross* reveals a darker, racially biased side to this (s)mothering. "There's no gringo alive," she tells her son's friend Rick, "who don't think he's better than ten *mexicanos.*" Later, behind Rick's back, she indicates her distrust of him and all gringos. "That Rick," she tells Johnny, "born a gringo, die a gringo." The

Mexican mother can't win in these films. Passive, obsequious ones raise weak Chicano males, active ones teach their sons to hate Anglos.

The Absent Father

Anglo families are complete and ideal, ethnic families fragmented and dysfunctional. The father's absence, from *Bordertown* to *La Bamba* (1987), is seldom explained. Once again, from the male-dominant point of view, the lack of an organizing paternal sensibility makes for an abnormal, structurally unstable family unit, subtly establishing the psychosocial reasons why ethnics are different from—and inferior to—the mainstream.

From the patriarchal perspective, the missing father is indicative of abnormal Oedipal development. Never able to identify fully with the father, the Chicano male cannot symbolically become like him, nor can he take his productive, "masculine" place in society. This interrupted transition from pleasure principle to reality principle, from the familial order to the social one, helps explain his antisocial behavior: Johnny Ramírez's sudden flash of violence in *Bordertown*, Johnny Monterez's short temper and Anglo paranoia in *Right Cross*, Angel's "murder" of the white girl in *Trial*. Instead of repressing his desire for his mother, the Chicano protagonist's mother love exists right on the surface. No wonder he is plagued by unfulfilled sexual and social relations and returns to her. Because of his arrested psychological development, the realm of (mainstream) language and culture is forever closed to him. From the phallocentric standpoint, he is relegated to "the half-light of the imaginary" [14] along with his mother.

This defective development results in two kinds of fatherless protagonists in Chicano social problem films: (1) the psychologically flawed ones, like Johnny Ramírez, who cannot succeed no matter how hard they try; and (2) the "salvageable" ones, less severe cases like Johnny Monterez in *Right Cross* and Chuchu Ramírez in *My Man and I*, who, evidently to compensate for the absence of the father, find an Anglo father surrogate to help them make the transition into the mainstream. For Johnny Monterez, it is his Anglo friend, Rick (Dick Powell), a happy-go-lucky sportswriter ("Help me!" Johnny pleads with Rick at one point). For Chuchu Ramírez it is none other than the president of the United States: wherever he goes, he carries a cherished letter from the chief executive with him that specifies Chuchu's place in American society. "The measure of your new country's greatness," the letter reads, "lies in its guarantee of justice and equality for all, and it counts on you to do your part to further that principle." For Chuchu, being a good American means being a patriotic "son"; his unquestioned ideological allegiance confers manhood.

Not coincidentally, the three Chicano male characters who are most well adjusted—Angel Obregón (Sal Mineo) in *Giant*, Tommy Cantanios (Lalo Rios) in *The Ring*, and Ramón Quintero (Juan Chacón) in *Salt of the Earth*—live in well-functioning (nonstereotypically portrayed) households. These films' break with Hollywood conventions (and the corresponding ideological baggage that goes with them) is indicative of the ways they operate to expose gaps in the dominant ideology rather than papering over them.

The Absent Chicana

Except for the protagonist's mother, Chicanas do not exist, and certainly not as someone our Chicano hero would be romantically interested in. The implied message: Chicanas are so inferior to Anglo women that they may be omitted from consideration altogether. Here the progressiveness of the exceptions only proves the rigidity of the rule. The most notable is Rosaura Revueltas's Esperanza in the independently produced *Salt of the Earth*. Sonny Garcia (Gail Russell) in *The Lawless* is an independent woman committed to helping her people, but her character deteriorates as she takes on the narrative function of guide/love interest for the Anglo editor.[15]

Besides *Salt of the Earth*, only two films depict an all-Chicano romance. To its credit, the entire narrative in *A Medal for Benny* is propelled by Joe's (Arturo de Cordova) attempts to capture Lolita's (Dorothy Lamour) heart. But the film's conclusion frames their union in dominant terms: Joe is most worthy of Lolita's attention when he becomes a proper American and joins the army to fight the "Japs" in the war. In contrast, for Tommy and his girl (Rita Moreno) in *The Ring*, the system is the problem, not the solution. They overcome numerous obstacles and gain a more mature relationship *despite* the system, not because of it. Finally, there is the interesting case of Juana (Elsa Cárdenas) in *Giant*, who marries into the Benedict family and becomes the only Chicana character in all these movies whose romantic involvement with an Anglo man goes unimpeded. (Johnny's sister has an Anglo boyfriend in *Right Cross*, but Johnny strongly disapproves of the relationship, and its outcome remains unclear at the film's end.)

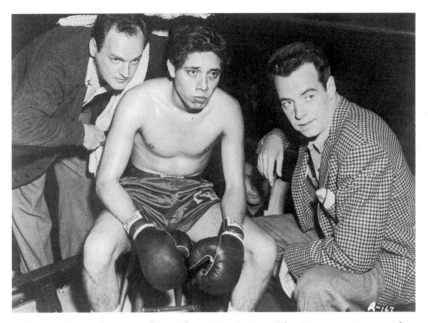

Lalo Rios as the young boxer from East L.A. in The Ring *(1952), one of the few Chicano social problem films to portray the Mexican American experience sensitively. (Photo courtesy of Luis Reyes Archives)*

The Alluring but Flawed Gringa

In light of the above, the protagonist's only option for romantic involvement is with an Anglo woman. But given the pattern of stereotypical inversion and Hollywood's trepidation about portraying interracial love stories, she is bestowed with severe emotional and psychological problems (Dale Elwell is a materialistic snob and a bigot, and Marie's sexual starvation drives her to lust and murder). As a result, the romance is sabotaged from the onset. By the use of an insidiously contorted self-preserving logic, Anglo patriarchy maintains its genetic "purity" in part by negatively stereotyping Anglo women as childish miscreants. Thus Chuchu's fascination with the troubled Marie (Shelley Winters) in *My Man and I* is both inexplicable (what could she possibly have to offer him?) and ideologically nonthreatening (as a marginal barfly, her mingling with and marrying a Mexican is of little consequence to the dominant).

The other impediment to cross-cultural romance is the male ethnic character's considerable psychological defects, already alluded to. In *Trial*, the most reactionary of the Chicano social melodramas, Angel Chavez (Rafael Campos) is convicted of killing a white girl. Though the movie never proves that he is guilty of homicide, the prosecution's case (and, ultimately, the movie's) is that he tried to rape her and she died of a weak heart. This reiterates the powerful patriarchal fear of Other male's violation of white womanhood. The male Other (re)presents two kinds of threats: (1) biological (his tainting of the dominant gene pool) and (2) sexual (always framed as his inevitable defilement of white women, never as his presenting the Anglo male with romantic competition for the Anglo woman). With a psychologically defective Chicano male, the impossibility of legitimate sexual union is rationalized and the dual threat is safely contained. As these convoluted narrative-ideological dynamics disclose, the real violation to white women comes not from the male Other but from patriarchy's degradation of them.

The Reductive Definition of Success

Even given the fact that in the American system the range of opportunities available to its minority members has been severely restricted throughout history, the options presented to the Chicano protagonist—succeed and die (morally or actually) or fail and live (in squalor though in moral equanimity)—are simplified in the extreme. This sort of absolutism is standard given Hollywood's wish-fulfillment narratives that define success—the quest to become the boxing champ of the world, or a Supreme Court justice—as an all-or-nothing proposition. Posed in such totalizing terms, however, the number of "successes" the American system allows in the movies is minuscule (one per protagonist per film), and these films reveal that both in and out of the movies achieving success is all but impossible for most people.

Hollywood has been expounding, explaining, and defending the exclusionist logic of this fable for decades, selling audiences the illusion of success even as they swallow the bitter pill of (preferred, safe) failure. Nevertheless, Anglo audiences can at least obtain pleasure from their identification with the Anglo hero's success. Mexican American audiences, on the other hand, must learn to identify with the Anglo hero in order to enjoy "the freedom of action and control over the diegetic world that identification with a [white] hero provides."[16] To the extent that such marginal viewer identification works, it justifies, celebrates, and naturalizes the WASP norm and becomes a means for Other viewers to approach the mainstream and internalize its values. But spectators from the margin are divided subjects, and at some point they must realize that they are different from the Anglo hero, producing alienation and estrangement in them and serving to exacerbate their marginality.

Hollywood's providing Mexican American protagonists in the Chicano-centered social problem films (save for *Salt of the Earth*) does not really improve the situation. A principal reason is that the heroes in these movies do not enjoy the sort of unbridled success available to Anglo protagonists. They get a greatly scaled-down version of Anglo success or they get failure. Johnny Ramírez cashes in and returns to East L.A. ("To do what?" we may well wonder as the film ends.) In *Right Cross*, Johnny Monterez injures his right hand swinging at his Anglo "friend." This ends his fighting career, but domesticates him (somehow ridding him of his bad temper, his inferiority complex, and his "paranoia" about the WASP system). In the conclusion of *My Man and I*, Chuchu is freed from jail and wins the heart of his beloved: a troubled, alcoholic blonde. Giving up his dream of a boxing career, Tommy in *The Ring* burns his cape and gloves in an oil drum in his backyard. With Lucy's help, he learns to be satisfied with life in the *barrio*. In the Hollywood cinema, Anglo protagonists succeed by succeeding; in the Chicano social problem films, Mexican American protagonists succeed by failing.

Finally, again except for *Salt of the Earth,* this either/or-ism denies Chicano characters the possibility of redefining success in less grandiose—and more personal and local—terms. Working in their neighborhoods or otherwise contributing to the incremental betterment of their people is seldom a "successful" option. Sonny Garcia's local activism in *The Lawless* is an important exception. But by and large there is no instance of Chicano characters redefining success in the positive, personal, and regional way that the protagonist in *Pinky* (1949, d. Elia Kazan) does when she decides to stay in her hometown and teach Black students at a nearby nursing school. Since there is no middle ground, no possibility for regional success, there is no mistaking the fact that from the dominant's point of view (given Hollywood cinema's definition of success), the Chicano's return to the *barrio* represents a Big Failure.

When an Anglo hero, from Will Kane (Gary Cooper) in *High Noon* to Deckard (Harrison Ford) in *Blade Runner,* turns his back on the system and retreats from it, it signifies the ultimate heroism—the rugged individual rejecting a contemptible system. But when a Chicano makes the same rejection, he doesn't ride into the sunset with Grace Kelly or discover a new Eden with Sean Young: he returns to the *barrio,* often alone. The Chicano couldn't make it in the big time, not so much rejecting the system as rejected by it. Clearly, WASP heroes have what it takes to succeed and have the added luxury of electing to accept or deny the system that allowed them that success. Other heroes have only what it takes to fail.

Given the constraints of the ideological patterns just described, it is obvious that the deck is stacked in significant ways against Chicanos in these films. Add to this the strictures of the Hollywood formula, which demands that an accessible hero find a happy resolution to the conflicts animated by the narrative, and we can appreciate why many of these social problem films deprecate the group they mean to celebrate. That *any* Hollywood film would ever attempt to tackle the Chicano "problem" is in a way amazing. That a few (*The Lawless, Giant,* and *The Ring* within the studio system; *Salt of the Earth* outside it) treated Chicanos humanely and contributed meaningfully to the discourse on American prejudice is astounding.

To be sure, much more work remains to be done with these films. Individual close readings are needed to investigate more fully the Anglo-centered films (Good Samaritan narratives,[17] more interested in their WASP heroes' redemption than in the fate of the Chicano characters) and the Chicano-centered ones (variations cut from the *Bordertown* template or about how Chicanos need to become "naturalized" to enter the mainstream).

It's also time for a full-blown appreciation of *Giant,* one of the most enlightened of all of Hollywood's wide-screen epics.[18] Its female protagonist allows it to question some of the key principles of the dominant ideology: patriarchy, the imperialistic bent of America's westward expansion ("We really stole Texas, didn't we?" Leslie tells Bick [Rock Hudson] the day after she meets him. "I mean away from Mexico"), racism, the class system, and the social construction of manhood. Most impressively, it argues that the betterment of Tejanos will come not by simply adjusting an existing system, but by intermarriage and the raising of Anglo consciousness. Dramatically, Leslie's aiding the impoverished Mexican American ranch workers is important, but ideologically it is secondary to the fact that Bick's son married Juana, that Bick now has a mestizo grandson, and that (even if it's only at a familial level) Bick rejected racism. *Giant* is a fascinating anomaly—a long, sprawling, big-budget movie made in the regressive 1950s that follows through on its liberal program and was a critical and box office success.

Beyond critical appreciations of well-intentioned films like *The Lawless* and *The Ring,* we need more social-historical research (along the lines of what has been done to explicate *Salt of the Earth*'s social and production history) to understand how these politically progressive productions came to be made at all. Finally, an area that urgently needs attention is the question of the spectatorship of ethnic and minority viewers, which could build profitably on the work of feminist, gay, and African American film theorists. If "in-built patterns of pleasure and identification impose masculinity as 'point-of-view,'" as Mulvey has argued,[19] then it follows that those same patterns impose a white, patriarchal, heterosexual, capitalistic, upper-middle-class, monogamous, English-speaking point of view as well. What do viewers from outside this perspective *do* when they watch a Hollywood movie? Richard Dyer's discussion of the relationship between gay men and Judy Garland is an excellent starting point for such an investigation.[20] In my discussion of the triangled viewer at the end of Chapter 2, I proposed my theory of spectatorship and identification. An associated issue is the mirrored relationship between the ethnic characters' success double-bind and the ethnic spectators' oscillation between Anglo identification and alienation.[21]

Finally, it is important that film scholarship itself not imitate the assimilation narrative. Commentators studying these films or dealing with issues related to people of color in the movies should not be shunted to the critical margin for doing so. Nor should these critics be asked to adopt current theoretical methodologies (criticism's dominant ideology) unquestioningly. Rather, it is hoped that their research will contribute to a true theoretical and critical pluralism, paving the way for film studies to become a richer, more complex field.

THE MARGIN AS CENTER

*The Multicultural Dynamics
of John Ford's Westerns*

John Ford's depiction of people of color is the most distressing feature of
his body of work. It has prompted a number of critics to take him to task
for his insensitive portrayals of ethnic minorities. An early attack came
from Robin Wood, who in 1971 noted (in "'Shall We Gather at the
River?' The Late Films of John Ford") the director's abstraction of Native Americans into savage threats to civilization as well as his paternalistic attitude toward them, which "continued basically unchanged"
from *Drums along the Mohawk* (1939) "right through to *Cheyenne
Autumn*" (1964).[1] This paternalistic streak was elaborated on a few
years later by Michael Dempsey, who challenged Ford's automatic ap-
pointment to the auteur pantheon.[2] Since then, many disparaging analyses of Ford's treatment of ethnic and minority groups have appeared.[3]

To be sure, Ford's paternalism and his condescension toward and
stereotyping of people of color are incontestable. Still, for all that, this
chapter will contend that it is a mistake to dismiss Ford too hastily as
one more racist filmmaker. It will propose that the films of John Ford
cannot be fully appreciated without taking into account his Irish heritage. Remembering that he was the son of Irish immigrants, surely something he never forgot, one begins to appreciate the fact that his films em-
anate from the position of that oppressed ethnic minority and that his
stories typically focused on marginalized outcasts. This made his cinema
far different from most Hollywood films, which centered on the WASP
mainstream as a matter of course and looked uncritically at assimilation.
Thus, counterbalancing Ford's stereotyping is a richly textured multicultural vision that is nuanced in comparison with the broad strokes
that characterized much of classical Hollywood's ethnic representation.

This multiculturalism is evident, I believe, in the majority of Ford's films, but it is especially pronounced in his Westerns. His frontier communities are filled with ethnics, in the more general sense that Ella Shohat speaks of ethnicity, namely, as a means of describing a wide range of disenfranchised outsiders, "a spectrum of identities and differences, all ultimately involving questions of inequalities of power."[4] Furthermore, within Ford's pluralistic multiculturalism, ethnicity includes not just the Irish, who are—understandably enough—Ford's Ur-ethnics, but also a host of socially (and geographically) marginalized Others, among them various tribes of Native Americans, Mexicans and Mexican Americans, women and African Americans, Slavs and Poles, Frenchmen and Italians, Swedes and Germans, poor whites and Southerners.

Ford's culturalism is multiple not only because numerous ethnicities are sympathetically represented, but because Ford shows ethnicity to be a hybrid property. Take, for example, the layered cultural identities and multiple affiliations of the kind Ford routinely portrayed with his Native Americans, who speak English, Spanish, and their Indian language and move freely across a permeable U.S.–Mexican border. Or consider the collective ethnicities of Elena de la Madriaga (Linda Cristal) in *Two Rode Together* (1961), who is born an aristocrat in Mexico, then, as a captive of the Comanches, lives as the wife of a warrior, is later "rescued" and sent to a U.S. cavalry fort, and finally, to escape the racism there, moves to California. Such depictions indicate that Ford regarded cultures not as autonomous, static, or fixed states, but rather as fluid, evolving, and organic ones that were inextricably intertwined.

Ford's films have a multicultural worldview rooted in the fact that, for him, ethnicity is the most important human attribute. It is the wellspring from which Ford's two cornerstone values, justice and tolerance, flow. Because, in his view, all that was good in the American experience originated from ethnicity, Ford was extremely suspicious of assimilation. He regarded it as an insidious trade-off involving the enforced erasure of one's cultural identity, as well as the adoption of the mainstream's rigid, intolerant, and merciless value system. Ford's skepticism about assimilation was part of his generally contradictory attitude toward America, which led him to critique the American mainstream even as he patriotically celebrated the nation as a whole. This conflicted perspective, I would argue, comes from the fact that John Ford, as the son of immigrants, found himself culturally suspended between Ireland's potato famine and the American Dream. Not surprisingly, a consistent theme in his Westerns is the tension between ethnics, who have been exiled to the social and geographical margin, and the elite WASP mainstream who drove them there.

This essay, then, is a multicultural examination of Ford's conflicted Westerns that privileges the fact that he was an Irish American filmmaker who had one foot in each culture, mainstream American and ethnic Irish.[5] This multicultural perspective, which positions Ford as an Irish American filmmaker who made ethnic films within the Hollywood studio system, brings at least three important aspects of Ford's Westerns into bold relief. First, several familiar Fordian motifs—the drunken brawling, the singing and dancing, the militarism—can be appreciated as expressions of ethnicity, rather than being dismissed solely as embarrassing directorial "touches." Second, Ford revealed his multiethnic sympathies, especially for Native Americans, Mexicans, and Mexican Americans, in subversive ways. Most significant are his subtle but effective manipulations of cinematic elements such as casting, characterization, music, and sound effects. Third, his consistent ethnic sensibility manifested itself in the form of a well-defined cultural narrative that ran just below the surface of a film's dramatic narrative. Within this cultural subplot Ford investigated the nature of ethnicity in America. But before getting to a discussion of all this, let me situate Ford as an ethnic filmmaker, look at the social position of the Irish in this country during Ford's formative years, and outline the ways in which his films are culturally distinct from most Hollywood movies of his time.

FORD AS ETHNIC FILMMAKER

Understanding Ford as a minority artist requires recalling the sociohistorical context from which he sprang, particularly the terrible discrimination the Irish endured during the director's formative years. Born to Irish immigrant parents in a farmhouse near Portland, Maine, in 1895, Ford grew up in a time when Irish immigrants were reviled in America. As the wholesale denigration of Irish immigrants retreats in time, it may be difficult to appreciate just how despised they were. But sociologist and novelist Andrew Greeley reminds us what it meant to be Irish in the last half of the nineteenth century and the first half of the twentieth:

> While the psychological degradation of the Irish was certainly no worse than that to which blacks have been subjected, it must also be said that from 1850 to 1950 there were no dissenting voices being raised on the subject of the American Irish; no one praised any aspect of their culture,

Two of the most successful Irish Americans in Hollywood film history: John Ford directing John Wayne in a scene from The Horse Soldiers *(1959). (Photo courtesy of Luis Reyes Archives)*

no one suggested that Irish might be beautiful, no one argued that their treatment was both unjust and bigoted.[6]

This hostile social climate notwithstanding, John Ford entered the social mainstream and found success there as one of the top Hollywood directors of the classical era.[7] Nevertheless, I would argue that his were minority-focused films. First, because they were made by a member of a denigrated minority group. Second, because their treatment of ethnics was unlike that of most classical studio cinema, in that they explicitly endorsed ethnicity, particularly immigrant ethnicity; they celebrated immigrant ethnics and their marginalized communities; they questioned assimilation into the WASP mainstream; and they sometimes valorized Native American, Mexican American, and African American ethnicities.

This focus on minorities and minority perspective was at odds with Hollywood's ideological raison d'être, namely, the promotion of the WASP mainstream. As a result, a built-in friction between Hollywood's "mainstreaming project" and Ford's counterhegemonic immigrant sensibilities is evident throughout his cinema. Hollywood's "America" was constructed to conform to the majority's utopian view of itself—white (from Western European stock), well-to-do, Protestant, and English-speaking.[8] Of course, Hollywood's attempts to present this coherent, upbeat America were never wholly successful—the socially repressed continually returned to knock on Main Street doors. Still, a generally positive—and exculpatory—portrayal of the WASP mainstream and a consistently derogatory—and disparaging—attitude toward various forms of Otherness did emerge. In contrast, Ford's films centered not on the dominant mainstream but on the immigrant, working-class, socially and geographically isolated margin.[9] And just as most Hollywood cinema used people of color to prop up its WASP self, Ford's films—especially his Westerns—used them to promote immigrant ethnicity over the eastern Anglo elite.

FORD AS NARRATIVE ETHNOGRAPHER

Ford's fictional American frontier, like the historical one, is a territory up for grabs, "a region," in the words of Gregory H. Nobles, "in which no culture, group or government can claim effective control or hegemony over others."[10] Consequently, it is in perpetual disequilibrium. The struggle to control it in Ford's films—as in American history—is a contest between the mainstream WASP establishment and the Native Americans (see Table 6.1). Squeezed between them at the margin frontier are the pioneer ethnics (the soldier-agents of the mainstream, who carry out its colonizing project, as well as the immigrant and working-class settlers).[11]

Let us examine each of these three main groups.

The WASP Mainstream

For Ford this WASP mainstream is the white Yankee elite, centered in the urban northeast. Rigid, hypocritical, and intolerant, they are self-righteously convinced of their social, moral, and racial superiority. This mainstream is typically represented at the frontier by a handful of arrogant colonizers, among whom Henry Fonda's Lieutenant Colonel

TABLE 6.1

Mainstream	Margin	Native
WASP establishment elite; represented in the West by colonizers and assimilated Westerners	European immigrants, especially the Irish (pioneers, settlers, soldiers) at the frontier	Native Americans

Thursday in *Fort Apache* (1948) is the archetypal example. They may also be social-climbing frontier folk who have adopted the mainstream's hard-hearted value system: for example, the self-righteous ladies of the Law and Order League who drive the prostitute heroine out of town at the beginning of *Stagecoach* (1939), and the similarly narrow-minded army officers and their wives at the fort in *Two Rode Together,* who insensitively query Elena about her sexual experiences as the woman of a Comanche warrior.

The money, power, and influence of the mainstream are corrupting forces rather than civilizing ones. That corruption is exemplified by the crooked banker Gatewood (whose wife is a leading member of the Law and Order League) in *Stagecoach.* Another example is Guthrie McCabe (James Stewart), the cynical, egotistical, and mercenary marshal in *Two Rode Together.* To enhance his salary he takes 10 percent of the profits of every business in Tascosa, showing that he has sold out to the capitalist cultural mainstream. Without a connection to their root culture, those in the assimilated mainstream have, according to Ford, no moral core. In its place they substitute self-serving capitalist traits (greed, materialism, careerism, legalistic rigidity, intolerance).[12] In short, if ethnics and minorities are sometimes stereotyped in Ford's films, the WASP mainstream *always* is, with its members consistently depicted as heartless, oppressive, and intolerant.

The Ethnic Margin: Betwixt and Between

Implicit in Ford's Westerns is a social caste system, enforced by the intolerant mainstream, that marginalizes immigrant ethnics and banishes them to the frontier. As Joseph McBride puts it, Ford's "characters are typically refugees from constricting societies (Europe, urbanized America) in which once vital traditions have hardened into inflexible dogmas."[13] The Mormons' exile to the desert wilderness in *Wagon Master* (1950) is emblematic of the way Ford's ethnics were cast out from the mainstream. He even illustrates their expulsion from the town by the sheriff and his armed deputies near the beginning of the film, a scene that echoes a similar one in *Stagecoach* in which Doc Boone (Thomas Mitchell) and the prostitute, Dallas (Claire Trevor), are exiled. A variation on this theme is Elena's self-exile in *Two Rode Together,* when she decides to go west rather than withstand the rampant racism at the army fort. Besides escaping intolerance, Ford's margin ethnics leave the cultural center for two other reasons: first, to increase their opportunities; and second, to find a space where they can openly practice their ethnicity, which is impossible within the tightly constrained, ethnically cleansed mainstream. So they gather at the river of the margin-frontier and show themselves to be in the main guileless and giving, raucous and lively, humorous and humane.

The Native: The Great Unknown

Often regarded as enigmatic racial Others, Native Americans in Ford's Westerns primarily serve to define the ethnics at the margin. Ford accomplishes this in two ways. The first is by using the treatment of peaceable Native Americans as a test of margin characters' sense of justice and tolerance. Those who treat them humanely—(Captain Kirby York [John Wayne] in *Fort Apache* and Captain Nathan Brittles [John Wayne] in *She Wore a Yellow Ribbon* [1949], the Mormons in *Wagon Master,* Lieutenant Jim Gary [Richard Widmark] in *Two Rode Together,* and the missionary Deborah Wright [Carroll Baker] and Captain Thomas Archer [Richard Widmark] in *Cheyenne Autumn*), or who can count a token Native American among their friends (Gil [Henry Fonda] in *Drums along the Mohawk*)—are Ford's heroes. Conversely, negative treatment of innocent Native Americans signifies villainy (Reese Clegg's [Fred Libby] violation of the Navajo woman [Movita Castaneda] in *Wagon Master,* the duplicitous Indian agents in *Fort Apache* and *She Wore a Yellow Ribbon,* the U.S. cavalry's killing of the innocent Look [Beulah Archuletta] in *The Searchers* [1956]).

A second function of Native Americans in Ford's Westerns is to serve as the social and racial boundary for immigrant ethnics at the frontier: the impenetrable racial-cultural "hard place," if you will, against which the immigrant pioneers are pressed by the mainstream "rock" of assimilation. In this sense, Native Americans in Ford's films serve to fix the cultural limits for margin ethnics. If the mainstream represents Ford's fear of what the margin ethnics will likely become via assimilation, the Native American is what they *can't* become—another race. Ford's settlers are therefore sandwiched between the ever-advancing colonizing mainstream and the Native American's inscrutable Otherness. Though they struggle to maintain an ethnic identity separate from both, Ford's immigrant pioneers discover that the effort is hopeless. Eventually they must choose between assimilation into the mainstream or life among the Native Americans, both of which are viewed as cultural deaths. Being caught between the devil of the intolerant mainstream and the deep blue sea of Native American Otherness is the subject of *Two Rode Together,* and the film graphically demonstrates the margin's fear of both. At the mainstream end of the spectrum, there is Elena's cruel treatment by whites at the army fort, a form of social death. A white woman (Mae Marsh) illustrates the cultural death at the Native American end for Ford's pioneer ethnics. Long thought to be dead, she is discovered living as a Comanche captive. But she requests that the investigating army officer, Lieutenant Gary, not change her record. "You'd rather be listed as dead?" he asks. "I am dead," she replies.

Yet, perhaps in appreciation of their ethnicity, there is a positive side to Ford's depiction of Native Americans. ("My sympathy," Ford once said, "was always with the Indians." [14]) Accordingly, Ford's Native Americans are culturally cohesive and, like the immigrant ethnics, struggling to maintain their culture in the face of the mainstream's genocidal onslaught. As such, they are a mirror image of the ethnics at the margin. Probably the best rendering of this cultural equivalence comes in *Wagon Master,* when the Mormons and the Native Americans each confront and tolerate the mysterious Other, locking arms and circling a flickering campfire in a Navajo dance.

Alongside Ford's three major social groups can be found two more Others who play an interesting, if minor, part in his Westerns: African Americans, and Mexicans and Mexican Americans.

African Americans: The Marginalized of the Margin

Rare in Ford's West, though more numerous than in classical Hollywood's West, African Americans exist at the racially segregated outskirts of margin society. Other than the grateful Blacks seen in *The Horse Soldiers* (1959) and what looks to be a lone Black cowpoke in the saloon in *Stagecoach* (who speaks Spanish!), they usually appear as faithful African American servants: Woody Strode's Pompey in *The Man Who Shot Liberty Valance* (1962), Daisy (Beulah Hall Jones) in *Drums along the Mohawk*, and Lukey (Althea Gibson) in *The Horse Soldiers*. Their narrative function, like that of the Native Americans, is to make explicit the tolerance—and thus for Ford, the heroic righteousness—of the ethnic margin. The exception that proves the rule, of course, is *Sergeant Rutledge* (1960), where Ford tries to make amends for this pattern of a marginalized depiction of African Americans.

Mexicans and Mexican Americans: The Hybrid Race

Mexicans and Mexican Americans straddle the line between the margin and the native in an interesting way for Ford. Mexicans in Mexico are typically light-skinned, upper-class, and well educated (the Mexican army officer [Alberto Morin] in *Rio Grande* [1950]; Emilio Fernández y Figueroa [15] [Antonio Moreno] in *The Searchers*). Mexicans in the United States and Mexican Americans, however, are usually darker-skinned in-habitants of the margin's fringes (Chris [Chris Pin Martin], the station master at Apache Wells in *Stagecoach;* the Mexican Americans on the streets of Tombstone in *My Darling Clementine* [1946] or in the cantina in Shinbone in *Liberty Valance;* Link's [Andy Devine] wife and children in *Liberty Valance*). As they approach the narrative's center stage, and particularly if they are female, they are frequently stereotyped as sneaky and untrustworthy (for example, Chris's wife Yakeema [Elvira Rios], who assists the *vaqueros* in taking the spare horses in *Stagecoach,* and the wily Chihuahua [Linda Darnell] in *My Darling Clementine,* who helps the tinhorn gambler cheat Wyatt Earp in a poker game). Occasionally, however, Ford allows them to step out of the background and break out of the stereotype (Pedro Armendáriz's characters in *3 Godfathers* [1948] and *Fort Apache,* Elena in *Two Rode Together*).

Interestingly, they are often conflated with Native Americans. This racial equation occurs both at the narrative level (with, for example, Yakeema in *Stagecoach,* the Thursdays' maid [Movita Castenada] in *Fort Apache,* the Navajo woman [Movita Castenada] in *Wagon Master,* and Chihuahua [whom Wyatt threatens to send "back to the reservation"]) and in his casting choices, when Ford cast Mexican actors as Native Americans (Movita Castenada in several films, Miguel Inclán in *Fort Apache,* Dolores del Rio, Ricardo Montalbán, and Gilbert Roland in *Cheyenne Autumn*). This could be seen as racial confusion or, as I will argue about the casting in *Fort Apache,* a fairly accurate rendering, since most Mexicans are mestizos, of both Spanish and *indio* blood.

FORD'S MARGIN MOTIFS

Thinking of Ford's films as emanating from the ethnic margin sheds considerable light on several of his recurrent motifs, which, when regarded solely as auteurist penchants, are at best quaint directorial tropes and at worst tiresome and repetitive self-indulgence. Let me focus on three of them—brawling and carousing, singing and dancing, marching and parading—to tease out their expressions of ethnicity.

Brawling and Carousing

In Ford's West, the marginals' ethnicity gives them ready access to emotional and sentimental human expression, which is certainly exemplified by the many instances of their drinking and fighting. These scenes of ethnic exuberance mark a major fault line between Ford's supporters and his detractors. True, the steady—some would say endless—stream of protracted boozing and fisticuffs can be tedious in the extreme and has been seen as stereotyping of the Irish.[16] But that is when it is seen from a mainstream point of view. From the margin's perspective, these actions are an oppositional carnival of ethnicity meant to disrupt mainstream sensibilities (in the narrative and in the audience too). For example, in *Stagecoach* the bombastic banker Gatewood (Berton Churchill) attempts to shame the drunken Doc Boone. "You're drunk, sir!" Gatewood tells him. But in a John Ford film drunks are never shamed. "I'm happy, Gatewood," Doc Boone replies cheerfully. "Boo!" These antics illustrate the freewheeling joy of being alive, which for Ford is another positive attribute that flows directly from ethnicity. Drunken revelry represents unabashed cultural contestation from the margin, a cinematic St. Patrick's Day festival that Ford employs as if to say, "We are Irish and proud of it, this is how we choose to act, and what are you going to do about it?" Moreover, these passages are Ford's litmus tests of assimilated conformity: characters (and, presumably, viewers) who show their impatience with them only reveal the degree to which they have sold out to the mainstream. The carousing of Ford's characters, therefore, presents a cultural polemic: the ethnic-less mainstream is inhibited and dull, the ethnic margin is loose and fun.

Singing and Dancing

Ubiquitous in Ford's Westerns, communal music serves multiple functions. First, of course, these occasions draw the ethnic community together and celebrate it as vital, unified, and uninhibited. For instance, right after the good citizens of Tombstone dedicate their unnamed church in *My Darling Clementine*, they immediately strike up the band and have "a dad-blasted good dance." Second, these parties are used to contrast the ethnics' unbridled self-expression with the WASPs' humorless reserve.[17] In *Fort Apache*, for example, there is Sergeant Mulcahy's (Victor McLaglen) playful attempt to spike the punch at the noncommissioned officers' ball, and his earnest—and therefore comical—efforts to "act respectable" ("We'll be the morals of decorum," he promises his master sergeant). Compare this with the unmistakable disgust on Lieutenant Colonel Thursday's face at having to dance to the barroom tune "Golden Slippers" with a noncommissioned officer's wife. Finally, Ford will use a dance to indicate the intrusion of insidious mainstream values into the frontier. Thus Lincoln's (Henry Fonda) unease at the upscale ball in *Young Mr. Lincoln* (1939), where he is told that he dances in "the worst way," contrasts with Mary Todd's (Marjorie Weaver) comfortable familiarity with high-society customs. In like manner, Ford uses the army officers' dance in *Two Rode Together* to proclaim the second coming of the Law and Order League. Indeed, one sign of the infiltration of mean-spirited mainstream values is the classical music that is played in the scene—the Blue Danube waltz has replaced the common reels, popular tunes, and saloon songs typically heard at Ford's ethnic dances.

Militarism: Marching and Parading

How can we reconcile Ford's distrust of dominant power structures with his rampant militarism, symbolized by his fondness for scenes of men marching in parades? From the perspective of the margin, such seeming contradictions find at least a partial explanation. First of all, there is a long tradition of ethnic militias and police and fire brigades in American history, stretching back to before the Civil War.[18] Thus it is important to note that in the experience of nineteenth-century immigrant groups, parading in uniform was a socially sanctioned way of expressing ethnic pride.

Second, military service has always been a viable way for America's disenfranchised to improve their lot. For many members of the underclass, the military is an opportunity: a good, steady job that pays a decent wage and raises one above dead-end alternatives such as poverty, crime, and exploitive manual labor. Before and during the Civil War it was common for military recruiters to meet boatloads of Irish immigrants just as they disembarked onto American soil.[19] "I stepped right off a boat and right into uniform," the military doctor (Sean McClory) says in *Cheyenne Autumn,* "and I had the good sense to stay there." Moreover, the military uniform is a sign of upward social mobility. The dignity with which Sergeant Major O'Rourke (Ward Bond) holds himself in *Fort Apache,* and his beaming pride in his West Point–educated son, Lieutenant Michael O'Rourke (John Agar), captures this well.

Third, the service can enhance an ethnic's self-image by leveling race, class, and ethnic differences. The reason two young officers from opposite ends of the social spectrum are able to vie for Olivia's (Joanne Dru) attentions in *She Wore a Yellow Ribbon* is that they are on more equal footing in the army than they would be in civilian life. (And in the end, it is the "commoner," Lieutenant Cohill [John Agar], not the WASP swell from the East [Harry Carey Jr.], who wins her affections.)[20] The first row of dancers in *Fort Apache*'s Grand March sequence is a prime example of military pluralism: the haughty Colonel Thursday links arms with the wife of the Irish sergeant major, and the sergeant major (Ward Bond) with Thursday's daughter (Shirley Temple). (There are real limits to this pluralism, which Ford probes in *Sergeant Rutledge.*)

Finally, military service implies patriotism, and it is an effective way for members of the underclass to demonstrate their love of country to a prejudiced mainstream. Unquestioning patriotism understandably becomes a core characteristic of Ford's soldiers' ethos, and they are devoted to a tradition that expands social and economic horizons for them and those like them. Much of the pride that the African American "buffalo soldiers" possess in *Sergeant Rutledge* derives from the loyalty they have for the institution that gave them a chance. "The Ninth Cavalry is my home," declares Sergeant Rutledge (Woody Strode) on the witness stand, "my real freedom, and my self-respect." Similarly, Sergeants Mulcahy (Victor McLaglen) and Quincannon (Dick Foran) gallantly lead their men in Colonel Thursday's suicidal attack on Cochise.

From this perspective, it is understandable why a second-generation Irish American director would celebrate militarism with a long cinematic parade of soldiers. The perspective also helps unravel one of the biggest mysteries in Ford's cinema, the transformation of Captain York (John Wayne) at the end of *Fort Apache*. Not only does York adopt the uniform, the manner, and, we suppose, the values of Lieutenant Colonel Thursday, a superior officer he was at odds with, but, as Robin Wood has noted, the film seems to endorse York's metamorphosis. But throughout the film, Captain York is portrayed as a professional soldier who obeys orders, regardless of how much he may disagree with them or dislike Thursday. York's transformation is consistent with his (and Ford's) loyalty to the institution, which ultimately prevails over any misgivings he may have had about his superior's judgment.[21]

Even so, and in keeping with Ford's conflicted attitude, there is a critique of the mainstream embedded within that ostensibly conformist conclusion. A happy ending for *Fort Apache,* which might have shown Captain York opposing and changing the system, would have falsified the workings of American assimilation as Ford understood them. Instead, Ford demonstrates the cultural and ideological co-optation of a decent man. It is a painful and disappointing ending—and that is precisely Ford's point. As Joseph McBride has written, with *Fort Apache* Ford shows "that an insane system may be perpetuated by noble men, and indeed, that it *needs* noble and dedicated men to perpetuate itself. . . . It is comforting to think that evil is done by beasts, monsters or 'pigs,' but profoundly disturbing to realize that it is done by human beings."[22] From a multicultural perspective, what we witness at the end of *Fort Apache* is the disturbing sight of Captain York's assimilation and his resulting complicity with the mainstream's program of genocide. As the son of immigrants, Ford may have been sympathetic to the military,[23] but he was not blind to its failings, nor to its dual role as the settlers' protector on the one hand and the mainstream's imperialist enforcer on the other. One of the more powerful aspects of Ford's cinema, consequently, is its ability to capture the double-edged sword of assimilation in America—opportunity and exploitation.[24]

MULTICULTURAL SUBVERSIONS
AND THE CHICANO AT FORT APACHE

Ford's stereotyping of Others conformed to Hollywood's representational poetics—then and now. As a result, it is hardly surprising that Ford's American Indians were handy antagonists and that he often stereotyped them. What *is* surprising is the number of times he either represented them respectfully or undermined the stereotype altogether. A modest example of the former is the narrator in *She Wore a Yellow Ribbon* complimenting the Indian warriors as "the finest light cavalry in the world." Furthermore, Ford's Indians are generally understood as victims of, at best, white America's shameless exploitation, and at worst, in Ford's words, genocide.[25] And Ford empathizes with them, to the point of occasionally seeing the winning of the West from their perspective. In *Wagon Master,* for example, the Navajo chief says he considers all white men thieves. This includes Travis (Ben Johnson), one of the film's heroes, who, though he denies it, is the man who once cheated the tribe in a horse trade. Another example is the Apaches in *Fort Apache* who are led by Cochise out of the reservation in order to keep their dignity in the face of demeaning treatment by the corrupt Indian agent, Meachum (Grant Withers).

These cases are obvious, and some have been discussed before. But there are more subtle and more telling examples of Ford's cultural subversions, especially in *Fort Apache*. I want to comment on how Ford cleverly uses basic cinematic components—casting, language, character development, music, and sound effects—to demonstrate his cultural sensitivity to Native and Mexican Americans.

In *Fort Apache*'s retelling of the defeat at the Little Bighorn, the Custer character is commanding officer Lieutenant Colonel Owen Thursday, who is not only arrogant and aloof but stubborn, stupid, and bigoted in the bargain. The film contrasts Thursday with Cochise (Miguel Inclán), who behaves with dignity and honor. For this role, Ford broke Hollywood's unwritten law about the casting of people of color (people of color who figure importantly in the narrative are played by whites; actors of color are allowed to play ethnic characters as long as they stay within the established stereotype).[26] Opposing or ignoring these rules, Ford cast the dark-skinned mestizo (Mexican *indio*) performer Miguel Inclán, one of the most distinguished character actors of the Mexican cinema, to play the nonstereotypical Cochise.[27] One final authentic touch in *Fort Apache* is Cochise's speaking historically correct Spanish (in addition to his Native American language), rather than broken "Hollywood Indian" English. Granted, these are small details, but there are enough of them to signal Ford's bucking Hollywood's stereotypical paradigm, and, more important, these choices endow Cochise and his tribe with a cultural specificity seldom seen in a classical Hollywood film.

Cochise's Spanish is interpreted by an army sergeant named Beaufort, played by Pedro Armendáriz—another top Mexican film star.[28] Ford gives us Sergeant Beaufort's cultural dossier piecemeal, so fixing his ethnicity is not easy. We see that he is accepted as an equal by the Irish sergeants (Dick Foran, Jack Pennick, and Victor McLaglen) at the fort, and that he participates in the sergeants' shenanigans (at one point their drinking gets them busted and jailed). Clearly, he knows the "army way" as well as any soldier. We subsequently find out that he was a major in the Confederacy (his nickname is "Johnny Reb") and served as an aide to Jeb Stuart. When he is handpicked by Captain York to accompany him into Mexico in search of Cochise, we discover he is fluent in Spanish. Still later, we learn that Sergeant Beaufort is Mexican Ameri-

Captain York (John Wayne, left) with his interpreter Sergeant Beaufort
(Pedro Armendáriz, center) entering Cochise's camp in Fort Apache *(1948).*
Armendáriz's character is arguably the most complex, interesting,
and well-developed Chicano in the classical Hollywood cinema.
(Photo courtesy of Luis Reyes Archives)

can. When he and Captain York pause at the Rio Bravo before entering
Mexico, York offers him a drink of whisky. Before taking a swig, Beau-
fort raises the bottle with a respectful glance toward Mexico and says,
"Por la tierra de mi madre" ("For the land of my mother").

Sergeant Beaufort's cultural hybridity makes him one of the richest of
all of Ford's secondary characters and arguably the most interesting and

finely drawn Chicano in classical Hollywood cinema. To fully appreciate this, it must be remembered how much Hollywood's classical cinema abhors ambiguity in plot or characterization. Clarity is paramount, and since the paradigm has little time to explain minor characters, the more simply they are presented, the better. Going by the strict rules of the paradigm, Sergeant Beaufort's rich ethnic background should have been greatly simplified or just dropped (and the part recast to eliminate any chance of viewer confusion). But by letting his elaborate ethnicity unfold as it did (and as it would in American life), Ford acknowledges— and illustrates—the multilayered cultural complexity of the American experience. It is sociologically honest filmmaking seldom seen in Hollywood cinema, before or since.

One last example from *Fort Apache* will illustrate how Ford undercuts conventional stereotyping to level differences between groups. It comes at the end of the film, when Lieutenant Colonel Thursday foolishly orders the cavalry into battle against Cochise. In preliminary skirmishes, Ford depicts the Indian warriors in stereotypical Hollywood fashion: their attacks are accompanied by high-pitched yelping on the soundtrack, the standard auditory sign denoting the barbarity of the Native American.[29] Here, as in most Westerns, this is contrasted with the U.S. cavalry's riding into battle as the bugler sounds the charge. Grandiloquent soundtrack music typically completes the genre's coded depiction of the cavalry's "correct"—and heroic—way of doing battle. Ford begins this way, but gradually peels away the cavalry's "civilized" features, together with Richard Hageman's triumphant movie music. First an officer's (George O'Brien) hat flies off his head. Then in quick succession, the bugler is killed, silencing the sounding charge, the regimental flag falls, and the music completely drops from the soundtrack (the rest of the battle is played without a note of either diegetic or nondiegetic music). Stripped of the magisterial signs of superiority, the horse soldiers yip and yelp just as the Native Americans do. By demonstrating that high-pitched war cries are not culturally specific to Native Americans, but simply the sounds made by warriors rousing themselves to enter battle, Ford dismantles a core stereotypical sign of Otherness in the Western, one that even he had used in *Stagecoach*.

DRAMATIC VERSUS CULTURAL NARRATIVES

The third major aspect of Ford's ethnic sensibilities is evidenced in two different narrative strands that are distinguished in the director's films:

the obvious dramatic narrative (the main plot, typically focusing on, say, rescue, revenge, or survival) and a parallel cultural narrative (Ford's persistent subplot, primarily concerning the interaction between mainstream and marginal cultures). Ford usually embeds the cultural narrative within Hollywood's requisite romantic subplot, so that the romance often contains a cultural dimension. Each narrative comes to its own resolution. As with most Hollywood films, the dramatic narrative is resolved first, and often satisfactorily, providing the obligatory Hollywood happy ending. Like the romantic subplot on which it is based, Ford's cultural climax comes last, and it qualifies the happy ending. The qualification is sometimes positive, idealizing the surviving community as having realized Ford's vision of multicultural harmony (for example, the similar endings of *Drums along the Mohawk* and *Rio Grande,* in which ethnics and Native Americans are joined together beneath the American flag). At other times the cultural resolution casts a disturbing shadow over the conclusion (as with Captain York's troubling assimilation into the mainstream in *Fort Apache,* or the end of *The Searchers,* which I'll discuss momentarily).

Sometimes (in *Fort Apache, 3 Godfathers, She Wore a Yellow Ribbon,* and *The Searchers*), Ford's subplot is strictly cultural and not romantic at all. In *The Searchers,* for example, Ethan's bringing Debbie back from the native concludes the dramatic narrative, and his exclusion from the margin in the film's famous last shot ends the cultural one.[30] One difference between the two narratives is that while the dramatic one always has an overt villain (Scar in *The Searchers*), the cultural subplot raises a cultural question. Because of the way morality stems from ethnicity for Ford, these cultural questions are moral ones as well. In *The Searchers,* the cultural question is, Can Ethan, the heroic representative of the margin, overcome his racism? To the extent that he doesn't kill his niece but brings her back to the margin community, he can. But Ethan's scalping of Scar shows that it is highly doubtful that his racial tolerance extends beyond his family. In the end, Ethan is isolated from the rest of the margin ethnics because the uncontrollable ferocity of his hatred of Native Americans threatens the margin's tenuous moral equilibrium, which is based on justice and tolerance.

Table 6.2 will help to distinguish between the dramatic and cultural narratives by giving the resolution of each. In addition, the table specifies the main cultural dilemma(s) that Ford poses in each film. Besides outlining the outcomes of the twin narratives in Ford's sound Westerns, it illustrates how skillfully Ford embroidered his cultural message onto fairly standard genre formulas.

TABLE 6.2

ilm	Dramatic Resolution	Cultural Dilemma	Cultural Resolution
tagecoach	Ringo confronts and kills the Plummers	Is there a place at the margin frontier for outsiders now that mainstream intolerance has infected the margin?	No. Ringo and Dallas escape into Mexico
oung Mr. Lincoln	Cass is exposed as the murderer	Should Lincoln stay in the margin or follow his ambition—and Mary Todd—into the mainstream?	Ignoring the devotion of Carrie Sue, Lincoln opts for Mary Todd, and mainstream success
Drums along the Mohawk	Colonists are victorious over British and Native Americans	Can mainstream Lana learn to accept the margin?	Yes. Lana becomes a frontier woman / multicultural harmony is established
My Darling Clementine	Clantons are killed	Can mainstream Clementine learn to accept the margin?	Yes. Clementine accepts the margin, will become the new schoolmarm
Fort Apache	Mainstream imperialist arrogance leads to massacre of soldiers	Should Captain York loyally obey orders or his (more tolerant) ethnic conscience?	York obeys orders, survives, but then assimilates into the mainstream
Godfathers	Bob saves the baby	Can Bob redeem himself after his attack on the ethnic margin community?	Yes. Bob redeems his robbery transgression against margin by assuming fatherhood and going to prison
he Wore a Yellow Ribbon	Captain Brittles avoids war with Native Americans ("No casualties, no Indian war, no court marshal")	Can Brittles serve two masters—the U.S. Army and his ethnic conscience— and avoid an Indian war?	Yes. Moreover, Brittles receives a scout's commission, returns to the margin's fold; multicultural harmony is established

(continued)

Table 6.2 (continued)

Film	Dramatic Resolution	Cultural Dilemma	Cultural Resolution
Wagon Master	The Cleggs are killed	Can the untolerated Mormons tolerate non-Mormon cowboys and a prostitute?	Yes. The cowboys and prostitute integrate into Mormon margin community; peaceful coexistence with Native Americans and multicultural harmony are established
Rio Grande	Children are rescued, and Trooper Yorke proves his manhood	Can mainstream Mrs. Yorke learn to accept the margin?	Yes. Mrs. Yorke adapts to the frontier; multicultural harmony is established
The Searchers	Debbie's return to margin	Can Ethan overcome his racism?	No. Ethan is separated from the margin
The Horse Soldiers	The Union strike force successfully completes its mission	Can Marlowe serve two masters— U.S. Army and his ethnic conscience— and carry out his raid on the South?	Unclear. Love of Northern Colonel Marlowe and Southern belle transcends cultural differences
Sergeant Rutledge	The dramatic conclusion is the cultural one: Hubble is exposed as a rapist-murderer, Rutledge is exonerated	Can a mainstream institution, the U.S. Army, overcome its racism and give an African American a fair trial?	Yes, but qualified by a romantic, not cultural, subplot: white romance rekindled
Two Rode Together	Romantic conclusion: Guthrie McCabe joins Elena on the stage for California	(1) Can McCabe overcome his racism?	(1) Yes. Romance transcends racism; McCabe rejects the fort's and the town's mainstream values, commits to Elena, and flees with her

Table 6.2 (continued)

Film	*Dramatic Resolution*	*Cultural Dilemma*	*Cultural Resolution*
		(2) Is there a place at the margin frontier for outsiders now that mainstream intolerance has infected the margin?	(2) No. Elena flees farther west, to the new frontier of California
The Man Who Shot Liberty Valance	Ranse reveals truth about who killed Liberty Valance, but it is rejected in favor of "the legend"	(1) Will Hallie choose Tom, the defender of the margin, or Ranse, the representative of the mainstream?	(1) Hallie, like Lincoln, chooses the mainstream; but at the end, she and Ranse resolve to return to Shinbone
		(2) Can Tom be a cold-blooded killer and the defender of the margin?	(2) No. Like Ethan, Tom is separated from the margin community
Cheyenne Autumn	Dramatic conclusion is the cultural one: the Cheyennes arrive at their ancient homeland and negotiate to remain there	Can the mainstream overcome its racism?	For the moment, yes. Romantic, not cultural, subplot: white romance rekindled

By viewing the films in such a schematic fashion, we can see clearly that, except for *Cheyenne Autumn* and *Sergeant Rutledge,* Ford's cultural focus is mainly on "his" (Western European) margin ethnics. Even the films ostensibly about people of color, *Cheyenne Autumn* and *Sergeant Rutledge,* follow this pattern. Particularly troublesome in both are the white romantic subplots that end them. The tired predictability of these films' conclusions suggests that one of the things that makes Ford's other Westerns special is their final cultural commentary, which is absent in both of these cases. Instead, these two films end by simply reverting to the standard Hollywood romantic subplot, which disappointingly shifts their focus to what should be secondary white characters. Because the final resolution in Hollywood cinema is so powerful ideologically, these two films' ultimate cultural commentary is made by what comes last— the white romantic happy ending. These conclusions imply that the

147

*Dolores Del Río (center) and Gilbert Roland as Native Americans in
Cheyenne Autumn (1964), Ford's last Western. As a critique of American
racism, the film is undermined by its shift of focus near the end to the romance
involving the schoolmarm (Carroll Baker, left) and an Anglo army officer.
(Photo courtesy of Luis Reyes Archives)*

films' true protagonists were the white characters all along. Ironically,
though they were meant to expose American racism, *Sergeant Rutledge*
and *Cheyenne Autumn* lack the cultural resonance that so many of
Ford's other Westerns have. And this suggests a paradoxical corollary:
Ford's films comment on race and culture most profoundly—and most
progressively—when their main plot is about something else.

CULTURAL PLOT FORMATIONS

In the remaining Westerns, Ford's cultural interest is mainly in the margin and its relationship to the mainstream. Based on the cultural dilemmas, their plots cluster around five discrete plot formulas.

The Conversion-to-the-Margin Plot

This is usually the story of a woman from the Eastern mainstream who
adjusts to frontier life and adopts tolerant ethnic-margin values: Lana

(Claudette Colbert) in *Drums along the Mohawk,* Clementine (Cathy Downs) in *My Darling Clementine,* Mrs. Yorke (Maureen O'Hara) in *Rio Grande,* and, the lone male, Guthrie McCabe (James Stewart) in *Two Rode Together.* Lana's transformation is the most fully elaborated and therefore the most emblematic of the three. A prim and proper woman from the Eastern establishment, she leaves her comfortable home and heads into the wilderness with her new husband, Gil. But on her first night in her husband's log cabin, she is startled at the sight of Blue Black (Chief Big Tree), a friendly Native American. She breaks down and begs to go back. "I'm going home," she cries. "I'm no frontier woman!" But she stays by her husband's side, perseveres, has a baby, and slowly adjusts to life on the frontier. The scene in which she tells Gil that they're expecting a second child marks her conversion to the margin. "I feel," she says, "as if I'd just begun to live all over again." And for Ford, by converting to the margin, she has.

The Assimilation-to-the-Mainstream Plot

In this story, a character succumbs to the lures of the mainstream (Lincoln in *Young Mr. Lincoln,* Hallie in *The Man Who Shot Liberty Valance*) or fails to straddle the line between margin and mainstream successfully (Captain York in *Fort Apache*). In these films, Ford reveals his tragic view of assimilation. Though probably unavoidable for Euro-ethnics, and though it may mean material success and maybe even improving the mainstream, assimilation always exacts a heavy price from Ford's characters. As I have discussed, it is made most disturbingly explicit at the conclusion of *Fort Apache,* when Captain York emulates Lieutenant Colonel Thursday. But the price of assimilation casts a pall over the ending of *Young Mr. Lincoln* as well.

In it, Lincoln's margin/mainstream cultural dilemma is cast as the tension between ambition and modesty, and it is made explicit in his speech at Ann's grave. "I don't know," he says. "I'd feel such a fool, settin' myself up as a-knowin' so much." Still, by the end of *Young Mr. Lincoln* he's well on the road toward mainstream success, which Ford sees as inextricably tied to assimilation and his tragic fate. The film's bittersweet ending arises out of the tension between the conflicting resolutions of its two narratives. The dramatic narrative concludes neatly with a triumphant celebration of American values: success is achieved by the talented lawyer from the margin, the real murderer is caught, and the American system of justice prevails.

But the cultural subplot is busy responding to the questions posed by

Lincoln's dead mother in Rosemary Benet's poem quoted in the film's prologue ("What's happened to Abe? / What's he done? / . . . Did he grow tall? / Did he have fun? / Did he learn to read? / Did he get to town? / Do you know his name? / Did he get on?"). Ford's film replies that he "got to town" and did indeed "get on"—he entered the mainstream and achieved success there. In the process, however, he forsook the margin ideal, represented by Ann Rutledge (and perhaps by Carrie Sue), and replaced it with the snooty representative of the mainstream, Mary Todd. Yes, Lincoln succeeds in the mainstream, positively affecting American history in the process, but he pays dearly for assimilating. For Ford, the life of Lincoln spells out the exacting terms of the American Dream's cultural bargain: mainstream success requires assimilation; assimilation means cultural, and sometimes actual, death.[31]

The Cultural Balancing Act

Two soldiers, Captain Nathan Brittles (John Wayne) in *She Wore a Yellow Ribbon* and Colonel John Marlowe (John Wayne) in *The Horse Soldiers,* are caught between allegiances to their ethnic values and allegiance to the military institution. In focusing on these soldiers' plights, Ford highlights the messy cultural politics of American imperialism, in which immigrant ethnics—in a test of their loyalty—are required to fight and kill first each other (in the Civil War), then, on the Western front, the Natives. From this perspective, the disconcerting story of Colonel Marlowe in *The Horse Soldiers* (who helps destroy the South in order to preserve the Union) becomes a sobering correction to the fantasy heroics of Captain Nathan Brittles, who so deftly, heroically, but improbably manages to serve two cultural masters at once in *She Wore a Yellow Ribbon.*

The Contamination-of-the-Margin Plot

This story focuses on the margin society to chart the results of its "infection" by the virus of mainstream gentility. In order to escape the encroaching hypocritical Victorian value system, the protagonists of *Stagecoach, Wagon Master,* and *Two Rode Together* are forced to retreat to a culturally healthier frontier. There are several implications of this, none of them favorable for margin-ethnics. The first is that the infection is irreversible. Mainstream values, once introduced to the frontier, mean the beginning of "civilization" and the end of tolerance, as we see in the treatment of Dallas, the Mormons, and Elena, and the reversion to the letter rather than the spirit of the law, as we see in the treatment of the Ringo Kid. The second is that mainstream assimilation is practically inescapable. It can be delayed, but we know what Elena and Guthrie may not: mainstream assimilation will eventually come to California too. The only way to save oneself from, in Doc Boone's ironic phrase, "the blessings of civilization" is to do what Ringo and Dallas do, seek refuge "across the border," outside the United States.[32]

The Cultural Redemption Plot

Three protagonists, Robert Hightower (John Wayne) in *3 Godfathers,* Tom Doniphon in *The Man Who Shot Liberty Valance,* and Ethan Edwards in *The Searchers,* "sin" against the margin by acting against Ford's cardinal values, justice and tolerance. These stories ask if they can be redeemed. Bob Hightower can, even though he robbed the Welcome town bank. Culturally and legally he is redeemed by rescuing a baby from a dying woman, saving the child at the price of his freedom, refusing to relinquish custody of the child, and serving jail time for his transgression. Tom Doniphon's crime, murder, is more grievous, and on top of that, he never seeks redemption. His punishment is to be excluded from the margin, like Ethan. If Tom's ostracism is less poignant than Ethan's, it is probably because it happens off-screen.

Ethan's cultural "sins" are the worst of all: his adherence to vigilante violence and vengeance, culminating in his scalping of Scar, and his racial intolerance. Having rejected the mainstream and loathing the Native, when he is expelled by the margin at the end of *The Searchers* Ethan becomes Ford's most tragic character. Without a cultural home, he is like the dead Indian warrior whose eyes he shoots out—doomed to "wander forever between the winds." In the character of Ethan, Ford crystallizes the triumph and tragedy of American history. Ford correctly sees—and shows—that settling the West required courage as well as savagery. In insisting that westward expansion involved both bravery and barbarity, the cultural conclusion of *The Searchers* is among the most emotionally unsettling and ideologically clear-sighted moments in American cinema.

I have endeavored to show that, as an Irish American, John Ford was an ethnic filmmaker. His films centered on the ethnics he knew best, the Irish and other first- and second-generation European Americans who, a century ago when Ford was growing up, were among the most socially stigmatized and marginalized groups in America. Because he depicted the fluidity and hybridity of cultures, his films were impressive, sometimes progressive—and sometimes even groundbreaking—examples of multiculturalism.

The progressiveness of Ford's cinema came from consistently taking the side of the oppressed against the mainstream. The problem in Ford's Westerns from a multiculturalist's standpoint is that for him, the oppressed at the margin were principally Euro-ethnics. Ford's overarching project was to elevate Irish and European ethnics above WASP elites, not to put people of color down. Unfortunately, in trying to accomplish the former he often ended up doing the latter. Since his first allegiance was to Euro-ethnics, Ford's multiculturalism never completely overcame his white ethnocentrism. At its worst, this resulted in his insensitive treatment of people of color, the oft-mentioned stereotyping and paternalism.

But Ford's multiculturalism was driven too by an obsession with justice and tolerance, which, at its best, offset his ethnocentrism. In his Westerns, this resulted in such counterhegemonic elements as his persistent critique of the mainstream and his ubiquitous cultural subplot. Moreover, as his career progressed, the cultural focus of Ford's films widened beyond class and ethnic discrimination to include racial prejudice. Paradoxically, though, his most direct attacks on prejudice, in *Sergeant Rutledge* and *Cheyenne Autumn*, were the least satisfying culturally and aesthetically. His multiculturalism and his ideological critique of dominant ideology were most powerful in his other Westerns, where he could play with and subvert familiar genre formulas. Because of his ethnic background, his cultural formation, and his adherence to justice and tolerance, Ford's Westerns were never "just" Westerns. Beneath the grandeur of their sweeping dramatic narratives, Ford's cultural subplots were busy asking the most fundamental American question: Could America ever achieve its inclusive ideal—malice toward none, justice and liberty for all?

SEVEN

IMMIGRANTS, ALIENS, AND EXTRATERRESTRIALS

Science Fiction's Alien "Other" as (among Other *Things)* New Hispanic Imagery

It's a movie image we've all seen: a mysterious craft gliding through outer space carrying a menacing passenger toward Earth. I am thinking of the very beginning of *Predator* (1987, d. John McTiernan), one of the hit movies of the summer of 1987, though the scene might be one from any number of science fiction (SF) films, either from the 1950s SF movie Golden Age or from the current SF renaissance. In the case of *Predator,* this unexplained Alien[1] invasion sets into motion yet another deadly confrontation between an extraterrestrial and a human hero called upon to save the world. Along with *Alien* (1979, d. Ridley Scott), *Aliens* (1986, d. James Cameron), and several other recent films, *Predator* is a good example of the traditional depiction of the Alien "Other" in American science fiction films—as a Destructive Monster whose sole purpose, it seems, is the eradication of human civilization. Additional examples of this type include remakes of two 1950s SF classics, *Invaders from Mars* (1986, d. Tobe Hooper) and *Invasion of the Body Snatchers* (1978, d. Phil Kaufman), as well as such films as *Life Force* (1985, d. Tobe Hooper), *Critters* (1986, d. Stephen Herek), *Night of the Comet* (1984, d. Thom Eberhardt), *Repo Man* (1984, d. Alex Cox), *Strange Invaders* (1983, d. Michael Laughlin), *The Terminator* (1984, d. James Cameron), *The Thing* (1982, d. John Carpenter), and some episodes of *Twilight Zone—The Movie* (1983), and extends to spoofs like *Ghostbusters* (1984, d. Ivan Reitman) and *Little Shop of Horrors* (1986, d. Frank Oz).

But a new, increasingly popular Other in SF films has begun to rival the traditional Destructive Monster for primacy as outer space Other: the Sympathetic Alien. This wise, understanding extraterrestrial was an oddity back in the 1950s when it appeared in the memorable form of

Michael Rennie's dignified Klaatu in *The Day the Earth Stood Still* (1951, d. Robert Wise). Now the Sympathetic Alien is so common a figure that in the last ten years roughly one-half of the SF Alien films have one figuring in their narratives. This inversion of the clichéd Destructive Monster formula was firmly established by characters in the most successful SF films of all time: the Aliens in Steven Spielberg's *Close Encounters of the Third Kind* (1977) and *E.T.: The Extra-Terrestrial* (1982), and the knowing Yoda and the kindly Wookie Chewbacca and the various friendly Alien cohorts in the *Star Wars* series. Several of the films Spielberg and Lucas have since produced, including *Harry and the Hendersons* (1987, d. William Dear), *Batteries Not Included* (1987, d. Mathew Robbins), *Gremlins* (1984, d. Joe Dante), and *Howard the Duck* (1986, d. Willard Huyck), have played variations on the Sympathetic Alien formula. In addition, sympathetic Others are major protagonists in *Enemy Mine* (1985, d. Wolfgang Petersen), *Cocoon* (1985, d. Ron Howard), *Iceman* (1984, d. Fred Schepesi), *The Last Starfighter* (1984, d. Nick Castle), *Short Circuit* (1986, d. John Badham), *Splash* (1984, d. Ron Howard), *Starman* (1984, d. John Carpenter), in the *Superman* movies, and let us not forget *Star Trek*'s distinguished Mr. Spock.

In this chapter I want to look at the extraterrestrial Alien as it has been depicted in SF films since the resurgence of the SF genre in 1977 (the year both *Star Wars* and *Close Encounters of the Third Kind* were released). I am looking for answers to several questions, among them: What does the Alien in these SF films signify? What does the introduction of the Sympathetic Alien mean? And in what way is the SF Alien connected to Hispanic imagery in American cinema? I will propose that these films fulfill an important mythic-cultural function by providing a cinematic arena for the unconscious reflection on the immigrant "question."

SF MOVIES AND SF MONSTERS

Several critics have commented on the significance of the outer space Alien in SF films. The Alien invader in 1950s SF films has been seen as a personification of the Bomb, that is, a representation of collective nuclear fear and anxiety about the uses of atomic energy. Some have said that the Alien Creature is symbolic of repressed sexual urges that threatens domestic tranquility.[2] Others speculate that the 1950s Alien Other is related to the Red Menace, "those massed hordes of Communists foisted on the American people by such venomous Red-baiters as Joseph McCarthy, Richard Nixon, and Billy Graham."[3] Still others have discounted this notion in favor of a broader, oppositional, possibility: that in terms of American culture, the SF Alien simply stood for "everything the center was not," basically "anything un-American, unfamiliar, alien."[4] What all of these speculations have in common is the recognition of a narrative pattern that identifies foreign intruders as threats to national order and socio-ideological coherence.

Since the 1950s SF Golden Age, however, it seems something else is afoot. Commentators on renaissance (post-1977) SF have noted a shift in both the form and the content of the movies and in the signification of the Other. Following Fredric Jameson, Vivian Sobchack, in *Screening Space,* posits that "new descriptions of contemporary experience have begun to emerge and dominate older ones" in the last decade. Among them is the practice of the figuration of "the cultural logic of late capitalism" in "the transformed poetics of the contemporary American SF film."[5] Peter Fitting takes a different tack, and sees recent SF as visions of a postapocalyptic future.[6]

Robin Wood, combining Marx and Freud, and building on Gad Horowitz's work, has found a way, I think, to link all these approaches by framing his discussion of the horror films' monster Other in terms of oppression and repression. Recognizing that "Otherness can be theorized in many ways and on many levels," Wood views the Other as functioning "not simply as something external to the culture or to the self, but also as what is repressed (but never destroyed) in the self and projected outwards in order to be hated and disowned." On a society-wide level, the Other exists as a projection of what the culture represses. That is, the culture projects onto the Other "what is repressed within the Self, in order that it can be discredited, disowned, and if possible annihilated."[7]

The Other may stand for different things. Wood lists some figurative versions of the Other as it operates within our culture. Among the groups and ideas that are viewed by our culture as Other are other people, women, the proletariat, children, deviations from ideological or sexual norms, and, more pertinent to this study, other cultures and ethnic groups within the culture. Citing examples from horror films, Wood proceeds to illustrate the "monstrous" embodiments of the items on his list.[8] What I want to do here, then, is to apply Wood's "other cultures" category to the SF Alien of the last decade. I will focus on other cultures as they are perceived to impinge upon national identity via immigration. I contend that these new extraterrestrial films are a culturally unconscious means of working out the whole question of immigration as it has emerged in the last several decades. Wood says that it is possible to say "that the true subject of the horror genre is the struggle for recognition of all that our civilization represses and oppresses."[9] My project is first to propose a correspondence between immigrants and SF Alien Others and, second, to analyze it with the hope of unveiling what we as a society repress and oppress in regard to immigration.

If these films are indeed working out the immigrant question, then the Aliens are symbols for immigrants. Since Hispanics make up the majority of all alien groups (naturalized, documented, and undocumented), it follows that science fiction Aliens present a radically new image of the Hispanic in Hollywood cinema. Because the Alien in SF movies stands for new immigrants in general, it is a polysemic image of the un-American Other, a signifier with a number of signifieds. Among them are a number of ethnic, national, and racial groups. What I want to do is investigate one signifier-signified pair, the Alien as Hispanic immigrant, in order to track the consequences of moving the cinematic representation of Latinos from stereotypes (in which group members are portrayed as one-dimensional characters) to distortion (where they are depicted as nonhuman Aliens). I want to amplify on this, but first let me turn to a discussion of our recent "immigrant problem" to see how the latest influx of aliens is affecting our sense of national identity and how it is that I contend that immigrant aliens are represented by Alien intruders in Hollywood science fiction films.

THE NEW IMMIGRANTS AND THE EXTRATERRESTRIAL

The total of 544,000 immigrants who are allowed legal entry to the United States each year is actually lower than the yearly number of legal immigrants who entered during the first two decades of this century, the years of heaviest immigration traffic in our history (8.5 million entered legally during the period 1900–1910 alone).[10] But to this need to be added the number of undocumented aliens residing here as well as the inflow of undocumented immigrants. The number of undocumented aliens living in the United States at any one time is difficult to pinpoint; the U.S. Census Bureau estimated in 1978 that the figure was anywhere between 3.5 million and 6 million.[11] The number of aliens who attempt illegal entry every year is similarly difficult to calculate. The statistics show that for the last several years an average of more than 1 million aliens per year entered the United States without proper documentation; nearly 5.8 million were apprehended by the INS in 1980–1985.[12] But these figures are confounded by three factors. First, those who are caught represent only a fraction of those attempting to cross (in 1980 one Border Patrol official in El Paso told me he estimated one in ten aliens attempting entry was apprehended). Second, yearly alien apprehension numbers are inflated since many aliens attempt border crossings more than once a year. Third, an unknown percentage of illegal immigrants enter the United States for short stays, then return home. Nevertheless, it is clear that the total number of immigrants coming to the United States in recent years is a formidable figure.

I want to suggest that among other things—because as Wood says, a culture's Other is not one thing but several Other things—the SF Alien is a figure for the alien immigrants who have been entering the country in increasing numbers for the past several decades. Among the historical events that helped to create this latest crop of immigrants I would isolate three moments:

1. Fidel Castro's rise to power in Cuba in 1959, which resulted immediately in three-quarters of a million immigrants coming to the United States, and other Cubans would continue immigrating to the present day; by the end of the 1970s there were more than one million Cuban Americans living in the United States.

2. The cessation of the *bracero* program in 1964. Begun during World War II to supplement the U.S. labor force, the *bracero* program had allowed Mexican nationals—hundreds of thousands of them by the 1950s, some say millions by the mid-1960s—to work legally in the United States. Shutting down the program closed what was at least a safety valve for Mexicans trying to get work in the Unites States, in effect forcing them underground.

3. The Immigration and Nationality Act of 1965, put into effect in 1968, which abandoned the quota system and had the effect of shifting the immigrants' place of national origin from Old World to Third World.[13]

My contention is that since the last great flowering of Hollywood SF in the 1950s, the movie Alien now symbolizes real-life aliens—documented and undocumented immigrants who have entered, and continue to attempt to enter, the United States.

Hispanics constitute the largest immigrant group. Of those naturalized in 1985, for example, 46 percent were Hispanics. In the same year, the percentage of Hispanics among deported aliens was 93 percent.[14] As

I have said, the SF Alien is a signifier with a number of signifieds. Among them are new immigrants in general and—since they are the largest group—alien Hispanics in particular.

Of course it could be argued that the new SF Alien also stands for Asians, too, or any other of the world's peoples that make up the new immigrant. But I will limit my discussion to the group most heavily represented among the new immigrants, and compare Hispanic's SF representations—as Alien Others—with their usual, stereotypical depictions. Recognizing that another similar essay could compare, for instance, Asian stereotypes and Alien monsters, I nevertheless deliberately restrict my focus to Hispanics for purposes of convenience and manageability. In the discussion of cinematic stereotypes, therefore, I will deal only with Hollywood's depiction of the Hispanic. Beyond mere convenience, comparing the traditional Hispanic stereotype—which has a long history in American cinema—with the new Alien provides me with a powerful critical dialectic that allows me to chart an interesting pattern of displacement and distortion, and gives me a way to resolve a troubling problem posed by the arrival of the renaissance SF Alien: Why have stereotyped cinematic representations of the Hispanic recently become so grossly debased?

NEW HISPANIC IMAGES IN AMERICAN CINEMA

Thus far we have noted a double representation change. One is the split in the symbology of the Alien in SF films, where the outerspace creature can now be either a traditional Destructive Monster or a newer Sympathetic Alien. A second is the distortion of Hispanic (and other ethnic group) imagery. The emergence of the Alien as a Hispanic image is significant. As we know, since the days' of silent cinema not just Hispanics but all ethnics have been dealt with in American movies mainly by stereotyping. Now an interesting distortion has occurred: Hispanics and other immigrant ethnics have become Creatures from Another Planet, Aliens that must be eliminated—either lovingly, by returning them to their native environs (*E.T., Close Encounters of the Third Kind, Harry and the Hendersons, Iceman, Splash, Cocoon*) or violently, by destroying them (*Alien[s], Predator, The Terminator, The Aurora Encounter, Critters*).

Where does such distortion come from and what does it signify? As I develop my argument I want to offer sociological, historical, psychological, and ultimately ideological answers. As a starting proposition, let me say that part of the answer is the perceived heightening of political and economic stakes placed upon the system by the new immigrant. The rise in the number of immigrants coming to the United States over the last two decades coincides with the gradual national realization of finiteness over the same period of time. From the native-born American's point of view, these new aliens are competition for a limited number of jobs and a dwindling reserve of social services. Stereotyped Hispanic images were common cinematic currency over a long period of our nation's history when the dominant Anglo majority *was not fundamentally threatened* by Hispanics, immigrants, or any other racial or ethnic minority group. Now the threat is palpable. The new Alien portrayal of the Hispanic immigrant is the symbolic correlative of a majority perception of the immigrant that is shifting from neglect to resentment. Such swings in the cognizance and treatment of immigrants by dominant groups in this country go back at least to the 1800s:

> During times of contentment and prosperity immigrants who did not conform were usually left to fend for themselves, but in times of emotional or economic adversity they have been victimized. Sometimes they have been labeled as the causes of the national difficulties; at other times they have stood in for elite groups as a more socially acceptable outlet for the release of high tensions.[15]

Anya Peterson Royce delineates different sorts of social dynamics between groups, based on power relationships and the changing nature of the stereotyping that results. She notes the shifts in the severity of the language used by groups as the power available to them is more competitively contested.[16] In the case of stratified social relations between a dominant group holding practically uncontested power over a subordinate group, the less powerful group is often typed along a spectrum of possibilities from harmless and childlike to dangerous. In the case of Hispanic film images, these correspond to the recognized stereotypes that I outlined in Chapter 3, running the gamut from the male buffoon and the corresponding female clown to a long line of slick Latin lovers, including alluring but treacherous half-breed harlots, as well as the sneaky *bandido*.

In the oppositional case of two groups competing for power and resources, however, stereotyping is different. The dominant group that once had autonomous use of now-contested power is naturally threatened, and its response tends to be hostile. Royce's example is the loss of power experienced by white Southern males after the Civil War, the rise of the Ku Klux Klan, and the increase in the number of lynchings of Blacks during that period. That violence mirrored dominant group confusion over "the breakdown of a world where everyone shared knowledge of the categories, stereotypes, and social rules—a world where each individual knew his or her place and did not challenge its appropriateness."[17] Certainly one factor that is perceived to threaten the Anglo-dominant American society's ordered worldview today is the increasing influx of immigrants. An upsetting aspect of the immigrant flow to the empowered majority is the severe strain it puts on the American melting pot ideal. Consequently, beyond threats to power, resources, and social order, there are also perceived threats to national well-being and psychosocial "order" in terms of the disruption of a nation's sense of ideological equilibrium and self-identity.

This antiforeign, pro-native sentiment has deep historical roots. "The spirit of American nativism," writes John Higham, "appeared long before the word was coined about 1840 and had its deepest impact long after the word had largely dropped out of common parlance." One later form of American xenophobia, "racial nativism," linked the Anglo-Saxon "race" with national greatness.[18] And for most of the nineteenth century the notion of the Anglo-Saxon as essential national ideal proved to be compatible with the founding ideals of humanity, democracy, and equal rights, fostering a general belief in the efficacy of immigrant assimilation. In fact, during the last three decades of that century, America's often-invoked mission was to serve as a shelter for the freedom-loving oppressed of the world. Emma Lazarus's fund-raising verse for the Statue of Liberty was emblematic of such feeling:

> Give me your tired, your poor,
> Your huddled masses yearning to breathe free,
> The wretched refuse of your teeming shore,
> Send these, the homeless, tempest-tost to me,
> I lift my lamp beside the golden door![19]

But, as Higham notes, there is condescension and contradiction in the invitation. In its self-congratulatory way, the poem expresses the belief that the immigrants yearn for a deliverance from oppression that only America can grant them, yet they are deemed "wretched refuse." The immigrant was perceived, then as now, as both boon and burden—and at times even a menace.

Ambivalent attitudes toward new immigrants stretch back at least a hundred years in American history, revealing a complex and painful tension. A nation that prides itself on having been founded and built by immigrants, that cherishes the diversity of its roots ("E pluribus unum"), and calls itself the melting pot of the world, is the same nation that has a well-documented record of antagonisms toward new immigrants, sometimes erupting into episodes of outright violence. This ambivalence continues to be played out today. Recent events provide numerous conflicted examples of the clash between official pride and existential concern that are centered, in one way or another, around the immigrant question. For example, there was the extended congressional debate over the immigration reform bill, lasting roughly six years, and resulting in the Simpson-Rodino-Mazzoli Immigration Reform Act of 1986.[20] There is the controversy surrounding the Sanctuary movement, the underground asylum program for Salvadoran refugees. Another example is the millions spent refurbishing the Statue of Liberty and the elaborate commemorative celebration for the statue harking back to the days of Emma Lazarus's poem and America's ethnocentric open-door policy. In startling contrast to this were the 1987 prison riots by about-to-be-deported immigrants, the Marielitos, protesting their forced return to Cuba.

Fredric Jameson posits the notion of a unitary political unconscious and calls for a kind of criticism that recognizes that "there is nothing that is not social and historical—indeed that everything is 'in the last analysis' political," a criticism that follows through and explores "the multiple paths that lead to the unmasking of cultural artifacts as socially symbolic acts."[21] In the realm of film, Thomas G. Schatz hypothesizes that genre movies operate "as socially symbolic acts" in a way similar to the Lévi-Strauss model of myth, namely "to provide a logical model capable of overcoming a contradiction."[22] Following in their footsteps is Peter Fitting, who, in his discussion of recent SF, sees the genre unconsciously addressing social "troubles":

> Like the manifest content of our dreams which can only emerge in heavily coded representations, these filmic images of the future are displaced signals from the social unconscious. Distorted so as to be unrecognizable, these indications of major troubles in our present, these signs of its fractures and contradictions work their way to the surface more easily in these less censored popular films, while the catastrophes of which they speak are not to be talked about in polite society.[23]

My position here is that one of the "major troubles" being addressed by the Alien SF movies is America's century-long melting pot dilemma. The immigrant question goes beyond the situation of an in-group competing with an out-group for resources. And it goes beyond in-group scapegoating of a politically powerless out-group (another possible cause of stereotyping[24]). The new immigrant "invasion" calls into question the very identity of the nation itself, and the rejection of the Alien in SF is projected, mass-mediated nativism. Viewed in this light, the SF Alien film since 1976 represents a forum for the national consideration of the "immigrant problem," though it is far from an open one, since it constantly comes to the same conclusion: the status quo can be maintained only by exclusion. Writing about the 1950s SF Alien, Judith Hess Wright says that those films built on fears of the intrusive and the overpowering and thereby promoted isolationism.[25] Extending that analysis to the SF films of today, that isolationist program takes specific historical shape in the advocacy of a closed-door immigration policy, which the 1986 Immigration Law sought to ensure. Today's SF film provides an arena for the negotiation of the pluralist–nativist tension; in order for this to occur, the immigrant takes the symbolic shape of the Alien.

This helps clarify the new figure of the Sympathetic Alien. The contradictory American position, that historically and officially honors its immigrant roots while simultaneously shunning new immigrants, produces a considerable measure of psychic guilt. This assimilationist–nativist tension is partially assuaged by the creation of the prescient, kindly-but-knowing Sympathetic SF Alien. Such characters allow the dominant group to appreciate the positive qualities of the intruders while at the same time recognizing their intrinsic (and irreconcilable) difference from us (and the U.S.). What we are made to realize through the appreciation–deportation narratives of Sympathetic Alien SF is that for all the space creatures' virtues they are still Aliens—a difference that makes not only a difference, but all the difference in the world. In narrative terms, this necessitates the Sympathetic Alien's leaving Earth and returning home. The Sympathetic Aliens in *Close Encounters, Cocoon, E.T., The Last Starfighter,* and *Splash* all return home, while the good Aliens in *Gremlins, Harry and the Hendersons,* and *Iceman* are returned to their natural habitat by human agents.

The Sympathetic Alien allows us to have it both ways: We can appreciate the aliens, and even learn from them. But in the end we must return to normality by sending *them* home—for their own good. Harry, E.T., and the Neanderthal man in *Iceman* are all returned to where they came from because they could not survive in the United States; for one reason or another their new Earth environment was life-threatening. In so doing the human heroes do the Aliens a favor—they are actually saving the extraterrestrials' lives. In terms of the immigrant question, this narrative resolution neatly blends both nativist sentiment and common humanity to rationalize deportation as more beneficial to aliens than to us. Deportation exists for the good of aliens, these films say; like E.T., aliens simply cannot exist (nor should they try) in our rarefied atmosphere. It would be best for all concerned—especially Them—if they left.

What will happen to aliens should they refuse to leave is illustrated metaphorically—and graphically—by the Destructive Monster SF films. Pushed to the ultimate limit by the Alien invasion, the human protagonists of these films do battle with the monster from outer space until it is eradicated. Aliens in Destructive Monster movies from *Alien* to *Predator* to *Blade Runner* are sucked into outer space, blasted to smithereens, or die a merciless, genetically engineered death. The message seems to be as clear and succinct as it is brutal: A/aliens, go home or die. Just as intriguing as the narrative formula that repeatedly eliminates the Alien in these films, however, is the process that accounts for the transformation of the Hispanic image in American films from the various human stereotypes into a Creature from Outer Space.

THE ALIEN AS DREAM-WORK

How do you go from a dream (in which the Hispanic is represented as a stereotype) to a nightmare (where Hispanic alien = Alien creature)? "The conditions under which a dream becomes a nightmare," Robin Wood says, "are (a) that the repressed wish is, from the point of view of consciousness, so terrible that it must be repudiated as loathsome, and (b) that it is so strong and powerful as to constitute a serious threat."[26] Having established the real-life external pressure immigrants place on national sovereignty and resources, as well as the internal psychological tension produced by the presence of the aliens (together with another threatening fact I haven't yet mentioned: Hispanics will soon become the national majority), the next step is to account for how the nightmare takes shape.

The psychoanalytic understanding of the Hispanic image's radical transformation from a human stereotype like the greaser bandit to a murderous Alien monster, and the basis for Wood's dream-to-nightmare progression above is provided by Freud in his discussion of the dream-work. A dream is wish-fulfillment; some dreams are undisguised wish-fulfillments, and others are less recognizable. "In cases where the wish-fulfillment is unrecognizable, where it has been disguised," Freud says, "there must have existed some inclination to put up a defense against the wish; and owing to this defense the wish was unable to express itself except in a distorted shape."[27] This dream-distortion Freud describes as a result of the battle between two "psychical forces" or "agencies" within the dreamer. "One of these forces," Freud writes, "constructs the wish which is expressed by the dream, while the other exercises a censorship upon this dream-wish and, by the use of that censorship, forcibly brings about a distortion in the expression of the wish." The first force presents the wish to the second force, which determines if that wish needs to be distorted before reaching consciousness. "Nothing," says Freud, "can reach consciousness from the first system without passing the second agency; and the second agency allows nothing to pass without exercising its rights and making such modifications as it thinks fit in the thought which is seeking admission to consciousness."[28]

This psychoanalytic schema can be applied to the case of Hispanic imagery in Hollywood cinema and SF films to provide an explanation for the dual, progressively distorted representation (stereotyped human to Alien creature) of Hispanics. Stereotyped versions of the Hispanic correspond to (relatively) undisguised dreams, serving to fulfill the wish of the dominant society to exercise control of Hispanics by belittling, ridiculing, and exaggerating them into the margin. Since in traditional Hollywood films the stereotyped representation of the Hispanic at least retains human form, as compared with the Alien extraterrestrial, the cinematic Hispanic stereotype achieves its marginalizing ends through only a modicum of distortion. The Alien Others, on the other hand, are fully disguised symbols for immigrants and Hispanics. Here the immigrant Other has gone through society's two-stage dream-work process of wish-fulfillment and distortion.

Freud links dream-distortion to the need of the dreamer to prevent anxiety or other distressing feelings,[29] and Wood says that the dream becomes nightmare when what is wished for is loathsome, powerful, and a serious threat. I speculate that the root cause of the cinematic distortion of the Hispanic goes far beyond concerns about loss of jobs or the drain on social services that the Immigration Reform Act sought to redress—though those material concerns are important. Something more fundamental is perceived to be at stake: national identity, the ideal of a unified, national "self." What Higham said about nativism in the early years of the twentieth century is applicable today:

> Nativism cut deeper than economic jealousy or social disapproval. It touched the springs of fear and hatred; it breathed a sense of crisis. Above all, it expressed a militantly defensive nationalism; an aroused conviction

that an intrusive element menaced the unity, and therefore the integrity and survival, of the nation itself.[30]

We distort through fear of losing our national self.

NEGATIVE AND POSITIVE STEREOTYPES

In linking the stereotype with the distortion for analytical purposes, it may be profitable to review the psychological mechanism of stereotyping. Sander L. Gilman uses developmental psychology to account for stereotyping, and his breakdown can be used as a model to delineate the traditional Hispanic stereotypes in Hollywood cinema.[31] His approach will also give us a way to interpret the distorted Hispanic Alien. Stereotyping, which everyone creates, has its origin in subjects at some time in early infanthood (from the age of several weeks to six months) and is linked to the child's growing awareness of the difference between self and world. When, to the child, self = world, control is absolute. As the child realizes that the world is much more than the self, anxiety arises because of the concomitant loss of control. As a coping strategy the child divides the self, and the world, into good (able to be controlled and anxiety-free) and bad (unable to be controlled and anxiety-full) halves. Next, the child distances the good self from the bad, creating an "us = good"/"them = bad" dichotomy. This psychic process is dynamic and situational, requiring the subject to redefine the boundary between self and Other according to stresses made upon the psyche. The Other takes on a protean quality, allowing it to take a myriad of forms as the situation warrants. The us/them anxiety is projected onto the Other to produce the stereotype.

Gilman explains the Other as both positive and negative. "The Other is invested with all of the qualities of the 'bad' and the 'good.'" Both positive and negative stereotypes exist. "The 'bad' Other becomes the negative stereotype; the 'good' Other becomes the positive stereotype. The former is that which we fear to become; the latter, that which we fear we cannot achieve." [32] This allows us to think of the standard Hispanic stereotypes in an interesting way—as negative or positive projections of dominant-group anxiety. We can arrange six conventional Hispanic stereotypes in two triad groups, based on gender. Each triad consists of a central positive stereotype and two negative ones: a positive center with two negative alternatives. For example, the two negative female stereotypes (the half-breed harlot and the clown) are opposed to the positive one (the dark lady). And the "greaser" *bandido* and male buffoon are opposed to the mysterious and magnetic Latin lover.

It is important to remember that whether negative or positive, these are still stereotypes—rigidly applied, crude, oversimplified representations of a group—and that even the positive stereotypes operate by marginalization. The dark lady and the Latin lover, while perhaps more tolerable to the dominant group and maybe flattering to Hispanics, are still flat, one-dimensional, generalized types, nothing more. Dolores Del Río was alluring, but aloof, detached, apart; Fernando Lamas was romantic, but like all Latin lovers the possessor of some special sort of sexual magic that differentiated him from the Anglo male. The result: both of these characters were just as distanced from the Anglo majority, by idealization rather than denigration, as their treacherous or clownish counterparts. All of this is of interest to us here because there are corresponding positive (the Sympathetic Alien) and negative (the Destructive Monster) extraterrestrials in 1970s and 1980s Alien SF.

SUPERMAN AND SPOCK: "NATURALIZED" ALIENS

Such Alien analogues of the established Hispanic stereotypes provide a framework to begin the analysis of those texts. For example, it gives us a way to account for such apparent anomalies as Superman and Spock, the Sympathetic Aliens who are not ushered out of our universe. First we must recognize the beneficial role of these two characters. Superman is a savior figure who rids the planet of world-threatening devastation. Mr. Spock, half-human, half-Alien, is clearly a less deific Other, though his contribution is still unique to the human crew of the Starship *Enterprise:* a combination of superior intellectual ability and calculated judgment.

These two likable and heroic figures function in much the same way as the Hispanic dark lady or Latin lover: they are characters imbued with special powers that set them apart from "normal" humans. And like the dark lady or the Latin lover they are allowed a place in Anglo society when they have demonstrated that the difference they represent has a potentially positive payoff. The Dolores Del Río characters in *Flying Down to Rio* (1933, d. Thorton Freeland) and *In Caliente* (1935, d. Lloyd Bacon) are so hotly pursued by the male Anglo protagonists because, though perhaps never expressed in so many words, they are like no other women in the (Anglo) world. Ricardo Montalbán's ChuChu Ramírez in *My Man and I* (1952, d. William Wellman) is allowed entry

166

to the Anglo world not when he becomes a naturalized citizen but only when he proves his value to the system (through hard work, productivity, determination, and mostly his unquestioning patriotic loyalty to the United States). Similarly, Sympathetic Aliens are allowed to stay if they can offer a unique service to the dominant majority—especially if they can protect humans from destructive alien forces. In *Blade Runner*, for example, Rachael, a Replicant herself, saves Deckard's life by killing another Replicant; Howard the Duck saves the world from the impending invasion of Alien "dark overlords of the universe"; and the android Bishop saves Ripley's life in *Aliens*.

Sympathetic Aliens' contributions are so uniquely beneficial that they not only are allowed to stay but are invited with open arms to stay. Once here, they will pass from acculturation to the desired (and only acceptable) end: "naturalization." Dolores Del Río's characters mentioned above don't have far to go: she is already an upper-class debutante in *Flying Down to Rio* and possesses all the proper high-class trappings in *In Caliente*. The narrative logic of ChuChu Ramírez's character is that he becomes a better American than a native-born citizen, and thus reminds the rest of us "what being an American is all about." Likewise, we are tickled when the half-human Spock finally and convincingly displays his appreciation—and application—of human qualities in *Star Trek IV: The Voyage Home* (1986, d. Leonard Nimoy). When he depends upon a "human" trait we recognize he is almost "home," almost one of us. One of the high points of the Superman films is Superman and Lois Lane's lovemaking. Viewers are made to wonder what they have wondered since the days of Rudolph Valentino—what must super sex with a super lover be like? Once again, as it was for the dark lady–Anglo male and the Latin lover–Anglo female pairings, sex is the great leveler of social barriers—extraordinary lovers have an automatic entrée to our society.

But afterward, it is expected that the A/alien will adapt and finally become a native. Thus, by *Superman III*, the Alien who is "more powerful than a locomotive" marries a divorced mother and settles down to earthling family life. The narrative trajectory of the *Star Trek* and *Superman* series allows us, then, to see a crucial immigrant/native trade-off. America will drop its isolationist barrier to get something uniquely valuable, be it a beautiful dark lady, a Latin lover, Mikhail Baryshnikov, or Superman. The Alien, in exchange for this acceptance, must do what generations of aliens have been called on to do for centuries—assimilate. That is, Superman, Mr. Spock, Howard the Duck, and the other naturalized SF Aliens must find a way to negotiate the exchange of original values, "such as personal loyalty to friends and origins, for social and ethical values that allow identification with the society of one's choice. Successful assimilation . . . means a real, if unacknowledged, rejection and repudiation of the family and friends with whom one grew up." [33] Thus for America, it becomes simply a matter of shrewd business, acquiring what you don't have in order to maintain power. Such gaps in America's nativism are never threatening because the end point of this process is the place where assimilation and co-optation converge. Howard the Duck becomes a rock 'n' roll star. ChuChu Ramírez becomes the ideal American; Superman fights for "Truth, Justice, and the American Way."

What we are made to see here is the way the psychological mechanism of stereotyping vaults us into the realm of the ideological. For cinematic stereotyping, because of the way it structures thinking, is hegemony. It does its work by generalization and repetition, creating a simplified—but comprehensive and "natural"—worldview. The Alien distortion is merely one more turn of that same screw.

THE TERMINATOR: (PRO)CREATING THE CORRECT FUTURE

On one level, *The Terminator* is a film about the radicalization of a woman. Sarah Connor (Linda Hamilton) goes from being a carefree single woman at the movie's beginning to a politically committed single mother by film's end. And so on the one hand the film is to be applauded for its progressive feminist narrative. But on the other, from the viewpoint of how the Alien is portrayed, how it functions in the narrative, and the manner in which "We" finally defeat "Them," there are enough disturbing elements to give one pause.

The Terminator is a fascinating variation on the time-travel theme. Its back-to-the-present narrative provides an excellent illustration of the way SF can provide, as Fredric Jameson says, a new slant on history, allowing us a perspective from which we become "conscious of our present as the past of some unexpected future rather than as the future of a heroic national past" [34]—though in the film the insurance of the proper heroic (and human) future requires the proper preservation and manipulation of the right sets of genes. Thus, *The Terminator* plants the seeds of its eugenic message early. The battle for the survival of the human race begins now. The prologue, appearing on the screen at the film's opening with the bleak landscape of the Alien-dominated future in the background (there are an abundance of human skulls amidst the rubble, crushed beneath the heavy treads of the Alien war machines), makes the racial stakes very clear:

> The machines rose from the ashes of nuclear fire. Their war to extermi-nate mankind had raged for decades, but the final battle would not be fought in the future. It would be fought here, in our present. Tonight . . .

We are in danger of being dominated—and exterminated—by Them. Our survival is precarious at best. It is a battle that cannot be put off any longer but must be waged immediately.

The Alien here, a futuristic *bandolero,* is a cyborg (Arnold Schwar-zenegger) from forty-four years into the future—a time when humans fight with their cyborg masters for survival. After years of fighting a revo-lutionary war against their computerized overlords, humans are finally winning. In a desperate move, the cyborg rulers send an unstoppable ro-bot warrior, a Terminator, back in time to alter history. If the Termina-tor can find and murder Sarah, he will prevent the birth of her son, who grows to be the rebel leader who spearheads the overthrow of comput-erized rule. This Alien is a fearful killer, described as "an infiltration unit, part man, part machine." It represents, we are told, a significant advance over previous cyborgs in that superficially it is human, though internally it is driven by a high-tech brain and microchip heart. Kyle (Michael Biehn), the rebel who is sent back in time to warn Sarah, de-scribes it well: "Underneath it's a hyper-alloy, combat chassis, micro-processor controlled—fully armored, very tough. But outside it's living human tissue: flesh, skin, hair, blood. . . . They look human: sweat, bad breath, everything. Very hard to spot." (This last sentence might be spo-ken by a Border Patrol officer looking for aliens along the U.S.–Mexico border, where distinguishing among resident Mexican aliens, docu-mented and undocumented Mexican immigrants, and native Mexican Americans can be difficult in the extreme.) Thus the threat of this film's Alien "race" is doubly pernicious: they are powerful and they look just like us.

The Terminator is, of course, an antitechnology fable. Warning of the potential terrors of the blind acceptance of new technologies, it is yet another instance of the familiar progress-run-amok SF theme. But the film is at the same time a paean of isolationism and racial paranoia. Schwarzenegger's cyborg is an "infiltration unit," built to in-vade—and destroy—human colonies. In one of Kyle's "flashbacks" (to his past, our future), he recalls a bloody incident at an underground human hiding place—an infiltrating cyborg brutally massacres an entire community. The Alien intruders of the future, once they have established their dominance, have a fascistic single-mindedness about achieving their goal of racial extermination. Indeed, Kyle's descriptions of the automated death camps of the technocratic future, in which humans are slaughtered night and day, conjures up frightful reminiscences of Nazi Germany. Yet the film invokes Nazism on the human side as well when the rebel counterattack relies on a disturbing combination of eugenics and the Christ story: Sarah and Kyle must mate in order to procreate the savior of the race.

The deeper structure of this survivalist narrative involves the construction of a workable response to the impending dominance of the Alien "hordes." One of the underlying threats alien immigrants have always posed to the native mainstream is not only their present numbers, but their procreative potential. This argument took formal—and acceptable—intellectual shape in the late 1800s when Francis A. Walker, president of the Massachusetts Institute of Technology and a leading economist, combined nativism, eugenics, Darwinism, and declining native birthrates to construct a racial basis for native American superiority in the face of the influx of what he viewed as unassimilative races. That century's new immigrants, "beaten men from beaten races; representing the worst failures in the struggle for existence," [35] would nevertheless be able, through uncontrolled reproduction, to defeat native Americans biologically. The answer to this, which only true racism was able to provide, was eugenics. In other words, native Americans, unable to compete numerically with the wave of immigrants, would have to offset the immigrants' procreative advantage by exploiting and maintaining their own (inbred) advantage—the "natural" superiority of the Anglo-Saxon "race."

Eugenics and anthropology added the needed theoretical basis for nativism at the end of the last century and the beginning of this one, and when that line of thinking reached the point at which it proclaimed one race superior to another, it resulted in racism. *The Terminator* illustrates a two-pronged answer to the alien invasion implicit in the logic of the racist argument: eliminating Them and maintaining Anglo-Saxon racial purity. The coming takeover by computers is not necessarily *the* future, but as Kyle puts it, "One possible future." The United States might survive in the face of immigrant infiltration, but only if it acts quickly. In the film's terms: if the right man and the right woman join sexually, the human race has a chance not only to create a future savior of the race, but also to maintain the racial purity needed to defeat Aliens. Today, to ensure the best possible future, vigilance is needed—eternal vigilance. As Sarah says to Kyle once she has fully comprehended the severity of the crisis and its irreversible human implications, "It'll never be over, will it?"

No. It will never be over because We have already let too many of Them in. And, as another cyborg Alien film, *Blade Runner,* shows, They are getting harder and harder to find and eliminate from our society.

BLADE RUNNER: A CRITIQUE OF NEO-NATIVISM

Blade Runner foresees a somewhat different future ahead in nearly the same time period (2019) as *The Terminator,* one in which humans still have an upper hand, but not the uppermost hand. That belongs to the powerful Tyrell Corporation, which runs things and creates this film's Alien Others, the cyborg Replicants. The Tyrell Corporation is the shape of twenty-first-century capitalism. "Commerce is our goal here at Tyrell," Mr. Tyrell says, speaking of the company's most cherished commercial venture, the Replicants. "More human than human is our motto" (more than a little reminiscent of General Electric's past and current catch phrases "Progress is our most important product" and "We bring good things to life").

The problem for Blade Runner Deckard (Harrison Ford), a specially trained policeman who executes Replicants, is the things Tyrell has brought to life. They become problematic because of the Tyrell Corporation's creation ethics. The Replicants—used as slave labor, for hazardous explorations, and for the colonization of other planets—are better humans than humans. "The NEXUS 6 Replicants," we are told at the film's beginning, are "superior in strength and agility, and at least equal in intelligence, to the genetic engineers who created them." When a group of renegade Replicants mutiny in outer space (the "Off World"), they are "declared illegal on earth—under penalty of death." Deckard's assignment, in the terminology of the Tyrell Corporation, is to "retire" the rebellious Replicants.

From our perspective, *Blade Runner* is a meditation on, and a critique of, nativism. Deckard is the next century's Border Patrolman, charged with the identification and extermination of Alien trespassers. As it is for Border Patrolmen today, the Blade Runner's job is the maintenance of national, cultural, social, psychological, and political unity and identity.

Blade Runner (1982) is set in Los Angeles in 2019. Deckard (Harrison Ford), a sort of futuristic Border Patrol agent, tracks down and executes human-looking robots, called Replicants, who rebel rather than be terminated. One of them, played by Daryl Hannah, lurks in the background of a room filled with life-size dolls.

He is paid to be able to distinguish Them from Us and to eradicate Them from our midst. Deckard's dilemma is very similar to that of the Border Patrolman played by Jack Nicholson in *The Border,* namely, how to uphold national identity in the face of the aliens' demonstrated humanity. *Blade Runner*'s main conflict is psychological: Deckard's inner tension between his job and his conscience. In this way, the film raises questions about the justice and humanity of America's policy of cold-blooded nativist isolationism.

For *Blade Runner* establishes well the Replicants' humanness. In part the Replicants could be said to be a combination of negative *bandido* and the superhuman Latin lover, though as the film progresses, they leave one-dimensional stereotyping as Alien bad guys behind and develop into complex characters. In terms of the Hispanic stereotype, the Replicant leader, Roy, could be compared with Raza, Jack Palance's revolutionary general in *The Professionals* (1966, d. Richard Brooks). Raza is first seen summarily executing *Federales* en masse. Later we voyeuristically watch as he makes passionate love to his woman. It is only in the last third of the film that we understand his motivation, which greatly softens his earlier, stereotypical actions. By film's end, he has left the stereotypical *bandido* behind and approaches a much more fully rounded characterization. So, too, Roy is at first presented as evil and menacing—an Aryan Destructive Monster, but by the end of *Blade Runner,* when he saves Deckard's life, his tragedy is clear: He is a superhuman who simply wants to be human.

The problem, just as it is in *The Terminator,* is Us (U.S.): what We have done and what We have allowed to happen (in the film's past, which is our present). Again, the film shows the fear of technology in the harrowing future that new tech will bring, of which the authoritarian Tyrell Corporation is only the most obvious sign. But it also shows the chaotic results of ethnic pluralism (that we are allowing to happen today). Simple communicative tasks are difficult. Deckard has trouble ordering food from an Asian street vendor. Gaff (Edward James Olmos), Deckard's assistant, speaks a street gibberish that Deckard tells us is a combination "of Japanese, Spanish, German, whatever." The teeming, multicultural makeup of the people in the streets is depicted as the dark side of the melting pot: chaos, filth, overcrowding, disorder. This technologized future world is a disintegrating Babel that shows the fearful results of an open-door immigration policy. Symbolically, our immigrant dilemma becomes the new century's aliens, the Replicants, a problem We created. The patronizing and condescending side of America's open-door policy resurfaces in the Tyrell Corporation's implied position on the rebel Replicants: We created them, We gave them a chance, and—their rebellion is the thanks We receive in return. In reality the chance the Replicants were given was the opportunity to be exploited. The Replicants are twenty-first-century *braceros.* Their lot is unpleasant at best, and they are intelligent and human enough to realize it. "Quite an experience to live in fear, isn't it?" Roy, the Replicant leader, asks Deckard just at the point when he could kill him. "That's what it is to be a slave." [36]

All they want, once introduced to Our life, is a chance to live it. "I want more life!" Roy tells Tyrell. And, of course, that is precisely what We cannot allow Them to have, not without risking our dominance. "You were built as well as we could make you," Tyrell responds. "But not to last," Roy replies. The designers realized the inherent danger of creating slaves "more human than human," and so built in a fail-safe

Deckard with his assistant, Gaff (Edward James Olmos), who,
Deckard says in voice-over narration, speaks a jumble of languages,
"Japanese, Spanish, German, whatever."

mechanism—Replicants automatically die in four years. What the turn-coat Replicants want is normal human mortality. *Blade Runner* asks the fundamental question of nativism: Why can't They stay? It asks us to consider how humane denying them "life" is. How humane was it to bring in Mexican laborers (by some estimates five million of them) during the twenty-two-year *bracero* program, then—when their usefulness was over—declare them, as the Replicants are declared in *Blade Runner*, "illegal on Earth"? How humane was it to accept the Marielitos with open arms, then round them up and attempt to send them back? Why must the Mexican *braceros* and the Cuban Marielitos be relegated to the "Off World"?

Blade Runner negotiates another aspect of the immigrant dilemma: the aliens' historically demonstrated ability to enrich Us/U.S. The underlying logic of the open-door policy and the grain of truth at the heart of the melting pot myth is that immigrants have contributions to make, beyond their immediate exploitability, contributions that can make Us better. "I've seen things you people wouldn't believe," Roy tells Deckard near the end of the film when, after winning their battle to the death, he inexplicably saves his pursuer's life. But we will never know what they have seen or what they might have to offer once we close the door. From that perspective, Their deportation is Our loss. This is nowhere more poignantly stated than in Roy's speech just before he dies the time-

Roy Batty (Rutger Hauer), the leader of the rebellious Replicants, first appears to be a menacing villain, but by the film's end becomes a sympathetic character and saves Deckard's life.

controlled death his genetic creator scheduled for him. Everything he knows, the sum of his experience, "All those moments," he says, "will be lost in time . . . like tears in rain."

Blade Runner exposes the human cost of the new nativism. By seeing the Alien Other in human terms, it once again forces consideration of how the long-range aims of immigration reform in this country conflict with the nation's cherished humanitarian ideals. True to one side of its generic roots, the film noir, in the end *Blade Runner* ruminates on the existentially inexplicable, raising more questions than its futuristic private investigator—or we as a society—are able to answer. Watching Roy "retire," Deckard sums it up in a sober voice-over: "All he wanted were the same answers the rest of us wanted—Where do I come from? Where am I going? How long have I got?"

The new immigrants, documented and undocumented, seek answers to the same questions. So do we. Can we, should we, allow the new immigrants "more life"? Deckard's escape with his lover, the Replicant Rachael, to a place where the difference between human and Replicant is meaningless, suggests the need to create a space for that alternative.

In addition to the ethical doubts that Deckard begins to have about his assignment, there is a romantic complication: he falls in love with a Replicant, Rachael (Sean Young).

ALIENS: TWO KINDS OF MOTHERING

Aliens is a film about mothers. In contrasting two maternal figures, Ripley (Sigourney Weaver), a nurturing "mother" of a space colony orphan, and the Alien queen mother, a mechanically efficient reproducing machine, it raises an intriguing question, as one critic put it, "How can a film both support and fear mothering?"[37] My own answer is that two different kinds of mothering are opposed: the First World, enlightened, "civilized" one, and the Third World, "primitive" one.

In terms of its depiction of women, *Aliens* is just as conflicted a text as *The Terminator,* though in quite another way. On the one hand it is progressive (not to mention refreshing) to have a female SF protagonist who saves the world from the monsters from outer space. Particularly if she is a woman like Ripley: bright and pragmatic, cool, resourceful, tough. And she is allowed personal growth. Ripley, the "new woman" in *Alien,* becomes the "new mother" in *Aliens,* and once again provides positive feminine imagery: She survives as a single mother in a man's world with an adopted child. Still, there is plenty in the film to offset the positive.

Two kinds of mothers confront each other in Aliens *(1986). Defending her lair, the foreboding Alien queen mother is a figure out of a nativist nightmare, ceaselessly procreating a steady stream of monsters.*

Ripley (Sigourney Weaver), the nurturing mother figure for a space colony orphan.

What is distressing about *Aliens* from my point of view is, first, its horrifying depiction of Alien (read Third World) motherhood. The giant Alien queen mother, the most foreboding monster in either film, is terrifying enough, but when it is so sharply contrasted with Ripley, the "civilized" mother, it has chilling implications. When we limit the analysis to Ripley, *Aliens* can pat itself on the back for its progressive leanings, Ripley being independent, caring, and responsible. But consider, as opposed to her, the Alien mother, down in her birth chamber, reproducing mindlessly, endlessly. She is a monster out of the nativists' worst nightmares, procreation gone mad, uncontrolled and unstoppable. Ripley's unforgettable cry, "Get away from her, you bitch," defends First World mothering at the expense of the Third World womanhood. In this light, the fact that a woman wipes out the Alien mother and her offspring is hardly cause for rejoicing. The film's positive feminist elements are overwhelmed by its imperialistic underpinnings.

It is not coincidental, I think, that Ripley becomes more resourceful and self-sufficient as the Alien menace heightens. The film will not allow Ripley's more liberated definition of womanhood to exist on its own terms, but only as a dialectical element, in direct opposition to the female Alien that threatens the existence of the human race. In outer space, with the survival of the race on the line, Ripley's portrayal of mothering is positive, especially when it is pitted against a perpetually procreating feminine Other. What awaits Ripley back on Earth, though? She will likely be dismissed as a "hysterical woman," just as she was at the beginning of the film, and will likely return to the same menial job she had been given. The feminism in *Aliens* is situational, opportunistic, and relative.

And so is its condemnation of capitalism in the person of the villainous Burke, the duplicitous Company man. One possible reading of the film's treatment of the treacherous Burke is a condemnation of capitalism. To me Burke seems more like the traditional stereotype of the capitalist businessman so common to film and television. Ostensibly, this stereotype is used to critique the system, but it actually deflects a more penetrating appraisal. One of the most popular narratives in media is the story of "bad" businessmen who receive their comeuppance, thereby conveniently shifting the blame to aberrations, in the form of corrupt individuals, rather than to the system that spawned them. Besides, Burke represents not so much clever capitalism as stupid greed. His error is one of discernment. He fails to see that the profit motive must take a backseat when survival of the status quo is on the line. Burke's fatal flaw is not his belief in the free-market system but rather his failure to recognize that for capitalism to operate it must first of all exist. He is a villain not because he is a capitalist, but because he is a shortsighted one: he fails to see that what is called for is a combination of capitalism and nativism's other face, isolationism—economic *and* biological Darwinism. With the death of Burke, capitalism does not suffer but in fact survives. It awaits Ripley on Earth, safe and unmolested.

By boiling everything—feminism, capitalism, mothering—down to a survivalist essence, *Aliens* demonstrates how extreme—and extremely conservative—measures can become natural in the face of the Alien threat. Ideologically, Ripley moves in just the opposite direction from Sarah in James Cameron's first film, *The Terminator*. Whereas Sarah shifts from a vague and uncommitted centrist position leftward, Ripley moves from left to right. Her political turning point comes, I think, in the scene (in this film the sex scene) in which she is instructed by a marine on modern weaponry. By the end of the film, when a low-angle shot captures Ripley emerging from the cargo bay, transformed into a superhuman forklift prepared to do battle with Alien Mother (it is here that Ripley calls her "Bitch!") the right has won Ripley's soul. She has become a female Rambo in space.

When it comes down to life and death, progressivism, feminism, and Third Worldism are quickly jettisoned political luxuries.

THE DANGERS OF SYMBOLIC DISTORTION

If these and other SF films are ways in which we as a society have been working through our immigration worries, there are a number of salient implications—all of them disturbing, some more than others. One, of course, is political. Unrestricted by mere planetary limits, American capitalism has bypassed multinationalism and leapt ahead to galaxy-wide proportions. The cultural imperialism evident in these films leaves no doubt that multinational capitalism—based on the American model— is the universal norm. "Mainstream SF's articulation of resemblance between aliens and humans," Vivian Sobchack says,

> preserves the subordination of "other worlds, other cultures, other species" to the world, culture, and "speciality" of white American culture. We can see this new American "humanism" literally expand into and colonize outer space, making it safe for democracy, multinational capitalism, and the Rolling Stones.[38]

Thus the Alien in *Starman* arrives on Earth singing the Rolling Stones' "Satisfaction" and the Aliens in *Explorers* (1986, d. Joe Dante) are vidiots, who speak in the language of American sitcom television.

Galaxy-wide cultural imperialism may be only a first step toward actual imperialism through military involvement. Seen through the aliens = Aliens lens, a film like *Aliens* may be seen as a metaphor for U.S. involvement in the Third World, specifically Latin America. The fit seems too neat to dismiss. The need to go There (a Company colony) before They invade Here is the film's underlying narrative logic. The need to help stop Them is strong enough in *The Last Starfighter* that in the end the young human pilot volunteers to leave Earth and join the intergalactic fight for freedom.

But it is the distortion of the alien immigrant into an Alien Other, and in the case of the Hispanic, the shift from ethnic stereotype to outerspace creature that raises the most distressing set of problems. Some stereotyping researchers have looked at the role of social perception and stereotyping as an important way to understand wide-scale, socially destructive behaviors (on the order of magnitude of genocide, for example, or the Holocaust). A starting hypothesis bearing on such horrible kinds of dehumanization is "that when members of one group think about members of another as intrinsically different—as categorically bad, unworthy, despicable—they are capable of inflicting great harm upon them." In this view, stereotyping constitutes "sanctions for evil," working to reduce restraint, and "may induce or justify acts that would be unthinkable to commit against members of one's own group."[39] In this light, the transformation of the alien immigrant into a nonhuman SF Other, most especially in the shape of a Destructive Monster, has frightful ramifications. Since we are all prone to stereotyping, "the participation in atrocities, to the extent that these are facilitated by stereotypes of the enemy or outgroup, is within the repertoire of many of us—as bystanders, at least, if not as perpetrators."[40] Dehumanization and stereotyping intersect at the point at which there is a loss of uniqueness and individuality. As one social psychologist—a survivor of the Holocaust—put it: "When a group of people is defined entirely in terms of a category to which they belong, and when this category is excluded from the human family, then the moral restraints against killing them are more readily overcome."[41] And indeed, one researcher's investigation of the My Lai massacre in Vietnam has noted how U.S. soldiers referred to people that were killed as "animals," "subhuman," and "insects."[42]

I am not making a doomsday prediction, only remarking upon some of the more destructive features of stereotyping that, I think, we need to be aware of. Siegfried Kracauer, in *From Caligari to Hitler,* his classic study of German cinema of the pre-Nazi era, never made what is for me the crucial link between the monsters of German Expressionist cinema and the Jews. In his discussion of the German monster films of his day, such as *The Golem* (1915, d. Henrik Galeen and Paul Wegener; other versions remade in 1917 and 1920, both directed by Wegener) and the six-part serial *Homunculus* (1916, d. Otto Rippert), both dealing with artificially created, destructive beings. Kracauer sees them as demonstrations of "a theme that was to become an obsession in the German cinema": the split in the German psyche between the horrible and the powerful. But he never ventures beyond that to speculate on what is most obvious: that those same monsters—particularly the Golem, which is a monster arising out of the Jewish ghetto, brought to life by a rabbi— are projections of socially unconscious dread of the Jew.[43]

From a completely different starting point, Vivian Sobchack comes to very nearly the same conclusion in her analysis of American SF films fifty years later: "The once threatening SF 'alien,' and Other," she writes, "become our familiars—our close relations, if not ourselves." She sees new SF Aliens as mostly nonhostile (a problematic proposition because in about half of the latest SF films they are hostile), and offers the proposition "that the 'aliens R U.S.'"[44] Though I agree with the way in which she sees conservative, mainstream SF as preserving the dominance of "other worlds" (particularly her slant on cultural imperialism in the postmodern world, which I mentioned above), still there is a demonstrable difference between human and Alien in both the marginal and the mainstream SF that she discusses, an important and a distorted difference. In seeing the difference between human and monster as only an internal schism (as Kracauer does), or as postmodern evidence of the strains within late capitalism (as Sobchack does), the distortion is neglected. By so doing, Kracauer never brings up the obvious fact about *The Golem:* the possibility that the creature that arises out of the Jewish ghetto is a fearful symbol of the Jew, one that must somehow be crumbled into dust, just as the Golem is at the climax of that film. Similarly, there are implications that arise out of the distortion of the Hispanic that are too frightening to brush over.

My purpose here is not to change the mental process of stereotyping (which is probably impossible) so much as to expose it. "The goal of studying stereotypes," says Sander Gilman, "is not to stop the production of images of the Other, images that demean and, by demeaning, control. . . . We need these stereotypes to structure the world."[45] What is important to remember is that in constructing Others, a society defines itself. The shape of those Others can reveal a wide range of constantly shifting social, political, and psychological tendencies. The SF Alien as immigrant Hispanic reveals a significant amount of stress within the dominant ideology. Cultural tension about immigrants, coupled with psychological guilt and fear, together with doubts about national identity combine to produce, as they have done in other times in our history, xenophobia, isolationism, and nativism. What is different—and what I wish to make us aware of—is the current cinematic shape of that fear: fear that transforms the greaser bandit into a terminating cyborg, the Hispanic harlot into a fertile, black Alien mother, menacingly reproducing monsters down in her lair.

PART THREE

LATINO SELF-REPRESENTATION

CHICANO AND LATINO FILMMAKERS
BEHIND THE CAMERA

The chapters in this section tell of only a small part of the Latino cinematic response to Hollywood stereotyping. In order to situate the documentaries that I analyze in Chapter 8 and the career of Robert Rodríguez that I cover in Chapters 9 and 10, however, it would be helpful to have a general understanding of the history of Latino directors in American film. While there is not enough room to do a full-blown history here, I can at least sketch out its main features.

The most organized and sustained Latino body of work has come from Mexican American filmmakers, who first began their radical Chicano filmmaking in the late 1960s in opposition to Hollywood's stereotyping. During that time Chicano filmmaking evolved from being ideologically oppositional to more mainstream practice, and it is to this history that I now turn.

CHICANO CINEMA'S THREE WAVES

The history of Chicano filmmaking may be thought of as a series of waves, each lashing out at Hollywood cinema in its own distinct way.[1] The First Wave (roughly from 1969 to 1976, or from El Teatro Campesino's *Yo Soy Joaquín* to Luis Valdez's *El Corrido*) was the radical documentary era. The cinematic expression of a cultural nationalist movement, it was politically contestational and formally oppositional. Recognizing that the Latino experience had been denigrated and stereotyped by the dominant cinema and that Latino talent was largely ignored by the industry, the First Wave turned its back on Hollywood and found inspiration in revolutionary Cuban documentaries. Fashioning itself as a kind of Third

World Cinema in the First World, its audience was *La Raza,* the Mexican Americans in the United States, and its goals were to: (a) decolonialize consciousness, (b) educate us Chicanos about our heritage, (c) give voice to our silenced history, (d) instill ethnic pride by celebrating our culture, (e) mold a self-determined identity, (f) expose the conditions of our oppression, and (g) mobilize La Raza politically, socially, and culturally.[2]

Among the beneficial results of First Wave Chicano cinema was the chronicling of *el movimento* (the Mexican American civil rights movement), the production of a self-affirming cinema, the genesis of Chicano cinema culture, and the establishment of a professional training ground where a number of Chicano filmmakers were able to hone their cinematic skills.

Second Wave Chicano cinema dates from 1977—the year of Esperanza Vasquez's *Agueda Martinez,* Jesús Salvador Treviño's *Raíces de Sangre,* and Robert M. Young's *¡Alambrista!*—and continues to the present day. Though the documentary impulse that spawned First Wave filmmaking remains in evidence, the politics of the Second Wave are rebellious, not separatist. Indignation still fuels the rhetoric, but the anger is channeled into more accessible forms. In part this was due to changes in the movement, the filmmakers, *La Raza,* and the greater American society. And it may have been partly a measure of the filmmakers' success at tapping mainstream funding sources (support to Chicano filmmakers came from, for example, PBS, the Corporation for Public Broadcasting, the American Film Institute, and the National Endowment for the Humanities). While this kind of institutional funding was welcome and helped legitimize Chicano film practice, it may have led filmmakers to soften their ideological message—which is not necessarily the same thing as compromising it.

A number of First Wave filmmakers continued the documentary tradition, and they were joined by new Second Wave documentarians (such as Daniel Salazar and Paul Espinoza) as well as by emerging Chicana filmmakers, primarily documentarians, such as Sylvia Morales (*Chicana* [1979]), Lourdes Portillo (*La Ofrenda* [1989]), and Susan Racho (*Garment Workers* [1975]). More recently, several women experimental film- and video makers, such as avant-garde videographers Frances Salomé España (*Anima* [1989]) and Sandra P. Hahn (*Replies of the Night* [1989]), have added significantly to the Second Wave corpus.

The Second Wave also marked the appearance of narrative films (the feature-length docudramas *Raices de Sangre* and *¡Alambrista!* were transitional works in this regard), which received the most attention from critics and audiences alike, both within and outside of *La Raza*. Some of these took the form of short subjects, such as Lourdes Portillo's *Despues del Terremoto* (1979) and Jesús Salvador Treviño's televised "Schoolbreak Special," *Gangs* (1988), which was nominated for an Emmy Award.

But many were feature-length: Luis Valdez's *Zoot Suit* (1981) and *La Bamba* (1987), *The Ballad of Gregorio Cortez* (1982, d. Robert M. Young, produced by Moctesuma Esparza), Jesús Salvador Treviño's *Seguin* (1981), and Robert Redford's *The Milagro Beanfield War* (1988). This last film was also produced by Moctesuma Esparza, a First Wave filmmaker who now operates within the Hollywood mainstream; he has also produced *The Cisco Kid* (1994) for Turner Network Television, *Selena* (1997), *The Disappearance of Garcia Lorca* (1997), and *Price of Glory* (2000). Gregory Nava has directed a significant body of work, stretching from *El Norte* (1982), to *A Time to Remember* (1988), *My Family/Mi Familia* (1995), and *Selena*. Others include Cheech Marin (*Born in East L.A.* [1987]), Isaac Artenstein (*Break of Dawn* [1988]), and Ramón Menendez (*Stand and Deliver* [1988]). Edward James Olmos's *American Me* (1992) and Taylor Hackford's *Bound by Honor* (1993), based on a script cowritten by poet Jimmy Baca, Carlos Avila's *Foto-Novelas* (a four-part, *Twilight Zone*–like miniseries broadcast on PBS in 1997) and his subsequent feature, *Price of Glory* (2000), and Jesús Salvador Treviño's miniseries for Showtime, *Resurrection Blvd.* (2000) are all evidence that Second Wave Chicano filmmaking is still a vital force.

But at the same time we are witnessing the dawning of a Third Wave, which began in the late 1980s. For the most part it consists of genre films, made either within the Hollywood system or, if not, adhering closely to the Hollywood paradigm. As such, Third Wave films do not accentuate Chicano oppression or resistance; ethnicity in these films exists as one fact of several that shape characters' lives and stamp their personalities. This does not mean that the films are consequently nonpolitical, devoid of commentary about Otherness, or that their makers have sold out. On the contrary, the critique mounted by some of these films at least may be just as pointed, if more subtle, than Second Wave films.

In Third Wave cinema, political content is embedded within the deeper structure of the genre formulas the filmmakers employ rather than being on the surface, where First and Second Wave filmmakers customarily placed it. For example, there is the aching sense of dissatisfaction with the system at the heart of Third Wave works as diverse as Jesús Salvador Treviño's episode for television's *Gabriel's Fire* ("The Neighborhood" [1990]) and Neal Jimenez's *The Waterdance* (which he scripted and codirected, 1992). There is also Jimenez's script for a sobering revision of the coming-of-age film in *River's Edge* (1986, d. Tim Hunter), which resists the hegemonic recuperation typical of the genre. More recently, Jesús Salvador Treviño has been series producer and director of *Resurrection Blvd.*, which effectively mixes boxing and family melodrama formulas. Another example is the playful blend of Hollywood genre and cultural myth in Robert Rodríguez's award-winning student short, *Bedhead* (1990) or the ideological critique that Rodríquez mounts in *El Mariachi* (1993), both of which I will discuss in Chapter 9.

OTHER LATINO FILMMAKING TRADITIONS

Of course, Chicano cinema is not the totality of Latino cinema in the United States. There is a rich tradition of Puerto Rican filmmaking based in New York that has been eloquently outlined by Lillian Jiménez. Similarly, Cuban American cinema made by Cuban exiles in the United States has, according to Ana López, also evolved in three filmmaking waves.[3] Like Chicano cinema, most of these films are not feature-length, the notable exceptions being the films of Cuban exile Leon Ichaso (*El Super* [1979], *Sugar Hill* [1993]) and Puerto Rican–born Miguel Arteta (*Star Maps* [1997], *Chuck & Buck* [2000]).

There is also a group of Latin American filmmakers who have found a place in U.S. feature-length cinema and form another noteworthy branch of the Latino filmmaking tree. These directors include Alfonso Arau (*A Walk in the Clouds* [1995] and a television miniseries remake of *The Magnificent Ambersons* [2002]), Luis Puenzo (*Old Gringo* [1989]), Guillermo del Toro (*Mimic* [1997], *Blade 2* [2002]), Luis Mandoki (*White Palace* [1990], *Born Yesterday* [1993], *When a Man Loves a Woman* [1994], *Message in a Bottle* [1999]), and Luis Llosa (*The Specialist* [1994], *Anaconda* [1997]). If none of these films has made particularly momentous progress in the name of Latino filmmaking, there is still something to be said for creating a critical mass of Latinos in Hollywood, which may, in the long run, form the basis for a more even-handed treatment of Latino ethnicity. The most notable films in this regard have been *A Walk in the Clouds* and *El Super*. Though the others have been mostly genre films, as Llosa demonstrated with the casting of

Jennifer Lopez in *Anaconda,* genre film provides a fertile ground for planting counterstereotyping subversions.

With this brief prologue, we can now proceed to examine two fascinating Latino cinematic responses. The first is a group of nonfiction films I call Mexican American border documentaries, discussed in Chapter 8. The second involves the career of Third Wave Mexican American filmmaker Robert Rodríguez, from his student film (*Bedhead*) to his first self-financed, low-budget (total cost $7,000) indie feature, *El Mariachi,* to his current children's adventure film *Spy Kids* (2001); I treat Rodríguez's career in Chapters 9 and 10.

EIGHT

EL GENIO DEL GÉNERO
Mexican American Borderland Documentaries and Postmodernism

Some scenes from my own personal border documentary:

Establishing Shots

The first house I lived in as an infant in El Paso, Texas, was on *la mera frontera,* as close as you could live to the U.S./Mexico boundary line and still be in the United States. The house was on West Main—the last residential street before Mexico (or the first, depending on one's perspective). Across the street a steep slope dropped down to the Rio Grande River valley, with Mexico on the other side. The Mexican hills facing us were in my earliest recollections bare desert, craggy and dotted with ocotillo bushes and the occasional maguey plant. By the time I graduated from high school those hills were crowded with dirt roads and huts, which belonged mostly to Mexican migrants to Ciudad Juárez. Many of these, no doubt, were awaiting their chance to cross *el río* to work and perhaps to live on *el otro lado,* just as my maternal grandparents, Jesús Morales Ramírez and Dolores Pérez, a professional gambler from Chihuahua and his wife, had done in 1913, during the height of the Mexican Revolution.[1] Today those hills are a bustling, established suburb of Ciudad Juárez, complete with a shopping mall and a soccer field down by the levee.

Geographically and sociologically, this was, for me, life on the U.S. southwestern margins.

Medium Shots

Like everybody else, I suppose, who grows up at the nation's fringes, I knew that I was in the United States but felt (and was made to feel) out of it. For one thing, you never saw yourself in the mass media. The homogenized, middle-class, *Leave It to Beaver/Father Knows Best* world depicted in television programs, magazines, and movies belonged to a cultural galaxy far, far away from the frontier where I lived. At the same time, I was clearly outside of Mexico, though there was no escaping my connections to it. I heard Spanish in my home and on the streets (though it was strictly forbidden in schools—"Speak English!" bellowed our Mexican American elementary school coach as we walked to the playground in double file). The music wafting out of the houses I walked by in the neighborhood ran the gamut from Javier Solís *rancheras*, to classics composed and sung by Agustín Lara, to *Nat King Cole Español*. When the kids commandeered the record player, you might hear Elvis Presley from the Jurados' house, Lesley Gore from the Navarros', or the soundtrack from *West Side Story* from mine; alternatively, Teensy Talavera might drop by to imitate Chuck Berry's "Nadine," or give us his rendition of the Beatles' "You Like Me Too Much."

It would be hard to find a briefer or, word for word, more telling description of this In/Out cultural feeling than what Pat Mora evokes in her poem "Legal Alien." I was fortunate enough to know her when she wrote it—we shared an office at the University of Texas at El Paso, where we were part-timers in the English Department. With her permission, I reproduce a portion of it here:

> American but hyphenated,
> viewed by Anglos as perhaps exotic,
> perhaps inferior, definitely different,
> viewed by Mexicans as alien,
> (their eyes say, "You may speak
> Spanish but you're not like me")
> an American to Mexicans
> a handy token
> sliding back and forth
> between the fringes of both worlds[2]

Caught between two cultural worlds, you internalize your In/Out existence. You tend to gravitate to the margins of groups you belong to.

You grow accustomed to watching ("I am used to being an observer," writes Cherríe Moraga[3]), and among the things you watch are the workings of the center from the margin. Because of that you replicate that "ex-centric" (to use Linda Hutcheon's term)[4] perspective in other arenas of your life. The disadvantage is that you feel perpetually alienated, decentered, and seldom "at home." On the other hand, since navigating between cultures is a necessary life skill, your "bordered" existence gives you extensive experience in the interpretation of cultures. For example, once you understand how you are being excluded from dominant discourses, what seems natural to others rings hollow and looks perversely constructed to you. Being on the fringe is a good place to begin analyzing the workings of dominant power structures, as Cherríe Moraga, Gloria Anzaldúa, Guillermo Goméz-Peña, Pat Mora, and so many other Chicano theorists, writers, and artists have discovered.[5]

Culturally and psychologically, this Inside/Outside condition was my border experience.

Close-up

As I came of age on *la frontera*, struggling to grasp my identity, I remember as a very young child—perhaps four or so—asking my older cousin, Lulu, what it meant when people said I was Mexican and American. (Beautiful Lulu, whose actual name is Carmen Fernández, lived in Los Angeles, had finished high school, and therefore knew *everything*.) I understand now that I was asking Lulu the most fundamental existential question: Who am I? To her credit, she gave me a very accurate answer: I was half Mexican because of my mother, Hortensia Ramírez Berg, and half German (mixed with strains of French and English) American due to my father, Gerald Berg. To a literal-minded young boy, however, this explanation only made things worse. Which half of me was which? And where precisely was the boundary line that split me into two halves? Did it run lengthwise, dividing me laterally into east and west halves? Or was I divided by an equatorial waistline into northern and southern hemispheres?

All this was compounded by the fact that, like Cherríe Moraga, I am *güero* and can pass for white. The question was, did I want to? One answer: yes, many times, because entering the Anglo comfort zone made things so, well, comfortable—for me and for my Anglo acquaintances. But not ultimately comfortable enough to forsake my Mexican heritage. Personally and existentially, then, a border runs through me. Gloria Anzaldúa describes the cultural tension I live with well: "The

My Hybridity, Part 1: The Mexican American side. My grandfather and grandmother, Jesús Morales Ramírez and Dolores Pérez de Ramírez, pose with their children in front of their new house in El Paso, Texas, in 1915, just months after moving there from Chihuahua. From left: My uncle Julio as a young boy, my maternal grandmother, my aunts Carolina, Margarita, and Maria; standing on the step, my grandfather holds the newest addition to the Ramírez family, my mother, Hortensia. The youngest, my aunt Chita (María de Jesús Ramírez), mentioned at the end of this chapter, had not yet been born.

struggle is inner: Chicano, *indio,* American Indian, *mojado, mexicano,* immigrant Latino, Anglo in power, working class Anglo, Black, Asian— our psyches resemble the bordertowns and are populated by the same people." [6]

I begin in this way partially to follow the trend of essays on post-modernism being autobiographical, but also because it illuminates my

My Hybridity, Part 2: The German American side, c. 1920. From left, my aunts Ruby, Velda, and Hazel, and my father, Gerald, pose for a photograph of the Berg children in Eldorado, Kansas. Their father, my grandfather Charlie, worked the oil fields throughout the Midwest, while my grandmother Ella raised the children, kept the household going, and baked the best apple pies in the world.

introduction to my own private multiculturalism, my own hybrid, postmodern formation that I thought was mine alone but which I now believe is shared by Mexican Americans in general. For years I thought these feelings were particular—and peculiar—to me, but now I see that the "living-on-the-edge" physical and emotional marginality, the Inside/Outside position, and the internal borderline describe significant features of the larger Chicano experience. They also describe important aspects of postmodernism. In fact, as I think about it, Chicanos must be experts at postmodernism, having experienced hybridity and divided subjectivity since the Treaty of Guadalupe Hidalgo in 1848. Since then, Chicanos have had to arrange their lives, their thoughts, and their language by negotiating the legal boundary line between Mexico and the United States. For a century and a half, Chicanos have lived layered lives made up of overlapping parts of two adjacent nations, two languages, two cultural traditions, two sides of a common frontier, a shared geography, and an interwoven history. Indeed, Mexican Americans may be postmodernism's ultimate decentered subjects, whose hybridity is an amalgam of many multicultural traditions, present and past, here and there, Mexican and American. It is precisely this composite, cross-cultural experience that Mexican American borderland documentaries capture so well.

My aim here is threefold. First, I want to sketch out the main characteristics of the borderland documentary genre, an established cinematic form utilized by Chicano filmmakers for more than two decades. This goal is something akin to what Craig Owens did in the early 1980s by bringing feminist theory and art to bear on postmodern thought. In his essay "The Discourse of Others," Owens sought "to introduce the issue of sexual difference into the modernism/postmodernism debate—a debate which has until now been scandalously in-different."[7] If I am successful in achieving my first goal, I hope to insert the issue of Mexican American ethnicity into the mainstream discussion of postmodernity, from which it has been scandalously absent. Now that the postmodernity of Mexican American literary artists has begun to be acknowledged,[8] a second goal is to include Chicano documentary filmmakers among the recognized ranks of Mexican American postmodernist artists. Finally, since these films represent the Mexican American postmodern existence and are postmodern works themselves, a third goal is to show how they exemplify Mexican American postmodernism, not just by the postmodern Chicano lives they document but also by the creative games they play with received history, mainstream Anglo culture, and cinematic tradition.

MEXICAN AMERICANS AND POSTMODERNISM

I have noticed, as a member of the academy (yet another institution where I feel Inside/Outside), that most postmodern theory acknowledges but deals reluctantly with the ex-centric. This in spite of the fact that, as Thomas Docherty admits, in a certain sense the discourse of postmodernism approximates the rationale of postcolonial criticism and is "the discourse *of* the periphery, a discourse which imperialism had strenuously silenced but which is now made available." [9] If this is true, then why aren't more—*any*—Mexican American scholars represented in the various anthologies on postmodernism? Why aren't they a more visible part of the debate on postmodernism?

It's not that Mexican Americans have not engaged in the debate—many have. To name a few, José Limón, Gloria Anzaldúa, Renato Rosaldo, Vicki Ruiz, Rafael Pérez-Torres, José David Saldívar, Cherríe Moraga, Guillermo Gómez-Peña, George J. Sánchez—enough, in fact, to have our own anthology on postmodernism. Enough, in fact, that Chicanos and other cultural critics of color could be driving postmodernism discourse instead of being relegated to the back of the theory bus. [10] At any rate, there is a range of response to postmodernism among these critics, not all of it favorable. Of them, José Limón has perhaps dealt most extensively with postmodernism and its effects—which he takes to be detrimental—in *Dancing with the Devil,* a study of working-class Mexican Americans in south Texas. Limón builds upon Fredric Jameson's conceptualization of postmodernism as the "cultural logic of late capitalism." Limón's view is that for Chicanos in south Texas, this is "a new form of capitalism that now wages war on lower-class Mexican-Americans and that may also be threatening the politics of moderation, compromise, and negotiation with the Anglo Other." [11] In this context, according to Limón, "postmodernism may be seen as the gradual decentering, fragmenting transformation" of what had once been, for south Texas Mexican Americans, a relatively stable sense of their history and their cultural past. [12]

Jameson's wary view of postmodernism, however, is not the only possible starting point. For other theorists the postmodern movement is—potentially, at least—more ideologically oppositional and less reactionary than in Jameson's estimation. Given these differing views, it is probably more beneficial to think not of a single postmodernism but rather of postmodernisms. The various branches may be roughly divided into two very different types, resistant and reactionary, as Hal Foster suggests:

In cultural politics today, a basic opposition exists between a postmodernism which seeks to deconstruct modernism and resist the status quo and a postmodernism which repudiates the former to celebrate the latter: a postmodernism of resistance and a postmodernism of reaction.[13]

It is the ideologically resistant variety that I am referring to when I talk about my own and Mexican Americans' postmodern formation, and it is this postmodernism of resistance that I see articulated so eloquently in the Chicano borderland documentaries. The Chicano postmodernist position they stake out is a very distant cousin of European or American academic postmodernism. But it is still postmodernism. Just as Toni Morrison says that "black women had to deal with 'postmodern' problems in the nineteenth century and earlier,"[14] so too, as these documentaries demonstrate, Mexican Americans have lived with realities that we now call postmodern—fragmentation, heterogeneity, hybridity, an ironic relation to the past, and a healthy skepticism about the master narratives of progress, liberation, and science—for the past 150 years.

Instead of Jameson's "cultural logic of late capitalism," then, what these documentaries describe is consonant with the oppositional idea of postmodernism put forward by Cornel West. West's position is that Jean-François Lyotard's *The Postmodern Condition* "is really a French reflection on the transgressions of *modernism* that has little to do with postmodernism in the American context." Instead, West subscribes to a postmodernism "in which political contestation is central." In this form, it can be recuperated for use within the American context, particularly by people of color. "In the United States," says West, "as Andreas Huyssen has emphasized, postmodernism is an avant-garde-like rebellion against the modernism of the museum, against the modernism of the literary and academic establishment." For West, postmodernism is a heterogeneous phenomenon "in which political contestation is central," and represents nothing less than "the revolt against the center by those constituted as marginals."[15]

These films portray a resistant form of postmodernism—what I would call "Mexican American postmodernism"—coherently and succinctly.[16] And just as José David Saldívar argues that the works of *norteño* musicians such as Los Tigres del Norte, Chicano rappers like Kid Frost, and writers like Helena María Viramontes and John Rechy are more perceptive than writings by many (mainstream) postmodern theorists, so too these filmmakers rank along with the aforementioned Chicano postmodernist artists as some of our leading postmodern thinkers.[17] As we shall see, among the things that the borderland documentaries show Mexican Americans resisting is one of the fundamental components of American dominant ideology: the cultural homogenization demanded by assimilation.

Of course, in a broad sense, all or nearly all Chicana/o filmmakers—whether they work in fiction or nonfiction cinema—are border documentarians, in that their films almost always refer back to our Mexican roots, directly or indirectly juxtaposing that heritage with their present American existence. But the kind of films I wish to single out are a group of Chicano documentaries that take as their subject what Américo Paredes identified as "Greater Mexico," a large territory located on both sides of the U.S.–Mexico boundary, including "all of the areas inhabited by people of Mexican culture—not only within the present limits of the Republic of Mexico but in the United States as well—in a cultural rather than a political sense." [18] Thus by Chicano border documentary I specifically mean such films as Les Blank's *Chulas Fronteras* (1976) and *Del Mero Corazón* (1979), Isaac Artenstein's *Ballad of an Unsung Hero* (1983), Héctor Galán's *Los Mineros* (1990), *The Search for Pancho Villa* (1993), and *Songs of the Homeland* (1994), Louis Hock's *La Mera Frontera* (1997), and Lourdes Portillo's *La Ofrenda: Days of the Dead* (1989) and *The Devil Never Sleeps* (*El Diablo Nunca Duerme* [1995]). These Chicano films are distinguished by their nonfiction form and their subject: the cultural history of Greater Mexico and the Greater Mexicans whose lives transcend the U.S.–Mexico boundary line. [19]

THE CINEMATIC DISCOURSE
ON THE BORDER AND IMMIGRATION

Not only are Chicano border documentaries distinct from other Chicano films, they are unlike most Anglocentric media treatments of the border and immigration. Since the mass media contribute significantly to the discourse of the border and immigration, it is important to understand how Chicano borderland documentaries break with the dominant media's perspective on the border. Specifically, we need to appreciate how they differ from Hollywood's typical treatment of the border, from border and immigration news coverage, and from contemporary immigration documentaries.

The major difference between these Chicano documentaries and the fictionalized studio-made border narratives lies in the Hollywood films' formative assumptions. In most Hollywood movies about the Mexican border, the underlying assumption is that Americans must be compelled to cross the boundary line—why else would they opt to leave their perfect life in the U.S.A.? People in the movies don't just go to Mexico, they have to be pushed into going there. Hollywood's "Mexi-go assumption," that Americans must be coerced into entering Mexico, means that in the movies there must always be an explicit reason for a character's heading for Mexico. Accordingly, the fundamental requirement of American screenwriters and filmmakers is to answer the central question for protagonists who venture south—Why are they in Mexico? [20]

A corollary to Hollywood's Mexican assumption is that few visitors to Mexico go there for cultural reasons. No one in the movies needs an excuse to visit and vacation in Western Europe, but how often do Americans go to Mexico to meet the people, to study Mexican art, history, or music, to sample the food, or to see the sights? Such activities would imply the possibility of learning something from Mexico and Mexicans, something Hollywood's ethnocentric prejudice typically denies even its most open-minded, liberal, countercultural characters. [21]

No—Hollywood's characters are forced south of the border. Typically they are running from the law (movie criminals always "head for the border," from William Bendix's thief in *The Big Steal* [1949] to the husband and wife team [Steve McQueen and Ali McGraw in the original; Alec Baldwin and Kim Basinger in the remake] who cheat their crime boss in both versions of *The Getaway* [1972, 1994]), or after someone on the run (Robert Mitchum in *Out of the Past* [1948] and *The Big Steal,* Jeff Bridges in *Against All Odds* [1983], the remake of *Out of the Past*). Or they might simply be looking for the kind of good time (alcohol in the days of Prohibition, gambling before Las Vegas, sex anytime) that can't be found in the United States (from the gamblers and revelers in *Bordertown* [1935] to the young kids headed for good times down south in *Losin' It* [1983]). They might come fleeing a romantic entanglement (Larry MacArthur [Pat O'Brien] in *In Caliente* [1935]) or hoping to improve their dwindling fortunes (like the down-and-out drifter Fred C. Dobbs [Humphrey Bogart] in *The Treasure of the Sierra Madre* [1948]). Then there are the disenchanted expatriots (the loser, Bennie [Warren Oates], in *Bring Me the Head of Alfredo Garcia* [1974]; Ron Kovic [Tom Cruise] in *Born on the Fourth of July* [1989]), for whom Mexico is a retreat. At any rate, in Hollywood films the border is a plot device, and the characters are driven to cross it. In contrast, the people in Chicana/o border documentaries voluntarily return to Mexico, either physically, or in their dreams and memories, or in their folkways (music, murals, food). Moreover, as opposed to Hollywood's south-of-the-border travelers, these willing border crossers do so almost entirely for cultural reasons.

Nor do these Chicano documentaries treat the border the way television documentaries or news stories do—as a leaky dike threatening to overflow into the United States, flooding the country with "illegal" aliens and destroying the American way of life in the process. These films are part of what José David Saldívar aptly calls "fundamentally colonialist discourses whereby U.S. Latinos are cast as an illegal outside force, an alien nation 'polluting' U.S. culture."[22] Or, as Ali Behdad puts it:

> The U.S.-Mexico border has been portrayed in the popular discourse as in a state of siege. As suggested by the titles of such journalistic reports as "Losing Control of the Borders" or "Invasion from Mexico: It Just Keeps Growing," the border is represented as a battleground where the Border Patrol strives to defend the nation by upholding its "border integrity" against "the swelling tide of illegal Mexican aliens."[23]

In fact, the Mexican American border documentaries exist in opposition to decades of such reporting. In the twenty-one years from Les Blank's *Chulas Fronteras* in 1976 to Louis Hock's *La Mera Frontera*, Chicano border documentaries span the most recent debate swirling about the issue of immigration. That is, they appear at a historical period bracketed on one end by the passage of the Immigration and Nationality Act of 1965 (enacted in 1968), which altered the quota system and had the effect of shifting the pattern of immigration to the United States from the Old World to the Third. On the other, more recent, end, there has been the passage of two hotly debated—within and without the Latino community—congressional measures: the Immigration Reform Act in 1986 and the North American Free Trade Agreement (NAFTA) in 1993, whose collective effects are still being sorted through today by Chicanos and by the society at large.[24] Among other things, the Chicano documentaries form an eloquent antinativist, counterhegemonic response to the dominant xenophobic discourse on Mexican immigration, a spirited corrective to the brand of alarmist journalism that typically portrays hoards of "illegals" storming the southwestern United States' border gates.

Finally, Chicano border documentaries have little in common with most immigration documentaries, those films that trace the diaspora of an immigrant group from their homeland to the United States. For example, there has lately been a spate of films on the Irish immigrant experience, like *Out of Ireland* (1994), *The Irish in America* (1997), and

In one of the most memorable scenes from Les Blank's Chulas Fronteras (1976), Los Alegres de Terán (Eugenio Ábrego, accordion, Tomás Ortiz, bajo sexto) sing a popular ranchera ballad, "Volver, volver," against the backdrop of Greater Mexico. (Photo courtesy of Brazos Films/www.arhoolie.com)

The Irish in America: Long Journey Home (1998).[25] On the whole, the narrative arcs of such immigrant documentaries balance the suffering of the diaspora with the triumph of later-generation descendants in America (in the case of the Irish, from the potato famine to the presidency of John Fitzgerald Kennedy). As such, they are assimilation success stories.

In contrast, Chicano borderland documentaries chronicle a longer, ongoing, more convoluted Mexican American history. The Chicano experience, unique among American ethnic group histories, is a mixture of colonizing conquest in the nineteenth century and diasporic migration—both to and within the United States—in the twentieth. Back in 1848, the first Mexican Americans did not move at all, but rather saw waves of Euroanglos, spurred on by Manifest Destiny, migrate to them. Afterward, as Rodolfo Alvarez has argued, the psychohistorical experience of post-1900 migrating Mexican Americans was distinct from that of other immigrant groups for several reasons. Among them was, first, the fact that the land the *mexicanos* came to was virtually the same as the land they left, a topographical similarity that underscored a legal truth—the entire southwest region was once one Mexican nation. Second, the border could be crossed quickly and effortlessly. European and

Hybridity, one of the fundamental characteristics of postmodernism, is the subject of Héctor Galán's Songs of the Homeland *(1994). Specifically, the film traces the century-long evolution of Texas* conjunto *music, a blend of Mexican* rancheras *and middle European polkas. At the microphone: one of the great artists of* conjunto *music, Valerio Longoria. (Photo by Al Rendón, courtesy of Galán Productions)*

Asian immigrants may have taken weeks to cross an ocean in order to arrive in the United States, a duration of time that allowed them to begin making the emotional transition from being *e*migrants to *im*migrants and to break ties with the old country and begin to deal with the new one. For Mexicans, the distance from the old country to the United States could be crossed in a matter of minutes.[26] Another crucial factor is the immigrants' proximity to Mexico, which means that it is more difficult for Mexican Americans to completely sever ties with their cultural homeland. Not surprisingly, then, as Rafael Pérez-Torres says, "Mexico—as a national or cultural icon—does at many levels remain significant for most individuals self-identified as Chicano or Mexicano or Mexican-American."[27]

Perhaps because of this singular immigrant experience, acculturation for Mexican Americans rarely resolves itself neatly into total assimilation. "I considered myself, since I was young, a Texas Mexican," says Tejano *conjunto* artist José Morante at the beginning of *Chulas*

Fronteras. Even José Limón, who sadly notes the loss of cultural memory in younger Mexican Americans of south Texas, reports that they do not "think of themselves as *Americans* in any ideological sense, although they are active participants in the less expensive aspects of American mass culture."[28] Along with resistant postmodernism, the Chicano border documentary interrogates the modernist notion of progress, embedded in the view of assimilation into the American mainstream as the supreme happy ending. Mexican American postmodernism is at odds with the dominant, totalizing version of assimilation, one that has required ex-centrics to renounce and/or forget their root culture in order to enter the U.S. mainstream. Instead, Mexican American borderland documentaries present a people redefining that totalizing notion of assimilation, a people who have managed to live in the United States as good, productive, and creative citizens without giving up their cultural ties to Mexico. Rather than celebrating the melting pot, these films redefine assimilation as fluid hybridization that does not require cultural amnesia. Mexican American assimilation is a cultural *mezcla* (mix) wonderfully symbolized by the border *conjunto* music heard in so many of the films, a blending, as the narration in *Songs of the Homeland* makes clear, of Mexican *rancheras* and middle European polkas.

THE POETICS OF THE CHICANO BORDERLAND DOCUMENTARY

In charting the characteristics of this documentary genre, I noted a rough similarity to those used to describe postmodernism, something that, as I have said, is hardly surprising. And the more I worked on this list, the more I realized that in describing the border documentaries I was at the same time delineating a variety of postmodernism I am calling Mexican American. Thus, as I discuss the characteristics of the Chicano borderland documentary, I am simultaneously defining Mexican American postmodernism. The Chicano border documentary, then, may be characterized by the following elements (all of which, in typical postmodern fashion, overlap).

"Double-Codings" and Contradictions

Using Charles Jencks's term, the films are packed with "double-codings"[29]—dualistic, double-edged, a "both . . . and" rather than "either . . . or" attitude, which often leads to contradictions. In Chicano letters, this attitude has been described before, perhaps most notably by Gloria Anzaldúa. In her article "La Conciencia de la Mestiza: Towards a New Consciousness," Gloria Anzaldúa defines the "new consciousness" as a hybrid "consciousness of the Borderlands" that results from "racial, ideological, cultural and biological cross-pollination." Though she doesn't say it in so many words, I think her proposal for our progressive future harks back to our collective past. From my perspective, I believe she is taking the best features of our 150-year-long postmodern experience and urging us to hold on to them as we face the future. In Jencks's words, she is advocating the use of a doubled-coded aesthetic that reads "the present in the past as much as the past in the present." [30] Note how Anzaldúa's words look forward while invoking the past, and do so with a plea to move beyond simple binary thinking:

> The new *mestiza* copes by developing a tolerance for contradictions, a tolerance for ambiguity. She learns to be an indian in Mexican culture, to be Mexican from an Anglo point of view. She learns to juggle cultures. She has a plural personality, she operates in a pluralistic mode— nothing is thrust out, the good, the bad and the ugly, nothing rejected, nothing abandoned. [31]

From the inventory of the unrejected occurrences of our collective plural pasts seeming contradictions will naturally arise, but they are accommodated. And the spirit of accommodation extends toward, well, everything: Mexico, the United States, the past, Mexican American identity. "What is there in me of my Indian past?" the female narrator in Lourdes Portillo's *La Ofrenda* asks, then immediately follows that with, "What is there in me of that conqueror of yesterday?" Beginning, interestingly, with a both/and rather than an either/or question, she proceeds to complicate it by adding more factors to the identity equation. As I will discuss in more detail later, Portillo's search in Mexico for clues to her Chicana identity amid centuries-old Mexican rituals of death uncovers complex, not simple, answers. She unearths a multicultural mix of influences, a hybrid synthesis of contributing cultures- -Spanish, *indio, mestizo,* gay, and American.

Hybridity

These documentaries, like Chicanos themselves, and especially Chicanos on the border, reflect the hybrid, multicultural sensibility that breaks down essential categories—nationalistic, linguistic, social, cultural, racial. In such a pluralistic context, writes Guillermo Gómez-Peña, "concepts like 'high culture,' 'ethnic purity,' 'cultural identity,' 'beauty,' and 'fine arts' are absurdities and anachronisms. Like it or not, we are attending the funeral of modernity and the birth of a new culture." [32] A perfect example of this hybrid identity is Pedro J. González, the subject of *Ballad of an Unsung Hero*, who was born in Mexico and fought for Pancho Villa in the Revolution, then became a media celebrity in Los Angeles, served time on trumped-up charges in San Quentin, was deported to Mexico, and finished his life in San Isidro, California. What does a term like "nationality" mean when applied to him? Greater Mexican culture transcends legal boundaries.

An Ironic Attitude toward History, Tradition, and Memory

Jencks talks about the ambiguous relation between the past and the present as one of the chief aspects of postmodernism. He refers to it as a sort of fragmented recollection. An example of this was provided by filmmaker Louis Hock in comments he made about the making of *La Mera Frontera*. During the filming, he had wanted there to be a meeting scene of all the survivors of the 1918 skirmish along the "Ambos Nogales," the two Nogales just across from each other on the Arizona/Sonora border. He hoped that they could all come together and tell their stories, and that he would then be able to arrive at some sort of consensus about what exactly had happened. But when he brought them together, the versions they told conflicted with one another. "You get these old timers, every time they tell a story—it's changed," one of them comments in the film. Significantly, though, there were no arguments. They were all perfectly at ease with their contradictions. Their recollections refused to cohere into neat History, or even into a typical Documentary Film Narrative.[33] Though that confounding scene never made it into the final film, the contradictory spirit of it and the sardonic sensibility toward History does.

All the borderland documentarians know the past, but also know that it has been constructed by the dominant culture. For example:

• They know that Chicanos' role in official history has been erased and, like Louis Hock in *La Mera Frontera*, debunk jingoist historiography (as I will discuss below).

• They realize that much of Chicano history has been ignored and, like Hock and Isaac Artenstein in *Ballad of an Unsung*

Hero excavate it, or in the case of Héctor Galán's *The Search for Pancho Villa,* reclaim it.

• They are versed in the Hollywood tradition and play with it, like Lourdes Portillo in *The Devil Never Sleeps* (1995), which is a postmodern variation on familiar film noir mystery themes (more below).

• They recognize that Chicano cultural memory is fading and, like Héctor Galán's *Los Mineros* and *Songs from the Homeland,* Les Blank's *Chulas Fronteras* and *Del Mero Corazón,* revive it.

The ironic attitude toward the past is well illustrated in the framing device of Louis Hock's *La Mera Frontera:* the "resurrection" of María Esquivel, a Mexican woman who was killed by U.S. troops in 1918 during the border uprising. In the film, María comes to life (in the form of Mexican actress Yareli Arizmendi) and begins interrogating the present, looking for traces of her existence. She finds few. Toward the end of the film, as she walks the streets asking people if they know María Esquivel, a Mexican man turns the tables on her and asks why should he know about her character's past? It's a wonderful, unrehearsed postmodern moment: the past interrogating the present confronted by the present interrogating the past. It's a postmodern spin on what Mexican Americans have learned about history: knowledge of the past depends on who is asking the questions and who answers them.

An Oppositional Stance

Chicano postmodernism questions not only the past but also the dominant political structures that marginalized *mexicanos,* that killed an innocent woman in *La Mera Frontera,* that deported Pedro J. González in *Ballad of an Unsung Hero,* and that supported the Mexican *macho* regime within which Lourdes Portillo's Uncle Oscar operated in *The Devil Never Sleeps.* In the border documentary the true villain is modernism—the belief in master narratives. The Chicana/o borderland documentarian cannot look back on the violence and oppression of the immigrant experience without scrutinizing such modernist notions as progress, democracy, freedom, and closure.

In fact, Louis Hock, it seems, fell into the trap of trying for the neat verities and the tidy happy ending of a historical master narrative when he gathered the survivors, and was shown empirically the futility of such an endeavor. So did Lourdes Portillo in *The Devil Never Sleeps.* For a master narrative to exist, it appears that there needs to be a "master" class which hammers the narrative into a shape that favors those it serves. So from this perspective, "master narrative" has at least three meanings: (a) the overarching story that resolves the contradictions and ambiguities of lived experience into an acceptable (i.e., unconflicted and unambiguous) ideological form; (b) the narrative of a dominant "master class," which places its members in a superior and privileged position; and (c) a narrative that also has the function of dominating ("mastering") marginalized classes.

Rather than subscribing to master narratives, the people portrayed by the makers of borderland documentaries have been victimized by various versions of them (Manifest Destiny, for example, is one, equal justice under the law another, and the melting-pot myth still another), and show how they have used cultural forms to resist those oppressive narratives. In these films the principal one is the Tex-Mex *corrido,* but Mexican Americans' creativity takes other forms as well, such as the inventive Day of the Dead commemorations of Bay Area Latinos that Portillo records in *La Ofrenda,* and, of course, there is the oppositional creativity of the filmmakers themselves. Thus, the borderland documentaries demonstrate that Mexican Americans relieved the psychic unease of their "bordered" existence in the way suggested by Gloria Anzaldúa— creativity.[34]

An Incoherent Narrative

The classical modernist artist's wholeness, symmetry, and unity do not correspond to the fragmentation, asymmetry, and complexity of Chicano existence, and the films reflect this well. Based on the formal qualities—the manner in which the films represent the fragmented nature of the Mexican American experience—they may be divided into two general types.

The first, and most traditionally "documentary," is represented by films such as *Chulas Fronteras, Del Mero Corazón, Ballad of an Unsung Hero, Los Mineros, The Search for Pancho Villa,* and *Songs of the Homeland.* The filmmakers structured these films by documenting the lives, cultural activities, and history of Greater Mexicans. What makes these films postmodern is not the form but the content: the lives of an utterly postmodern people, Mexican Americans torn between two cultures that molded them.

The other, more radical type of borderland documentary is postmodernist in both form and content: *La Ofrenda: Days of the Dead, La*

Mera Frontera, and *The Devil Never Sleeps* (*El Diablo Nunca Duerme*). These films are doubly oppositional and subversive. First, because like the traditional borderland documentaries, they depict the hybridity of their Greater Mexican subjects. Second, because the filmmakers play with the conventions of the documentary form in depicting those lives.

LA OFRENDA: THE FRACTURED NARRATIVE

An illustrative example of the postmodern form I'm referring to is the narrative structure of *La Ofrenda.* The film begins in Mexico, to which filmmaker Portillo returns seeking an understanding of her *mestiza* roots by investigating the rituals of *el día de los muertos* (the Day of the Dead).[35] As I alluded to earlier, she uncovers hybridities that complicate rather than simplify her quest: a spirit world that shadows people's material existence, rituals that combine Roman Catholic and ancient *indio* traditions, celebrations that add layers of identities by the use of costumes, masks, and role playing, and cross-dressing that blurs gender distinctions. Then, in the midst of this ethnographic excavation project, the film takes a remarkable turn. It shifts to the San Francisco Bay Area, where Portillo lives, and begins looking at the ways the Day of the Dead is celebrated there.

The move is unexpected and cinematically and narratively unmotivated—nothing in the Mexican half of the film forecasts the necessity of doing a comparative study of *el día de los muertos* in the United States. And for that reason it may seem jarring to some. But, I would argue, for the unassimilated Mexican American, the move is smooth and natural and makes sense *culturally* because it mimics the back-and-forth cultural shifts that Mexican Americans make dozens of times daily. Moreover, it matches the back-and-forth culture-hopping operations that Mexican American viewers (at least *this* viewer) do as they watch the film, comparing the Mexican there with the U.S. here. Though its abruptness and its lack of foreshadowing place it outside the poetics of the classical documentary tradition, Portillo's narrative leap adheres perfectly to the logic of Mexican American postmodernism.

LA MERA FRONTERA: THE RETURN OF THE REPRESSED PAST

We have already mentioned one important way that Louis Hock's *La Mera Frontera* typifies Mexican American postmodernism: the incredulous view of the past that reveals how little we know—or are allowed to know—of it. Let me now discuss briefly how he achieves this formally, how he invokes investigative journalistic techniques while at the same time undermining them. To begin with, Hock's borderland documentary

Director Lourdes Portillo spends the first half of La Ofrenda: Days of the Dead *(1989) in Mexico, seeking an understanding of her Mexican roots by studying traditional Day of the Dead rituals. "What is there in me of my Indian past?" the female narrator asks. "What is there in me of that conqueror of yesterday?" (Photo courtesy of Xochitl Films)*

blends a fictional (if historically based) character, played by an actress, with the traditional investigative journalistic format and comes up with a new form: the historiographical documentary. That is, *La Mera Frontera* is about how history is—and has been—written. This is done by exposing and thereby subverting the fundamental modernist assumption of purportedly "objective" journalism—that the truth is unitary and knowable, requiring only an enterprising and informed reporter to arrange it into a coherent narrative.

Thus, part of the film looks like a traditional talking-head documentary, with old witnesses recounting the border battle of 1918. But then Hock introduces his star witness, a resurrected María Esquivel, an innocent casualty of the fighting. Her interrogation of the survivors exposes the way documentary reportage constructs the past and the uncritical way that that method is accepted as History. For instance, one central element in creating a typical documentary's coherent historical

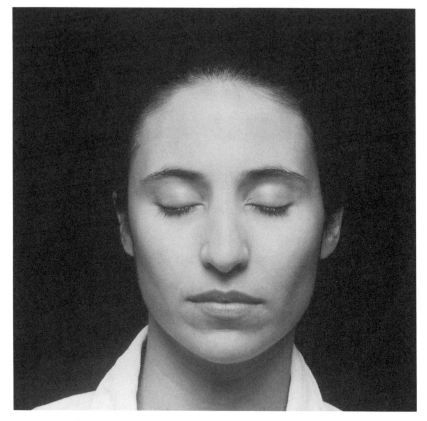

Louis Hock's La Mera Frontera *(1997) "resurrects" María Esquivel (played by actress Yareli Arizmendi), a young Mexican woman killed by U.S. troops in a border battle in 1918. As the film's organizing sensibility, she interrogates survivors of the skirmish in search of her place in history.*
(Photo courtesy of Louis Hock)

version is the narration: the person who speaks the narration writes history. The fact that María commandeers the narration makes her—one of history's lost victims—the film's organizing sensibility. The past is seen through the eyes of one of history's forgotten victims.

Not surprisingly, achieving coherence is elusive for her. After hearing several versions of what happened all those years ago, María comments on the fragmented historical narrative she is able to assemble. Speaking for all those left out of official, received histories, she says, "I could only see what was missing."

THE DEVIL NEVER SLEEPS: CHICANA FILM NOIR

The narrative formula of a typical Hollywood film noir has its usually male protagonist, such as the world-weary Sam Spade (Humphrey Bogart) in *The Maltese Falcon* (1941), investigating a crime and getting mired in a web of deception. Indeed, one of the genre's most notable characteristics is its grim worldview: the status quo is thoroughly corrupt. This depravity is personified by the protagonist's romantic interest and temptress, the treacherous femme fatale. Given this gloomy moral landscape, there are generally two narrative outcomes. In the happier one, the investigator resists temptation (barely, as in *The Maltese Falcon* and *Chinatown* [1974]) and survives. In this case, survival is the most that anyone can hope for and serves as the happy ending. In the downbeat version, as in *The Postman Always Rings Twice* (1946, 1981), or director Billy Wilder's disturbing *Sunset Boulevard* (1950), or Lawrence Kasdan's later homage to those films, *Body Heat* (1981), the protagonist surrenders to and is destroyed by evil. All in all, because of its uncompromisingly bleak look at contemporary American society, film noir is arguably Hollywood's most subversive genre.

But there is another, less common, type of film noir, a fusion of the above two. The result is a dual-protagonist narrative exemplified by films like Billy Wilder's *Double Indemnity* (1944) and Robert Siodmak's *The Killers* (1946). In these films, there are two male protagonists: the man who is tempted by the femme fatale and an investigator on the trail of the crime.

Ideologically, these films have it both ways. The standard noir corruption narrative is a bleakly fatalistic view of the American system, saying that the system stifles opportunity along class lines. Accordingly, the only way for an average Joe to achieve success, defined as sex and money, is to succumb to temptation and break the law. But this critique is neutralized by the investigation narrative, which—ideologically and dramatically—provides a far more positive resolution. What the insurance company investigators in both *Double Indemnity* and *The Killers* uncover is similarly sordid stories of men who capitulated to evil and got what was coming to them. Since the detective's solution concludes both films, it conveniently counters the criticism of the status quo in the noir half of the movie. The investigators' explanations proclaim that the system does work after all—if you play by the rules. This is affirmed by the experience of its working-class gumshoe, whose perseverance demonstrates that success in America—redefined in moral rather than material or sexual terms—is the result of hard work and is therefore actually class-blind and attainable.

Lourdes Portillo reactivates this hybrid film noir formula in *The Devil Never Sleeps* to look at the Mexican status quo, but replaces the ideological happy ending with ambiguity and doubt. The twin protagonists are Portillo herself, as the documentary detective, and her favorite uncle, Tío Oscar, who has mysteriously died in Chihuahua. "I had to go to Mexico," she says, using one of the more familiar film noir conventions, voice-over narration, "to find out what really happened" to her handsome, gregarious, and extremely successful relative. Looking for clarity and closure, she is frustrated at every turn. At the same time, her investigation takes her deeper inside the shadowy labyrinth of Mexican *machismo* without bringing her closer to solving the mystery of her uncle's death.

Because Oscar was a prominent businessman and politico, the basic facts of the case are immediately obscured. The first account of his death, published in the local newspaper, says that he was found dead of a heart attack in his bedroom. But that is just an awkward public relations cover for what the family knows actually happened: Oscar's body was discovered in a pool of blood early one morning at a health club with a fatal gunshot wound to his temple. The police, who, as Portillo records on camera, are initially unable to find Oscar's file for her, write it off as suicide. And, to be sure, there are rumors to support this interpretation. One that surfaces is that Oscar killed himself because he knew he was dying of cancer. Another that turns up later is that Uncle Oscar was gay and turned the gun on himself when he realized he was dying of AIDS.

But Portillo uncovers other noir-like facts that point to murder. "It's easy to have someone killed in Mexico," reflects Portillo once she begins entertaining the possibility, "like Pancho Villa and more recently, [PRI presidential candidate] Colosio." Among the suspicious clues, for example, is a business deal that went sour, followed by some animosity between Oscar and his partner. Then there is his second wife, Ofelia, the film's femme fatale. Twenty years his junior, she is described by Oscar's relatives as an unscrupulous gold digger. Is it just a coincidence that Oscar wrote his two children out of his will only a week before his death, leaving his entire fortune to Ofelia? Finally, there is an estranged son, banished from the household by his father after being accused by Ofelia of making sexual advances toward her.

Unlike Hollywood's dual-protagonist films noir, in the end Portillo fails to crack the case. Consequently, the film comes to a philosophical rather than a dramatic climax. In an honest concluding voice-over, Portillo admits that, for all her digging, she knows more but understands less. Her reflection on the investigation is a lucid definition of the postmodern condition:

> I came back to Mexico with the naive idea that if I pursued all the clues and found out all the facts, I'd uncover the truth. Just like in the movies. Did Oscar commit suicide or was he killed by a hired assassin? Maybe I'll never know. The only thing I'm sure of is that by his own choices he contributed to his destiny. The family still holds tightly to its secrets, and once again I realize there are no clear answers, no simple solution to life's mysteries. Just half-glimpsed truths and tantalizing questions.

Portillo comes to Mexico with a modernist goal and leaves with a postmodern insight. In the process, her documentary film noir exhibits an array of postmodern techniques: it is self-reflexive (there is never any attempt to hide the filmmaking process), hybrid (mixing family home movies with talking-head interviews and snippets from Latin American *telenovelas*), mistrustful of history (she questions hers and everyone else's memories—a skepticism that spills over into the interviews, so that it's hard to give anyone complete credence), and incoherent (unable as it is to arrive at closure). But, because it mirrors the fragmented Mexican American point of view, it is coherent in its incoherence (achieving what Jencks calls postmodernism's "disharmonious harmony"[36]) and is, for all its red herrings and narrative dead ends, altogether intelligible. It makes perfect postmodern sense.

Unfortunately, the implications of the sense it makes for Greater Mexicans are doubly disturbing. To begin with, Portillo's documentary film noir is as critical of the Mexican system as Hollywood's fictional noirs are of the American status quo—and for many of the same reasons. We see—and here, the fact that the investigator is female and Chicana is crucial—from the life Oscar lived that the Mexican system is sexist, patriarchal, and corrupt. The primary message for Mexican American viewers is that, for all their nostalgia about their roots, they can't easily go home again. What's worse, with Mexican Americans marginalized from both the U.S. and the Mexican systems, they have no home. From this perspective, *The Devil Never Sleeps* is a persuasive postmodern treatise on Mexican American alienation, illustrating how we are caught betwixt and between, unable to fit in on either side of the border.

Sitting beside the camera, Lourdes Portillo directs The Devil Never Sleeps *(El Diablo Nunca Duerme, 1995). Portillo also serves as the film's on-screen investigative reporter, looking for clues to her uncle's mysterious death. By making herself the documentary's private eye, she gives a new Chicana spin to Hollywood's classic film noir formula. (Photo courtesy of Xochitl Films)*

DOMINANT AND MEXICAN AMERICAN POSTMODERNISM

My title is "El Genio del Género"—the genius of the genre, which, as I see it, comprises two key elements, one aesthetic, the other philosophical. In analyzing borderland documentarians' cinematic aesthetics, it becomes clear that they are practicing the aesthetics advocated by Gómez-Peña, namely, "to embrace more fluid and tolerant notions of personal and national identity, and to develop models of peaceful coexistence and multilateral cooperation across nationality, race, gender, and religion. To attain this," Gómez-Peña continues, "we need more and better information about one another." [37] Border documentaries are busy making and disseminating transcendent multicultural information.

Philosophically, let me try to reconcile the seemingly different views of postmodernism held by José Limón and myself by suggesting that they are not really as antithetical as I have possibly cast them. Remembering that there are different varieties of postmodernism, we may think of it as a cultural and aesthetic process whose ideological effects depend on who participates in it and how. I agree that the postmodernism that comes out of the U.S. mainstream is, on the whole, Jameson's "cultural dominant" and contains the cancerous effects of late capitalism. When it arrives at the social margins it is ideologically leveling. This mainstream postmodernism creates, in Limón's words,

> a world in which the human subject is no longer just alienated, thus presuming some lost agency and purpose, but rather *decentered* and *fragmented*, incapable of conceiving mission, agency, purpose. It is a world "liberated" from feeling and from history, conceived as an informing past, a world whose primary self-representational style is the no-style of what Jameson calls *pastiche*—the random piecing together of any and every thing into representations without motivation or motive in the world.[38]

This discussion comes halfway through Limón's *Dancing with the Devil*. Afterward, Limón looks at "folkloric practices—indebted to tradition—among marginalized working-class Mexican-Americans in south Texas and possibly elsewhere" as forms "of a continuing, if repressed, war with a late-capitalist urbanized 'Anglo' culture of postmodernity." Through these forms, border Mexican Americans seem "to maintain a centered historical subjectivity, a creative sense of critical depth against these new, flattening, fragmentary pressures" of the dominant culture.[39] In my scheme, this resistance is what I have called Mexican American postmodernism. As Limón's ethnographic work shows, and as the borderland documentaries depict, it lives on in the lives of Mexican Americans, in their music and food, joking and dancing, language and poetry, criticism and filmmaking. *Postmodernism from the mainstream is brutalizing and dangerous; postmodernism from the margins can be defiant and liberating.*

Lastly, a word about Mexican American theory building. Chicano cinema was born thirty years ago with documentaries, and in the beginning the filmmakers themselves, in their manifestos, were the first Mexican American film theorists.[40] It appears that Chicano filmmakers continue to be among our foremost cinematic and cultural philosophers. The films by border documentarians display, describe, and define Chicano postmodernism and proclaim that Mexican Americans, having lived the postmodern condition since 1848, are old hands at postmodernism and are using it as an antihegemonic tool.

Final Freeze Frame

This article was written during the time that my Aunt Chita, whose full name is María de Jesús Ramírez Sánchez, suffered a series of debilitating strokes that left her confined to a foster home bed in El Paso. Some of the ideas I have expressed here first came to me at her bedside, as I stroked her head or held her hand. Going through her possessions as I cleared out her house, I found evidence of her ample expertise at Mexican American postmodernism. On her bookshelf, for example, James Joyce sat next to Amado Muro (his collection of short stories inscribed to her by Amada Muro, his wife, a personal friend), and Shakespeare's complete works leaned against Arturo Islas's *The Rain God* (personally inscribed "To Chita" by the author—his father and my aunt grew up in the same neighborhood). Her record collection was similarly eclectic, and juxtaposed Hadyn concerti with Agustín Lara, Michel Legrand and Juliette Greco with Jorge Negrete and Javier Solís, and included, of course, *Nat King Cole Español*.

To an inquisitive but naive kid growing up on the border, Aunt Chita gave the best gifts—unexpected yet fitting, and reflecting her expansive tastes. My two favorites were both Christmas presents: an album of calypso music from the Virgin Islands, whose wry, risqué lyrics and funky melodies I can recall to this day (quite a remarkable recording to give a nine-year-old!),[41] and Dag Hammarskjöld's introspective and darkly existential *Markings,* whose penetrating meditations helped me to look beyond superficial signs of prosperity ("Never let success hide its emptiness from you," Hammarskjöld wrote, "achievement its nothingness, toil its desolation").[42]

I guess the most important thing I learned from Aunt Chita was to resist marginalization by expanding your horizons, which could then lead to independent thinking. That is, she taught me how to achieve creative agency, which, I would say, is the essence of Mexican American postmodernism.

Aunt Chita died while I was writing this page. To thank her for "hybridizing" my thinking, I lovingly dedicate this chapter to her.

APPENDIX: DISTRIBUTORS OF THE CHICANO
BORDERLAND DOCUMENTARIES

Ballad of an Unsung Hero (1983)
The Cinema Guild
1697 Broadway, Suite 506
New York, NY 10019-5904
(800) 723-5522, Fax: (212) 246-5525

Chulas Fronteras (1976)
Added to the National Film Registry in 1993
Del Mero Corazón (1979)
(Both films included on the same video)
Cost for video copy: $30 + $3 postage and handling
Arhoolie Productions/Brazos Films
10341 San Pablo Ave.
El Cerrito, CA 94530
(510) 525-7471
Credit card orders: 1-888-274-6654

Los Mineros (1990)
The Search for Pancho Villa (1993)
Songs of the Homeland (1994)
Galán Productions
5524 Bee Caves Rd.
Austin, TX 78746
(512) 327-1333
See order form on Internet: www.galanproductions.com

La Ofrenda: Days of the Dead (1989)
The Devil Never Sleeps (*El Diablo Nunca Duerme* [1995])
Xochitl Films
981 Esmeralda St.
San Francisco, CA 94110-5207
415-642-1614

La Mera Frontera (1997)
Louis Hock
Visual Arts 0327
University of California, San Diego
La Jolla, CA 92093
(619) 534-2915
lhock@ucsd.edu

NINE

ETHNIC INGENUITY
AND MAINSTREAM CINEMA

Robert Rodríguez's Bedhead *(1990)*
and El Mariachi *(1993)*

Columbia Pictures' distribution of Robert Rodríguez's low-budget independent first feature, *El Mariachi* (1993), shortly after signing him to a lucrative two-picture contract, marks a significant break with two decades of Chicano cinema. As I've said already in this book, this New Wave is much more mainstream than earlier Chicano filmmaking and far less overtly political, and its appearance raises some interesting issues for Chicano cinema.[1] The key one for me is this: Is it possible for ethnic or otherwise marginalized filmmakers to enter mainstream media institutions and maintain their ethnic identity? Or is co-optation inevitable? As I have argued elsewhere[2] and have shown in Chapter 3, although mainstream filmmaking typically resists changes—much less challenges—to dominant norms and forms, film history has demonstrated that impressive interrogations of the status quo are possible from within.

Nevertheless, Hollywood remains an especially risky place for minority filmmakers. In their quest for the broadest possible appeal, producers typically eliminate ethnicity. During one of Rodríguez's early visits to Hollywood, one Disney producer urged him to direct an English-language remake of *El Mariachi*. Revise the script to make his protagonist "less ethnic," he was advised, and change the hero from a Mexican singer to an Anglo rock guitarist.[3] One way to counter such attitudes is to slip progressive politics into mass-mediated genre formulas—as Cheech Marin once put it, "so that they [viewers, but, presumably, producers as well] don't taste it, but, they get the effect."[4] It's not a bad tactic. As Armond White has noted, speaking of recent African American cinema, there is much to be said for films that choose not to "objectify their politics as an issue" but instead make their subversive statements "inherent in the very presentation of character and setting, and in the manipulation of images."[5]

These sorts of manipulations will require the employment of a sophisticated filmmaking aesthetic by Chicano cineastes, and knowing readings by us. Chicano critics' primary job, it seems to me, is to discern to what degree—if at all—New Wave Chicano filmmakers have stirred the tangy zest of ethnicity into their films. This is the question I now ask of Robert Rodríguez's award-winning student film, *Bedhead* (1990), and of his low-budget mainstream hit, *El Mariachi*.[6]

BEDHEAD: COMING-OF-AGE
GENRE MEETS MEXICAN MYTH

Bedhead, a family comedy narrated by an adolescent Chicana, Rebecca (Rebecca Rodríguez), is a Mexican American version of the familiar preteen subgenre. A variant of the teen coming-of-age films, the preteen flick most often tells a childhood empowerment narrative that transforms a victimized and/or powerless child into a self-actualizing, self-sufficient agent.

Typically in these films, children confront adulthood and are chastened by it (*My Girl* [1991]), or are contaminated/adulterated by it (*To Kill a Mockingbird* [1961]; *A High Wind in Jamaica* [1965]; *Empire of the Sun* [1987]). Sometimes the youths actually manage to defeat it (*Night of the Hunter* [1957]; *Home Alone* [1990]; *Home Alone II* [1992]; *Dennis the Menace* [1992]; *Free Willy* [1993]) or at least hold it at bay (*E.T.* [1982]). Stephen King has often utilized this narrative trope, and interesting variations occur in several films based on his works: *Children of the Corn* (1984) and its sequel (1993), *Stand by Me* (1986), and two made-for-TV movies, *It* (1990) and Stephen King's own *Sometimes They Come Back* (1991). In King's hands, the adolescent liminality narratives become horrific tales about the powerlessness of childhood that have two outcomes. In one formula (*Stand By Me, It,* and Stephen King's *Sometimes They Come Back*), adult corruption is a deadly force. In the reverse, revenge variation (*Children of the Corn*), the children viciously strike back at the grown-up world at large.

Like the teen coming-of-age movies, ideologically most of these preteen films negotiate between childhood idealism and adulthood compromise, between, that is, innocence and hypocrisy. The critique that this ostensibly oppositional genre assembles is effectively contained, though, when biology overcomes the kids' burgeoning counterideology: the children grow into adults and eventually assimilate into the mainstream.

Bedhead *(1990), Robert Rodríguez's award-winning student film, tells the story of Rebecca (Rebecca Rodríguez), who acquires special magical powers.*

The similar endings of *Rebel without a Cause* (1957) and *Home Alone* (1990), in which children and parents embrace despite unresolved differences, illustrate how the genre as a whole manages, in the final analysis, to preserve the status quo's conservative agenda by domesticating the children and incorporating them into the system. The formulaic happy ending occurs despite ample evidence that adults have forsaken their ideals and made the mainstream a moral wasteland.

Bedhead cuts against the generic grain in a likable, lighthearted way. True to formula, Rebecca is terrorized by her big brother, David (David Rodríguez), who knocks her down and causes an injury to her head. Mysteriously, though, the blow endows her with supernatural powers. Now she turns the tables on him, and gets him to kiss her feet, literally. But when she overplays her hand, ties him to her bike, and begins dragging him around the neighborhood, she falls and is injured again. Recovering in her hospital bed, she reflects on the day's experiences, realizes that she has received a precious gift, and resolves to exercise it discreetly— except when it concerns David. To keep him perpetually off balance, she displays her power one more time when he comes to visit. Spooked, he

*Rebecca's nemesis is her older brother, David (David Rodríguez), who takes
great pleasure in taunting and tormenting her.*

rushes out of the hospital room in a panic. In a final close-up, Rebecca
smiles into the camera and the film ends.

Some of Rodríguez's critique of the system is obvious. For instance,
he takes potshots at the nutritionally poor American breakfast. The
kids eat "Little Dog's Big Cacotas" cereal (the translated name would be
"Little Dog's Big Big Shits"), a breakfast food that, according to the sun-
burst blurb on the box cover, contains all of "1 essential vitamin." But,
beyond such easy targets, Rodríguez's interventions modify the genre
considerably and alter its conservative tendencies. The most prominent
change, of course, is his choice of a Chicana protagonist. That alone
transforms it into a progressive story of the raising of a young girl's consciousness in reaction to her brother's sprouting machismo. Enlightened
and liberated, she playfully—but effectively—exercises her newfound
sorcery, tests its limits, comes to terms with it, and learns how to deploy
it strategically. In doing this, Rodríguez not only creates a counterhegemonic Chicano variation of a well-known Hollywood subgenre, he
also revises the culture-specific myth of La Llorona.

As I discussed in *Cinema of Solitude,* one way to think of the narrative of *mexicanas* who buck the patriarchal system is to see it as a variation of the age-old Mexican myth of La Llorona.[7] Probably a mixture of European and Aztec tales, the Llorona myth is the narrative of a woman betrayed by a macho. In some versions, her lover takes their son away from her. In others, she kills the child in retaliation for being abandoned. In either case, she returns to haunt the male order, either as a ghost or as a madwoman. What I detected in the Mexican films that I analyzed was a series of women descendants of La Llorona who challenged patriarchy and consequently threatened the system. Rodríguez continues the tradition of cinematic Lloronas by placing the myth in a contemporary, middle-class Chicano context.

David is a Mexican American macho-in-training who torments Rebecca endlessly. The last straw is his ruining the one doll—this Llorona's child—she had salvaged from his wholesale destruction. David has stripped off the doll's clothes and combed its hair straight up in a stiff "bedhead" hairdo. ("Bedhead" refers to the unruly look of one's hair when rising in the morning. David is so lazy that not only does he spend the whole day with a bedhead, he has developed it into a style.) Significantly, he has disfigured the doll by painting swastikas (what else?) on its face.

Rebecca feels the "awesome surge" of her newfound mystical powers.

223

Suddenly Rebecca can make David do anything—even kiss her feet.

After Rebecca begins to notice "the awesome surge" of her antipatri-
archal powers, she realizes that the reach of her ability is unlimited. "I
could bring peace to the Middle East," she muses, "or become the first
Mexican American female president of the United States." But first,
playing Llorona-Delilah to David's macho Samson, she must get rid of
David's bedhead and deflate his oppressive masculinity. Washing (cleans-
ing?) him with a blast from a water hose, she douses his bedhead. When
that fails to flatten his stiff hairdo, she "loses it" and becomes "a complete de-mento."

What's clear from *Bedhead*'s ending is that adulthood will not rob
Rebecca of her powers because what she has acquired—in narrative
terms, magic; in symbolic terms, a raised consciousness—is beyond the
reach of ideology. *Bedhead*'s coming-to-consciousness narrative over-
whelms the genre's assimilationist coming-of-age formula and instead
of ending up a co-opted adolescent, Rebecca becomes a spy within the
system—patriarchy's, machismo's, and David's worst nightmare. When
the film is read in this way, a couple of things are worth noting. First,
because there is so much cultural layering in *Bedhead*, it's a good bet
that only a Chicano filmmaker could have made it. Second, the more a

viewer is aware of the interplay among Mexican, Mexican American, and American cultural elements in *Bedhead*, the more the film's progressiveness reveals itself.

EL MARIACHI: HYBRID EXPLOITATION FILM

For his first feature-length film, Rodríguez devised a taut, economical plot. A wandering minstrel dressed in black (Carlos Gallardo) arrives at a small Mexican border town. Carrying only his guitar in its case, the mariachi hopes to find a job singing in one of the local cantinas. Instead, he is mistaken for a hit man, Azul (Reinol Martínez), who also wears black, uses a similar guitar case to carry his weapons, and is in the midst of a bloody battle with the local drug racketeer, a North American called Moco (Peter Marquardt). The more the mariachi tries to stay out of harm's way, the more trouble finds him. Only Domino (Consuelo Gómez), the manager of a bar owned by Moco, befriends him. After both Azul and Domino have been killed by Moco, the mariachi trades in his guitar for one of Azul's pistols and confronts Moco and his gangsters in a final showdown.

Analyzing *El Mariachi* is a more complex task because of its mixed genre heritage. It's a *mezcla* of two exploitation genres, the Mexican

In El Mariachi *(1992), a warrior adventure genre film, a traveling musician
(Carlos Gallardo) arrives at a Mexican border town
and is mistaken for a hit man.*

narcotraficante film and the transnational action genre I call the warrior adventure film. Rodríguez adopted the mode of production from the first and adapted the narrative strategies and highly charged kinetic style of the second. Because he intended his film for the Spanish-language video market, and because Mexico's *cine fronterizo* (border film) provided a model for Rodríguez's frugal moviemaking strategy, it's appropriate first to discuss the influence of that Mexican film cycle on Rodríguez and his production of *El Mariachi*.

El Mariachi *and* Cine Fronterizo *Mode of Production*

Border films have flourished on the lowest end of the economic and aesthetic Mexican moviemaking scale for decades. The *narcotraficante* film, a Mexican police genre, is the most popular type of *cine fronterizo*. *Narcotraficante* films boomed from 1979 to 1989, when at least forty were made.[8] Arriving at a precise number is difficult because of their ephemeral mode of production (most were made by small, independent production companies, which sprang up overnight), their choice of media (some were shot on film, others on video), and, for some, their non-traditional distribution pattern (many bypassed theatrical exhibition, opting instead for release to Spanish-language home video markets in Mexico, Latin America, and the United States).[9]

This type of cinema was spawned by political, economic, and industrial conditions of the 1970s. It was then that, for all intents and purposes, the state took control of Mexican film production and forced independent producers out. Some of them found a highly profitable alternative by making low-cost films along the U.S.–Mexico border. They created close-knit enterprises that cut expenses by relying on family members for their labor pool, eschewing studio sets in favor of location shooting on ranches owned by relatives, and using whatever props were at hand. Initially, these productions were shot in the United States in order to avoid the expense of hiring union workers. A further cost-saving measure was the housing of cast and crew on the same ranches where the films were being shot. To trim costs still more, producers sometimes filmed two movies simultaneously. Each film typically took three to four weeks to shoot, at a cost of $50,000 to $85,000.[10]

In effect, what Rodríguez did was to streamline this lean, super-efficient production system to its cost-effective essence. As has been widely publicized, he was his own one-person film company, performing the creative duties (writer, director, director of photography, sound recordist, and editor) as well as the more labor-intensive ones (grip, gaffer, property master, and coproducer). He made *El Mariachi* for just over $7,000, shot it (on film) in fourteen days, and edited it on video. Not surprisingly, the U.S. press praised Rodríguez for his provident production ethic but failed to acknowledge his adherence to a well-established, low-overhead Mexican filmmaking tradition. And even in relation to that modest industrial practice, what Rodríguez did is still astounding: He made a quality feature film for one-tenth the budget generally regarded as appropriate only for inferior-quality films.

El Mariachi *as Warrior Adventure*

Narratively, *El Mariachi* is in the tradition of a species of the transnational adventure film—the warrior adventure genre—rooted in the Hollywood Western, which has blossomed because of a series of cinematic cross-pollinations between Asia and Hollywood. Principally, the genre includes Hong Kong martial arts adventures, low-budget U.S. variations on Hong Kong's kung fu themes, and Hollywood blockbuster actioners. As one martial arts critic has put it, their common defining feature is a protagonist who possesses and displays his fighting capability.[11]

One tracing of this genre's lineage would begin with Hollywood Westerns, which influenced—and were influenced by—Japanese samurai films. Both of these in turn influenced the Hong Kong martial arts films produced by Run Run Shaw in the early 1970s. An international market for such films was clearly identified with the U.S. success of films like Bruce Lee's *Enter the Dragon* (1973), which grossed more than $100 million here.[12] After that, Hong Kong and U.S. martial arts action films boomed.

The stage was set by the martial arts set pieces in the James Bond films (for example, *Goldfinger* [1964] and *Diamonds Are Forever* [1971]). Hits like *Billy Jack* (1971), *Cleopatra Jones* (1973), and *Cleopatra Jones and the Casino of Gold* (1975) featured heroes expert in hapkido. They paved the way for Chuck Norris, who starred with Bruce Lee in *Return of the Dragon* (1973) and began his own series of low-budget, independently made warrior adventures in the late 1970s. Other martial arts stars such as Steven Seagal and Jean Claude van Damme followed in the same vein. The high-rent, Hollywood blockbuster side of the genre includes such films as *First Blood* (1982), *Rambo: First Blood Part II* (1985), *Lethal Weapon* (1987), *Die Hard* (1988), and *Total Recall* (1989). In Hong Kong, two recent variants have evolved: John Woo's hyperviolent gangster movies and Jackie Chan's kung fu comedies.

THE WARRIOR ADVENTURE NARRATIVE

Although this transnational genre has proliferated to the point that it exists in numerous story variants, from crime dramas to police thrillers to war adventures, it is possible to distill a basic narrative and identify its essential elements: [13]

1. The genre centers on a *lone male protagonist* who possesses *special physical skills*. In the Hong Kong kung fu films and the Norris-Seagal-Van Damme spin-offs, this is the mastery of martial arts. Sometimes this is combined with police/commando/military training, in everything from Jackie Chan's *Police Story* (also known as *Police Force* and *Jackie Chan's Police Force* [1986]) to all of Seagal's films, *Lethal Weapon,* and *Die Hard.*

2. Like many a movie hero, *this genre hero adheres to a personal code of justice and morality, which he directs toward altruistic ends.*[14] "As a policeman, I fight crime for justice," says Jackie Chan's guileless hero in *Police Story,* a principle to which all warrior adventure heroes subscribe. The society that the hero rescues can be local, regional, or global. In *Above the Law* (1988) and *Hard to Kill* (1990), Steven Seagal contains threats posed by urban gangs; in *Die Hard,* Bruce Willis saves the executives of a Japanese company held hostage by international thieves (disguised as terrorists) in a Los Angeles skyscraper; in *Under Siege* (1992), Steven Seagal saves the world from nuclear destruction.

3. *The protagonist undergoes a severe test, involving a loss.* Often this comes in the form of an assault that nearly kills him, or kills a loved one, or both. In *Hard to Kill* (1990), hit men murder police detective Seagal's wife and leave him for dead.

4. *Revenge motivates his physical rehabilitation,* wherein he regains the special abilities he once commanded. Steven Seagal awakes from a seven-year-long coma in *Hard to Kill* and puts himself through a strenuous rehab regimen. Secret agent Mike Locken (James Caan) in Sam Peckinpah's *The Killer Elite* (1975) is similarly rigorous in his comeback training.

5. He is also *spiritually rehabilitated,* converting to or reaffirming his belief in some strain of Taoism, Buddhism, and/or Confucianism that promotes the sacredness of all life and underpins his martial arts prowess.[15] Sometimes an older male serves as philo-

sophical mentor and martial arts coach; sometimes the hero goes it alone. In Bruce Lee's *The Chinese Connection* (1972), several elements are combined as the hero avenges the death of his fighting teacher.

6. After recovering, *the hero confronts and defeats the ruthless villain (usually a drug lord) in a violent and spectacular duel to the death*. An important distinguishing feature of these films that separates them from adventures like, say, the Indiana Jones movies, is the climactic showdown. In the climax of the Indiana Jones action adventures, Jones triumphs by enduring a test and withstanding a powerful spiritual force that eliminates the bad guys. In the warrior adventures, the hero always fights to vanquish the villain and a host of his goons. The fight is a protracted, graphically violent, highly ritualized, and carefully choreographed set piece.

GENRE AS SYSTEMS OF VIEWER EXPECTATION

That the narrative I have sketched out may be applied to a wide variety of films, ranging from Bruce Lee's *Fists of Fury* (1971) and Sam Peckinpah's *The Killer Elite* to several of Steven Seagal's films, *Lethal Weapon*, and *Total Recall* points to several possible classificatory stumbling blocks I'd like to address. First of all, is this a genre at all, or merely a familiar revenge narrative?

To answer, we need a working definition of genre. I'd suggest one that posits genre as not simply a body of similar films but, as Steve Neale argues, also—and equally—

> specific systems of expectation and hypothesis which spectators bring with them to the cinema, and which interact with films themselves during the course of the viewing process. These systems provide spectators with means of recognition and understanding. They help render films, and the elements within them, intelligible and therefore explicable. They offer a way of working out the significance of what is happening on the screen: a way of working out why particular events and actions are taking place, why the characters are dressed the way they are, why they look, speak and behave the way they do, and so on. . . . These systems also offer grounds for further anticipation.[16]

The films of the warrior adventure genre share an array of narrative elements, not only the revenge plot. And while one or another of them may be present in Westerns, war films, detective films, and films noir, most if not all of them are present in this genre. Furthermore, the manner in which the elements are combined by the warrior adventure activates a set of specific audience understandings, expectations, and anticipations that are satisfied exclusively by this genre.

A second issue is the amount of narrative overlap between this genre and the others I've mentioned. Since this is an international genre, a certain amount of blurring is to be expected. Moreover, overlap is a problem only if one considers genres to be separate and discrete categories, which I don't. The case of warrior adventures only serves to point out that genres are seldom if ever absolute categories, only patterned narrative responses to a cluster of interconnected social and ideological dilemmas. I agree with Robin Wood, who stresses the interrelatedness of genres and opposes regarding them as discrete and fully autonomous categories.[17]

Third, if this is a distinct genre, does *El Mariachi* belong to it? Yes, for several reasons. Its narrative contains most—perhaps all—of the genre's distinguishing elements: the loner hero who is alienated when he encounters a hostile, corrupt society and who becomes a warrior as a result of this confrontation; the loss, albeit at the very end, of Domino and of the use of his hand because of a bullet wound; the reliance upon a cultural tradition as his spiritual guide; and finally, the climactic showdown with Moco. (The revenge element may also be present. It could be what motivates his transformation into a warrior at the very end, but we'll have to wait for the sequel to be sure.)

Additionally, the presence of several motifs and iconographic indicators supports the inclusion of *El Mariachi* in the warrior adventure genre. For instance, there is the hero in black, the color traditionally worn by martial arts warriors (made explicit by the title of Chuck Norris's *Good Guys Wear Black* [1979]). There is the wandering protagonist, a characteristic trope that harks back to the beginnings of the genre, in both Eastern (*Yojimbo* [1961] and *Sanjuro* [1962]) and Western (*Shane* [1953]) incarnations. There is a subtle reference, at one point, to martial arts weaponry. Trapped in his hotel room, the mariachi pulls a morning star (a spiked ball on a chain) from a decorative set of medieval arms on the wall and swings the ball around as if he might use it as a *nunchaku*, the hinged weapon used by martial arts fighters. (Typical of the film's continual cutting against the generic grain, the mariachi never uses it as a weapon, but he does use it as a hook to slide down the wire and onto a speeding bus.) Finally, there is the de rigueur heightening of fighting noises on the soundtrack. (There were more hints in *Bedhead* that Rodríguez was an aficionado of martial arts cinema: the ex-

True to the genre's conventions, events compel the peaceable guitar player into becoming a gun-toting avenger.

aggerated *SNAP!* on the soundtrack when Rebecca commands the garden hose into her hands; the fighting position Rebecca assumes as she experiences the surge of her awesome powers.)

At this point a table of key narrative elements might help to summarize the genre's distinctive features, distinguish it from other, similar genres, and explain why I include *El Mariachi* in the warrior adventure genre. In this graphic form, it can be seen how closely *El Mariachi* resembles the warrior adventure narrative. And, among other things, the genre comparisons reveal why some films, like the Indiana Jones action adventures, don't belong to the warrior genre, though others, like *First Blood* and *Rambo: First Blood Part II* do.

Genre as Industrial Formula

In identifying and defining the genre, we should not lose sight of the industrial understandings that coincide with an audience's, for, I would argue, it is precisely when narrative formula, audience familiarity, and industrial practice merge that a genre's existence is confirmed.[18] As evidence for the existence of the warrior action genre as an industrial formula, let me return to the Hollywood producer who told Rodríguez that his protagonist was "too ethnic." Remember, this was in the spring of 1992, after Rodríguez had signed with the powerful ICM (International Creative Management) agency but before he had committed to

TABLE 9.1

Warrior Adventure Genre: Key Narrative Elements

Genre or Film	Wandering, Alienated Hero	Loss	Revenge Narrative	Spirituality	Weak/ Corrupt Society	Duel to Death
Warrior adventure (martial arts)	X	X	X	X	X	X
Action adventure (Indiana Jones)	Wandering, not alienated			Judeo-Christian; not invoked by Jones		
Detective (Maltese Falcon)	Alienated, not wandering	Partner's murder hardly affects him	Loyalty more than revenge		X	
Film noir (Postman)	X					
Western	X	Sometimes (e.g., Anthony Mann's Westerns and John Ford's The Searchers)				X
War				Patriotism		
First Blood; Rambo	X	X	X		X	X
El Mariachi	X	X	Perhaps at end	Ethnicity as cultural memory	X	X

Note: Films referred to are The Maltese Falcon (1941); The Postman Always Rings Twice (1946; 1981); The Searchers (1956); First Blood (1982); Rambo: First Blood Part II (1985); and El Mariachi (1993).

any studio, and about a year before the release of *El Mariachi*. The producer was one of various studio executives courting Rodríguez. At that point *El Mariachi* was deemed stunning but unmarketable because it was in Spanish. For Hollywood, films in foreign languages exist only as source material for potential American films. Hence French hits like *Three Men and a Cradle* (1985) and *La Femme Nikita* (1990) become *Three Men and a Baby* (1987) and *Point of No Return* (1993). By such ethnocentric, imperialistic reasoning, a Hollywood remake—in English—of *El Mariachi* should obviously be Rodríguez's first project. Besides wanting to "de-ethnicize" Rodríguez's hero, the producer suggested a revised plot. When a drug deal turns sour, the Anglo hero, a rock guitarist, is beaten to a pulp and left in the desert to die. Fortunately, he is found and nursed back to health by an aged Native American medicine man, who imparts the wisdom of his warrior ancestors to the recovering protagonist and trains him to fight. The hero tracks, finds, and destroys the drug-peddling bad guys.[19]

Beyond the insensitivity of the "too ethnic" remark—which, purely as market-savvy advice, may have been dead accurate—what's interesting about the producer's proposed story line is how closely it resembles the genre narrative I just outlined. This genre obviously existed in the executive's mind as a distinct narrative with an established, well-understood pattern of understandings, expectations, and anticipations. Moreover, this pattern offered a way to gauge the marketability of Rodríguez's film. From this producer's perspective, the main plot problem with *El Mariachi* was that it varied too much from genre conventions, which would frustrate viewer expectations and likely result in a box-office dud.

Let me conclude this section by returning to Neale, who believes that genres are "best understood as *processes*" characterized by repetition and variation, stasis and change. This "process-like nature of genres manifests itself as an interaction between three levels: the level of expectation, the level of the generic corpus, and the level of the 'rules' or 'norms' that govern both."[20] What's so interesting about *El Mariachi* are the ways it plays with all three levels. But before I discuss that, let me briefly set out the ideological dynamics of the genre.

Warrior Adventures: From Narrative to Ideology

A celebration of untrammeled male power, the warrior adventure genre negotiates between the solitary exercise of sanctioned violence on the one hand and the common good on the other. When, the genre asks, can an individual act violently and autonomously? Answer: when society is seriously threatened. In order that the hero's unrestrained vigilante justice not endanger the community it is supposed to preserve and protect, the genre presents a desperate situation. The evil is potent and menacing; society is either so weak it can't defend itself or so corrupt that it's part of the problem.

Any genre, be it a Western, a film noir, or a kung fu adventure, that has as its starting point a disintegrating society and the hero's reliance on an idiosyncratic code of behavior—as opposed to shared mores—implies a social structure whose moral center has not held. What's made of that ideologically varies from genre to genre. In film noir, for example, corruption is the dark side effect of capitalism; society is a collection of alienated individuals given over to instant gratification. In this genre, however, the weak society supplies the justification for vigilante violence. With the Visigoths at the gates, authorities—and audiences—have little choice but to dispense with civil liberties and allow the hero to trample on individual rights so that he can save society. "I'll give you every dope deal," says detective Gino (Steven Seagal) in *Out for Justice* (1990) as he bargains with his supervisor for permission to embark on a personal, police-subsidized vendetta. "Just give me a shotgun and an unmarked."

Naturally, the genre's sanctioned vigilantism makes it disturbingly conservative.[21] Because of the reductive way the genre frames the lawlessness-versus-order issue, there is a pressing need for a champion. And not just any hero will do—this is no time for amateurs. What's called for is a contemporary Hercules. Thus the regressivity of the narrative is underscored by the casting. In both Hong Kong and Hollywood varieties, the actor who plays the hero is physically exceptional. In the martial arts films, he is a highly trained athlete who has made his body into a lethal weapon. In the Hollywood variant, actors like Sylvester Stallone and Arnold Schwarzenegger are, literally, supermen. Why not, these films ask again and again, turn things over to the likes of them?

El Mariachi's *Oppositional Genre Variations*

El Mariachi makes some fascinating contestational responses to this inherent conservatism. Let's look at some of the ways that Rodríguez's film cuts against the generic grain.

PROTAGONIST

The fact that the hero is a Mexican is a crucial difference. Any hero presents a locus for viewer identification and empathy. Given the lopsided number of Anglo male action heroes in film history, simply providing audiences someone other than a white male focus for their rooting interest is necessarily positive (the same is true for the Hong Kong films). Beyond that, though, there is the ordinariness of Rodríguez's hero, and of the actor who plays him.

With the way the genre works, even if the character has no special physical skills, we know that the actor does and that it will only be a matter of time before the narrative devises an excuse for him to take off his shirt and display them. This is what was so intriguing about the variation *Die Hard* almost presented—Bruce Willis's hero wasn't another martial arts hard body, he was just an average Joe. Except, of course, that he wasn't—he was an experienced and very resourceful cop. In *El Mariachi*, though, the guitar player (and Carlos Gallardo) really doesn't have any special physical powers. He is truly what *Die Hard*'s hero nearly was—a man thoroughly unprepared for the mayhem that comes his way.

Since the guitar player is clearly not a man of action, his unpreparedness undercuts one element of the genre's veiled fascism—that is, the notion that only a superhero can successfully handle the evil that threatens. Rather, the mariachi's skills are art, culture, and morality, and, in this film, they are enough to overwhelm Moco.

MASCULINITY/MACHISMO

El Mariachi redefines heroism and masculinity in sharp contrast to the genre's established norms of manhood. A hero need not have the physical capabilities of a Mr. Universe or a martial arts master, nor does he need to be looking to save the world (and prove his masculinity); he can simply be a balladeer looking for a receptive audience. How often do we get to see a hero who lives for his art? How many action heroes could say, as the mariachi announces proudly to Domino when he first meets her, "My voice is my life"?

But he's faced with an uncaring world. No one wants a mariachi, and the first bartender he encounters shows him why—he already has a one-man techno band. The bar musician, wearing a sequined sombrero as his sole cultural marker and banging out noises on his electronic keyboard, is a sad remnant of a rich musical heritage that includes Agustín Lara, Jorge Negrete, and Pedro Infante.

Of course, the other, oppressive side of that illustrious Mexican movie tradition was its accompanying machismo. But *El Mariachi*'s antimacho hero effectively counters that. He neither drinks nor smokes, and the film is knowing enough to make a running gag out of it. The bartender has to look long and hard to find the mariachi a soft drink in his cooler overflowing with beer, and even Domino shoots the mariachi a questioning glance when he requests a soda. What sort of macho doesn't drink or smoke? In relation to reigning norms of masculinity in the United States, Mexico, and in the genre, the mariachi is unique: a male who does not depend on external signs—the pumped-up body, the hard-drinking lifestyle, the phallic weaponry—to confirm his masculinity.

But just as the town does not welcome a singer, neither does it comprehend a man who does not exhibit the conventional markers of manhood. In fact, it's the naturalized dominance of such signifiers of masculinity, and the mariachi's lack of them, that gets him into trouble. No one is prepared to believe that he is a male without any traditional indicator of masculine power—that he is a different kind of male. Therefore, the mariachi's guitar case is misread as his masculine sign—assumed to be Azul's trademark arsenal—and he is mistaken for the hit man. Being an antimacho in a macho universe is a very risky proposition.

SPIRITUALITY

One of the warrior adventure genre's more troubling aspects is its depiction of Eastern mysticism. The hero's spiritualism endows him with inner tranquillity, but all too often it is debased and simplified into a motivational linchpin that rationalizes his wreaking havoc and maiming foes. Tao is his license to kill.

El Mariachi is more reverential and less manipulative with the guitar player's spiritualism—his devotion to his cultural roots. Because he's not looking for a license to kill, his belief system can be more than facile motivation. For the mariachi, culture, memory, and tradition connect him to his familial past (the tradition of singing in his family that stretches back to his father and grandfather) and with his Mexican musical heritage. Additionally, they provide him with a coherent credo and a moral basis for his explicit critique of global capitalism.

WEAK/CORRUPT SOCIETY

In keeping with genre conventions, *El Mariachi*'s border society is thoroughly corrupt. Everybody is on the take: the cops, the bartender, the hotel clerk—even Domino is beholden to Moco. After the first sequence, law enforcement is absent. Bodies pile up, but the police never appear. However, *El Mariachi* posits a specific source of the social depravity, namely, the United States and high-tech "progress." "Technology," the mariachi ruminates at one point, "has crushed us, robbed us of our culture, turned us into machines."

Thus the locale in *El Mariachi* is not just another sleazy border town. It's a town that's sleazy because it borders on the United States, whose relentless technology and ruthless market system have combined to destroy Mexican culture. Again, the scene that best exemplifies this is the musical "performance" by the one-man band. It's played for laughs, but beneath the comedy lurks the tragedy of the First World erasure of the Third.

CRIMINAL MILIEU

The most corrupt and treacherous figures in the compromised world of this genre are the drug-peddling villain and his gang of thugs. *El Mariachi* conforms to the convention and never whitewashes the drug racketeering so prevalent along the U.S.-Mexico border. But it's clear about where to fix the blame for it. Here again the critique is specific and directed—the drug-running kingpin, Moco (does he know his nickname means "snot"?), is a gringo. Thus, in *El Mariachi,* drug trafficking is the logical extension of corporate America's international expansionism and exploitation. Drugs and technology are two sides of the same global market-driven, cultural-imperialistic coin.

It's interesting to note, for instance, how the structure of Moco's drug operation, where a gringo owner oversees Mexican laborers, mirrors that of *maquiladoras,* the assembly plants that (mainly) U.S. industries own and operate along the Mexican side of the border. Promoted in the mid-1960s as a boon to U.S. industry and a helping hand to unemployed Mexican workers, they quickly boiled down to institutionalized exploitation. Mexican workers were typically paid salaries that, with peso devaluation factored in, were one-twelfth the U.S. minimum wage; in the late 1980s this amounted to about $3.30 per day.[22] Moco's borderland gangster is, like all movie gangsters, the shadow of a successful capitalist businessman. In this context, it's fascinating that the action in *El Mariachi* is in effect triggered by a worker's revolt over a salary dispute: Azul comes to get the money that Moco failed to pay him.

If Rodríguez bent the familiar genre formula nearly to the breaking point, and overturned a number of its more regressive elements as he did so, the question that's begged is how and why the film was released by a major Hollywood studio. Had the film languished on some producer's shelf, there's a good chance it never would have been released. But Columbia Pictures decided to enter the film in selected festivals in the fall of 1992, and it became a favorite with audiences at Toronto and Telluride, and won the Audience Award at the Sundance Film Festival. Hoping that the film's unqualified festival successes would translate into healthy box-office revenues, the studio released *El Mariachi* as Rodríguez made it.

The numerous press stories that covered the festivals and the film suggest two reasons why those early audiences were so taken by the film. First, its low cost—the fact that the film was made for seven thousand dollars raised interest and curiosity, and, perhaps more important, engendered audience sympathy. The second reason was the film's engaging, highly energetic style. Filmmaking on a shoestring may have initially drawn audiences, but it was the accomplished and compelling film that viewers actually saw that won them over. Let me conclude, then, by analyzing Rodríguez's formal style in *El Mariachi* and speculating on its generic and ideological implications.

Rodríguez's Aesthetic: Creating from Constraints

Recognizing cinema's fundamental link with motion, the warrior genre makes movement its subject. Its style is a combination of acrobatic bodies in motion and a camera eagerly moving to capture them. Films of this genre offer the same pleasures as the films of Harold Lloyd, Douglas Fairbanks, and Buster Keaton, where carefully choreographed gags were combined with fluid camera movements.

Based on the sort of spectacle they (can afford to) mount, warrior adventure films may be divided into two classes: the dozens made at the bargain-basement level and the relatively few Hollywood blockbusters. Because of their lower budgets and meager resources, the cheaper films rely on basic cinematic techniques, and this has had a liberating effect. A style that requires only a movie camera, an active imagination, and a keen cinematic sensibility, that relies mostly on what the camera lens can record and the body can do, rather than on the endless artifice that technology can concoct, is a brand of cinema that has divorced quality from money. As Rodríguez puts it:

> Money has nothing to do with making a good movie or telling a good story. . . . You have problems on the set when you make a movie all the time. You can solve them one of two ways: real quick, with money, or creatively. Which makes your movie better? . . . a movie . . . is a creative endeavor. So sometimes you can actually be forced to be more creative when you have no money. And that can only make your movie better. You end up being more creative than you even intended. And we did that a lot here [with *El Mariachi*].[23]

One advantage of coming from the margins is that living there prepares minority filmmakers to be adept at creating from the materials at hand rather than from cash. For *El Mariachi*, Rodríguez tailored his script to what was available: a bulldog and a turtle, a school bus and a black motorcycle, two bars and the exterior of a brothel, a ranch, a swimming pool, and a freestanding porcelain bathtub.

Even though Gallardo is a game performer, he is not the equal of a Fairbanks, a Keaton, or a Jackie Chan. But Rodríguez more than compensates for that with his kinetic cinematic style. It is characterized by short takes (most shots are only a few seconds long) edited together in rapid-fire succession. His furious tempo is reminiscent of Sergei Eisenstein's staccato montage and the jump-cutting brashness of the French New Wave. Combining that with Rodríguez's shot selection (which favors close-ups and extreme close-ups), his playfully moving camera, and his use of speeded-up action for comic effect yields a formal style somewhere between Mack Sennett's herky-jerky slapstick and Sam Peckinpah's elegiac lyricism. Rodríguez approximates the cinematic frenzy of the Bruce Lee–Jackie Chan tradition via his indefatigable style.

When the best of the Hong Kong and low-budget American films like *El Mariachi* are contrasted with the Hollywood blockbuster variations, the cinematic difference is dramatic. It's a battle between ethnic ingenuity and high-dollar tricks. The blockbuster's heavy reliance on costly state-of-the-art special effects is, in a sense, one more conservative element. The sorts of effects associated with Hollywood warrior movies—computerized image enhancements and dazzling pyrotechnics—shift the emphasis away from human dexterity and toward technological expertise; that is, away from physical stunts people perform with their bodies and toward technological effects that only Hollywood can provide—and afford. Expensive effects thereby reinforce the ideological thrust of the genre, illustrating the ideological message that we can't do it ourselves—"it" being everything from solving social problems to making movies. Someone better financed, more experienced, and more powerful should be in charge of that.

Ultimately, *El Mariachi*'s most progressive element and its greatest achievement may well be the effective and entertaining way it says no to all that. What Rodríguez championed with his making of *El Mariachi* is creativity over wealth. What his film bemoans is the loss of cultural memory in the name of progress. What it calls into question is dominant notions of masculinity, heroism, the U.S.–Mexico border, and, finally, cinema. You can hardly be more provocative or more subversive than that.

TEN

THE *MARIACHI* AESTHETIC GOES TO HOLLYWOOD

An Interview with Robert Rodríguez

ROBERT RODRÍGUEZ FILMOGRAPHY

Short Films

Bedhead (1990): d., sc., d.p., ed.

10 Minute Film School

10 More Minutes (Anatomy of a Shootout)

Features

El Mariachi (1992): d., ed., co-p., sc., d.p., sound ed.

Roadracers (1994): d., camera op., co-sc., ed.

Desperado (1995): d., sc., p. (co-p. Elizabeth Avellan), ed., Steadicam op.

Four Rooms (1995): "The Misbehavers" d., sc., ed., camera op.

From Dusk Till Dawn (1996): d., ed., camera op., Steadicam op., sound rerecording mixer

The Mask of Zorro: left in preproduction phase

The Faculty (1998): d., ed., sound rerecording mixer, camera op.

From Dusk Till Dawn 2: Texas Blood Money (1999): direct-to-video feature, co-executive producer

Robert Rodríguez directing on the set of Spy Kids *(2001) with his assistant for the day, his son, Rocket. (Photo by Rico Torres, courtesy of Dimension Films)*

From Dusk Till Dawn 3: The Hangman's Daughter (2000): direct-to-video feature, co-executive producer, co-story

Spy Kids (2001): d., ed., writer, producer, sound mixer, visual effects supervisor, camera op.

As you can see from his filmography, Robert Rodríguez has been busy since *El Mariachi*. For this book, I wanted to bring our knowledge of his career up to date. In particular, I wanted to address some of the more problematic representations in his work, especially in films like *From Dusk Till Dawn*. And I wanted to discuss the absence of Latino representation altogether in *The Faculty*. But instead of writing another critical essay covering this ground, I thought it would be better to hear him talk about these issues, to hear his side of the story. I wanted the filmmaker himself to talk about what he has done and why he has done it.

Robert Rodríguez is one of the more successful of the wave of young directors of the last seven or eight years, and to date arguably the most successful Latino director ever to work in Hollywood. Because they were made so cheaply, all his films have made money. *Four Rooms* may have been a critical bomb, but Rodríguez's segment, "The Misbehavers," was the most successful, and it was the project that allowed him to edit and to have final cut on future films. And he managed to leverage the directing of *The Faculty* for Miramax into a multifilm deal in which he has virtually complete creative control. The first of these, the children's adventure *Spy Kids,* he was busily editing at the time of this interview.

The basic questions that I wanted him to address are important ones: What is it like for a Latino director working in Hollywood these days? What is the responsibility of a Latino filmmaker in Hollywood? How can a Latino filmmaker, one who is proud of his heritage, balance being true to his ethnicity and satisfying the needs of a large, profit-driven media industry? Could someone like Rodríguez, who began his career with his low-budget *Mariachi* filmmaking aesthetic, continue making films with that same guerrilla mentality? Or would he, by agreeing to work within the media mainstream, be forced to conform to Hollywood's ethnically cleansed paradigm? Said another way, though he may have entered the mainstream hoping to change it, there is always the danger that it will change him. Put bluntly, has Robert Rodríguez sold out to the system?

We talked in his editing suite, which is in a converted garage at his home outside of Austin, Texas. When we first sat down at his editing station, he showed me some of the sequences of the film and explained how the editing on this film was made more complex by the four hundred special-effects shots. He had just gotten back from a trip to the special-effects house to coordinate some of the shots.

Typically, he edits all night and sleeps from early morning to midafternoon. Then he gets up, plays with his three sons, Rocket, Racer, and Rebel, and takes care of odds and ends until it's time to begin editing again. Besides the editing computer monitors, he keeps a Mac laptop on the desk, and to the left of the monitors there is a large high-definition television. He plays a film, some on DVD, some on video, as a sort of "visual background" while he edits.

He popped in Alfred Hitchcock's *Vertigo* (1958) to show me how it looked on high definition. Together we marveled at how sharp Hitchcock's film looked with the latest technology. I remarked on the color design, in, for example, the scene in the restaurant where Madeleine's (Kim Novak) green dress explodes against the red walls. He talked about the compositions, such as the one of Scottie (James Stewart) and Madeleine under the Golden Gate Bridge when she tries to commit suicide by drowning.

Lining up a shot on Spy Kids. *Opting to direct, script, and co-produce
(with his wife, Elizabeth Avellán) his own film, he turned down offers to direct
films such as* Superman, Wild Wild West, Planet of the Apes, *and* X-Men.
"I'd rather do something I created myself," Rodríguez says. "On Spy Kids
*I have final cut and I can do anything I want." (Photo by Rico Torres,
courtesy of Dimension Films)*

His favorite editing films, he said, were *Heavy Metal* (1981) and
Glengarry Glen Ross (1992). "I'll be editing away, and then when I'm
waiting for an effect to be rendered on the screen, which takes a long time,
I'll turn over to see what's going on in the movie," he said. "With [*Heavy
Metal*] there's either some cool music going on, or a nice graphic, or
something funny happening [in *Glengarry Glen Ross*]." Our conversation gradually drifted toward the topics I wanted to cover for the interview, but when I turned on the tape recorder, it was he who asked the
first question.

ROBERT RODRÍGUEZ: When do you write?

CHARLES RAMÍREZ BERG: I try to write first thing in the morning.

RR: That's what I heard. I tried it. I'm just not a morning guy, you
know.

CRB: I'm not either, but once you have children, then you become a
morning guy.

RR: I just don't like getting up in the morning.

CRB: I don't either.

RR: And it's hard to write fiction, you know, because there's just a blank page. So it's really discouraging to try and write because you don't want to face the blank page. You'll do anything to avoid writing. You'll go clean your toilet before you write. So I finally figured it out. I've done the most writing this year because of a trick I've figured out.

CRB: And what's the trick?

RR: The trick is you gotta find something worse than writing. [*Laughing*] That's it, that's the trick.

CRB: I found it too.

RR: What's your thing?

CRB: Grading papers.

RR: Well, see, you got that! But I don't like getting out of bed in the morning. I'm not a morning person, so I just love lying in bed for thirty or forty minutes. You know, you're just rolling around, trying to avoid getting out of bed. Especially since our bed's real warm, and we keep the bedroom cold in the summer.

So I pull this out [*indicates a Mac PowerBook laptop*]. And as soon as I wake up, instead of just lying there dozing, I put this on my lap, turn it on, half asleep, and I write. And I focus so easily. Since that light's coming from the screen, I zero in on it. So you're not even thinking about anything. And I'll lay there for three or four hours, writing, and not get up. So I think to myself, "Hey, at least I'm not getting up, I'm just laying here." If I were to get up, and go get coffee, I would find ten other things to do. Once I get up, that's it.

But when I'm in bed, the ideas are really good. I may lay there with no idea of how I'm going to approach a story, and an hour later I've got all this good stuff. And I think, "Wow, that never happened when I used to work at night!" I never had any good ideas, because I'd be falling asleep.

CRB: Your energy level is another thing—I find that I have much more energy in the morning. And if you start early enough, by noon you're done.

RR: Yeah, I quit sometimes after two hours, happy that I got so much done.

CRB: And the rest of day is yours. And the other thing is, I think you have to figure out how to fool your critic, so your critic doesn't show up. And the way I do it is, early in the morning my critic is still asleep.

RR: Everything's still asleep.

CRB: Well, I'm finishing this book on Latino images in Hollywood film. And one of the essays, I don't know if I've ever showed it to you, is on *Bedhead* and *El Mariachi.* And one of the reviewers of the manuscript said that you've made other films since then, and there's been some criticism of some of your Latino portrayals after that. So then I thought, why don't I let you talk about the films and let you address those issues in your own words. Let the filmmaker comment on his work.

Because of our previous conversations, I know you're aware and conscious of these things—

RR: Sometimes . . . [*laughs*].

CRB: For example, I've heard you say before that you would rather do genre movies and interweave the ethnicity than be known as an ethnic filmmaker.

RR: Well, I feel fortunate to have the background that I do because you can borrow from all that, and use it to give your films and your ideas a distinctive flair.

For example, take this movie, *Spy Kids.* It could very easily be an Anglocized, *Home Alone*–type movie, but anyone who has watched it so far really notices the colors and the flavor and the feel. I remember when the studio first read the script, they said, "So where does this family live?" And I said, "It's fictional. Somewhere along the coast of Mexico." And they said, "So they're *Mexicans?*"

But for me it was using Latin America to give it a Latin feel. So it's not a British James Bond, it's like a Latin James Bond. Most of it takes place in Latin America and Mexico because it's somewhere else. I mean, somewhere you don't get to see in the movies. And I get to highlight that to give it a different flair.

And it's great for me because I can put all kinds of stuff in it that I grew up with. So for example, there's a scene in here where another kid speaks Spanish. The Spy Kids take off with their special rocket shoes, and another kid sees them and tells his parents, "*¡Quiero zapatos como esos!*" ["I want shoes like those!"] And his parents say, "You've got enough stuff." And it'll be in Spanish and subtitled, so you'll know you're in Latin America.

CRB: So it's a different starting place.

RR: A different starting place. And it's nice seeing really cool, heroic characters who are named the Cortez family. Carmen and Gregorio Cortez. And it's great being able to do that in a very mainstream film. And I hope that one of the audience's reactions is that there will be kids going around wanting to be Carmen Cortez. And I like being able to do that without being overly preachy about it.

Rather than doing it as a niche film, for a niche Latino market, instead I want it to play to everybody. And have them identify with the

*Robert Rodríguez directing his young stars—Alexa Vega, who plays Carmen
Cortez, and Daryl Sabara, who plays her brother, Gregorio ("Juni").
(Photo by Rico Torres, courtesy of Dimension Films)*

characters. So I want to fool the audience into seeing the movie, and
have them enjoy it, and not even have them realize that this is also about
a Latino family. I started to do that with *Desperado.*

CRB: I think you started in *Bedhead.*

RR: *Bedhead?* I don't think it was ever specified. Well, Rebecca did
say that she could be the first Mexican American president of the United
States. But that was the only time you really knew that they were Mexican American.

So even back then, I guess, I was just going for something more mainstream and including us [Mexican Americans] in there, as if to say,
"We're mainstream." That's all the statement it needs.

CRB: But in *El Mariachi* there was another statement. The drug dealer,
the bad guy, Moco, was an Anglo. And also your portrayal of the border was interesting because it seemed different from the typical Hollywood treatment of the border. In it the border seemed like a lived-in place.

RR: Uh-huh. Well on *El Mariachi* I just used the local townsfolk,
and the town. I didn't build any sets or anything, because it was so low-
budget. So it had a real feel of the border because it *was* the border. But
in *Desperado* the border didn't seem as real because I had to import a

lot of talent, a lot of SAG [Screen Actors Guild] actors, so it felt more artificial.

CRB: In your mind was *Desperado* a sequel to *El Mariachi*?

RR: It was a weird thing because all along I was always going to re-make *El Mariachi*. Then when Columbia released the original, I thought, "Now what am I going to do? I've been working on *El Mariachi* for all this time." So I thought, "Let me write a sequel because not that many people would have seen the first one." So it wasn't a sequel and it wasn't a remake. It was kind of in between.

To be honest, I didn't really know what it was. In fact, it wasn't even going to be made and then suddenly it was being made, because of the turnover in the head office at Columbia. I had written it a year and a half before and didn't even look at it again. Then we got a green light and I didn't rewrite it. We just started shooting it. So it was one of those weird things. I remember shooting and going, "Oh, I didn't even rewrite this thing after I wrote it a year and a half ago. And there's a bunch of problems with it." But I just wanted to get something made so I could show people that I could do a studio film and go on to other projects.

CRB: But the drug lord changed from an Anglo to a Latino.

RR: Yeah, that was always the idea. I wanted it to be like one of those Mexican soap operas, where you had the family connection between the two brothers [the *El Mariachi* character, played by Antonio Banderas, and his drug lord brother, Bucho, played by Joaquim de Almeida]. And that got very weird, because he was going to be played by Raúl Julia, who suddenly passed away just before we were going to shoot his part. So I had to rewrite that character very quickly, in about a week, and I took a lot of the family stuff out. And in the final film the relationship didn't make a whole lot of sense.

CRB: How do you think it would have been different if Raúl Julia had lived to play that part?

RR: I think in the original script the relationship between the brothers was woven in better. I just ended up having much less time to shoot de Almeida, so I cut out a lot of stuff to have it make more sense.

CRB: Did you write it with Raúl Julia in mind?

RR: Oh, yeah! And Antonio even said he acted it with him in mind. Julia wasn't going to come shoot until the last two weeks, and we'd already shot most of the movie when he passed away. And up until that point that's who Antonio and I had been picturing as Antonio's brother. I was looking so forward to it. I only talked to him on the phone, and he read it and he told me, "I love it! It reminds me of the *The Threepenny Opera*." [Early in his acting career, in 1978, Julia was nominated

for a Tony Award for his portrayal of Macheath in a Lincoln Center production of *The Threepenny Opera.*]

I guess for the first *El Mariachi* I wanted to make him an Anglo because I thought that film was just going to be a Mexican video movie for
the Spanish-language video market. So I thought, why have another
Mexican bad guy? Let's make him an Anglo bad guy, that would be more
fun. Make it as if he had just showed up at the border, did a drug run
to Mexico, escaping the law, then took over and became a drug bandit
leader. Nobody really wants him there, but he's the boss because he's
smart and ruthless.

So I didn't want to repeat that in the second one. In *Desperado*, I
wanted the mariachi character to kill somebody that would make him
not want to kill anymore. I needed to end that somehow.

CRB: I notice that you do a lot of interesting things with ethnicity. I
mean even here in *Spy Kids*, as you've said, this family doesn't have to
be Latino for the story to work. And Antonio Banderas doesn't have to
be the actor who plays the kids' father, but you're doing it and that says
something to the audience. Earlier in your career, for example in *Roadracers*, there's the character of Donna [Salma Hayek, in her first major
U.S. feature film role] and when her boyfriend, Dude [David Arquette],
takes her home, we see her Anglo parents. And Donna and her parents don't seem to go together. But you didn't explain it, that's just her
family.

RR: Yeah, it's like mixing up the pot. And that family looks more like
what we look like in this country—we're all mixed up ethnically.

CRB: And the same thing with your segment, "The Misbehavers,"
in *Four Rooms*. You have a Latino father, an Asian mother, and Asian-
Latino kids.

RR: Yeah, but in *Four Rooms* what happened was I knew Antonio
was going to play the dad. Then I wanted to find two Latino kids, but
also wanted to find the best child actors for the parts. So I thought I'll
find the best kid actors, then I'll cast an actress for the mother who looks
like their mother. So I thought about Isabella Rossellini, I thought about
Irène Jacob, who was in *The Double Life of Veronique*. But the little
girl who was best was a little Asian girl, so I picked an Asian actress
[Tamlyn Tomita] to play the Asian mom. I really wanted to make it look
like a family.

So I did the same thing in *Spy Kids*. I knew Antonio was going to be
the dad, then I cast the two kids, and based on that I needed a redhead
mom. So I found Carla Gugino and dyed her hair red, and I had my mom.

CRB: And in this film, what ethnicity is she?

Rodríguez on the set with the "spy parents," Carla Gugino and Antonio Banderas. (Photo by Rico Torres, courtesy of Dimension Films)

RR: It doesn't really come out in this movie, but in the next movie she's going to be identified as either Polish or Hungarian. She's going to have spy parents who show up in the sequel, so there'll be a lot more about her family in that, but I'm still working on it.

CRB: So your strategy is to cast someone like Antonio, and you make an ethnic statement that way.

RR: Well, *Spy Kids* stemmed out of *Four Rooms*. I came up with this story when I was doing *Four Rooms*. I just loved the way this family looked, and when they were dressed in tuxedos and they looked like little James Bonds. And I had this idea—what if Antonio and his wife, who is Asian, what if she was Michelle Yeoh? And have them be two spies as parents, because I never really said in *Four Rooms* what the parents' job was. So then I thought, they could be spies, and they could get captured, and the kids have to save them. And that would be a great way for me to do a *Bedhead*-type action film.

And, also, going back to casting Antonio, I think directors, especially writer-directors, find someone who's a projection of themselves, because so much of themselves goes into the characters. So John Woo used Chow-Yun Fat, who doesn't look anything like him, so you think that's his projection of himself. For Martin Scorsese it was Robert DeNiro. So

I tell people that Antonio is a very, very good projection of me—he's humorous, he's dashing, everything that you wish you could be, you know? But I'm also very much the character of Floop [Alan Cumming] in *Spy Kids*. There's a lot of me in that character. He's always making something. But you find yourself in a lot of the characters, in the little boy [in *Spy Kids*] too. So you project yourself into everything.

CRB: What about *From Dusk Till Dawn* and the criticism that film got?

RR: What criticism did it get? I don't even remember.

CRB: Well, for one thing, all the Mexican women are vampires, and that's how Mexican women have been portrayed in the movies, as vamps, as women who will use and abuse men.

RR: That's how it was in [Quentin Tarantino's] script. And the way I looked at it, I tried to add more of the matriarch-type myth. So that the one who was running the whole show, the queen bee, was a woman. And I based Salma's character [Santanico Pandemonium] on a figure out of Aztec mythology, a goddess with a skull head and snakes. There was a vampire cult that believed that they had to kill to keep the sun shining. We found, you could say, vampires in Mexican history, this blood cult. And that's where I got the image of the snake woman. I added the snake dance because the image of that goddess was full of snakes and she was the queen of that cult. So I wanted to make like that bar was actually a temple where they would do this.

CRB: So that's the meaning of the last shot.

RR: That's the meaning of the last shot. That's how they kept the world going. And that over the years, they needed ways to attract victims, so the temple evolved into a biker bar. And they'd bring in the bikers and they'd kill them. And when I told it to Quentin, he thought, "That's such a cool idea that they decided to turn it into a bar as a sneaky way to attract customers and have plenty of victims."

CRB: So it was a way of victimizing the Anglo bikers. If you look at it that way, it's the revenge of the Latina on oppressive white males.

RR: Yeah, that was basically what it was. It's not really explained, but that's how I sort of backstoried it. And in the third sequel we showed the origin of Salma's character. It's called *The Hangman's Daughter;* my cousin and I wrote it. And it shows how she was born in that temple, but her father takes her away from it, but she returns and she meets her mother there, and her mother's mother. And she becomes Santanico and the keeper of the temple.

So I guess on face value, people can go, "Oh, look, it's the same thing, it's Latina women being stereotyped." I guess they could see it that way.

"You can't kill her." Santanico Pandemonium (Salma Hayek), the leader of the vampire cult in From Dusk Till Dawn *(1996), who disappears but doesn't die. (Photo courtesy of Luis Reyes Archives)*

I based it on the requirements of the script that Quentin had written, and I just sort of changed it a little bit to make it more based in Mexican history. And more about the women.

CRB: So does Santanico die in the film, do you think?

RR: No, she smiles and kind of disappears. You can't kill *her*. We always had another ending where all the vampires would get up and say, "That was a rough night, rougher than usual."

CRB: So let's clean up for tomorrow.

RR: Yeah. [*laughing*] So we used the actor Danny Trejo in all the sequels, he showed up at the bar. He was a constant. It was a way of saying, he's been there forever.

CRB: What about *The Faculty?*

RR: Well, that was a deal I made with Miramax. They asked me if I'd do *The Faculty.* And I said "No, I want to do *Spy Kids.* I want to do my own scripts." But they insisted, saying *Spy Kids* wasn't ready yet. But I said, "There's a time limit on *Spy Kids.* Someone could get that idea and run and make it right away." And they said, "There's more of a time limit on *The Faculty,* because these teen movies are going to be dead by next year. So we have this Kevin Williamson script, and you can shoot it and have it out by next November, and then you can shoot *Spy Kids.*"

So I made them a deal. When that company wants something bad, you can really put them over a barrel and get anything you want, anything your heart desires. So I thought, what can I ask for? I wanted to make my own stuff, but I didn't want to have to pitch a story to them each time. I didn't want to be at anyone's mercy. So the deal was, I would direct one film for them, and they would do *four* films for me, pay or play.

CRB: So *The Faculty* was the film for them?

RR: Yes. And the other four would be two family films, *Spy Kids* and *Bedhead,* and two others. One's a science fiction movie, and the other's a Stevie Ray Vaughan movie. And *Spy Kids II* isn't even in that deal. So I still conceivably have three more pictures to do after that. And pay or play means that even if I turn in the scripts and they don't like it, they have to pay me anyway. Everything, directing fee, editing fee, everything. That's a lot of money. But they want to do everything I do.

In fact, I wrote another script for Carlos Gallardo [the actor who starred in *El Mariachi*]. It's a *Mariachi*-type movie, it's supposed to be shot in that style. It's called *Curandero,* set in Mexico, an action movie where he's a folk healer. So I wrote it really fast for him, basing it on his father and my *huecero* [medicine man] grandfather. And I wrote it for him to direct and star in, and I'll produce it and maybe edit it. Really low-budget. And I wrote it in four days because I kept telling him I was writing it and never did, and he called and I told him it was ready and he could have it the following week. So I wrote it that weekend. So I went to Miramax and told 'em, "Guess what I did this weekend?" And I pitched them the story, and they wanted it. Right now Carlos is shooting it on Hi-8 just to get practice. So I have a good relationship with Miramax because I make huge movies for very little money for them.

CRB: So, getting back to *The Faculty,* it was still a movie about outsiders, the teens, and about different kinds of aliens, the space invaders and the teachers.

RR: That was in Kevin Williamson's script.

CRB: You didn't add things?

RR: It wasn't anything I was going to work on and try to change, or add like an ethnic spin to it. I mean it was not that kind of movie. It was a very commercial, get-it-out-there, *Scream*-type teen movie. So I didn't change it at all. When I work with another writer, usually I know, just having written stuff myself, you don't realize what's on the page until you've shot it. You really want to stay faithful to the script, and not screw around with it too much because there might be ideas there that you haven't really seen until you're editing the film. So I didn't mess around with that very much at all.

But even so, I liked it. I've always liked John Carpenter's *The Thing*, so I thought to myself, if this is the movie I do for them, it's not so bad. This will be my B-movie horror flick, and it won't take too long. And I wasn't finished with the script for *Spy Kids* yet, so it was worth doing.

And now that I'm set, it's much easier. Miramax is much more excited about *Spy Kids* than they ever were on *The Faculty*. This is a general audience movie, and that's new for me. The earlier films were for limited audiences and that's what I liked about them. I liked making under-the-radar-type movies that weren't expected to do very well, and if they did, it would be a nice big surprise. But other than that, they'd just be decent little films that still made money because they were made so cheaply.

I still get all sorts of offers because I'm a young director who's very cost-conscious. They bring me projects before they take it to the A-list directors because they know if they get one of those guys on, it'll be $150, $160 million budget and forget it—it's so hard to make any money off of them at that point. To do my own stuff, I turned down *Superman* before it went to Tim Burton, which was going to star Nicolas Cage, and then the plug got pulled because it got too expensive. *Wild Wild West* was brought to me, and *Planet of the Apes* that James Cameron is producing. *X-Men*. And I passed on all of them.

CRB: Why?

RR: Well, you're going to give these projects all your good ideas and you don't own any of it. You're only a director for hire. You're really only working for the studio, who will tell you what to do, and lead you around like a monkey on a chain. I'd rather have something I created myself. On *Spy Kids* I have final cut and I can do anything I want.

CRB: Was the struggle over final cut what had you drop out of *The Mask of Zorro*?

RR: *Zorro* was really difficult because there were two studios involved. It was the last movie Amblin was going to do before it became Dreamworks. And as Amblin, it had been tied in to TriStar. And TriStar had

253

already sunk a lot of money in previous incarnations in pay-or-play deals, so they were already $16 or $20 million in the hole and nothing had been done yet. So they couldn't take it to Dreamworks, which is where we tried to get it, so that it would be easier and not have to deal with two studios, constantly pulling you back and forth. So when it became time for everyone at that studio to get fired, I said, "I'm not going to wait for another regime to come in and wait, who knows, another eight months." So I just left and came back home.

CRB: Did you have any input on the script? One of the best things about that version of Zorro was that at last the hero was a Mexican, and not a Spaniard.

RR: Well, that was already in the script, and it's what I liked about it. I thought, "This is cool, a Mexican Zorro!" I wanted to take it even further that way, and make him a Mexican bandit running around, you know, like Joaquín Murrieta.

But one of the problems was that they had half a script. The writers, who were good, were pulled off to work on *El Dorado*. And the studio didn't want to spend any more money on the script of *Zorro*. So they said, "It doesn't matter, we'll fix it internally." So I said, "What does *that* mean?" Well, what it means is that you all sit around and figure out the rest of the story and the script. That didn't make any sense to me.

It was really funny. In a strange way it was kind of wonderful to hear all these people who make a lot of movies act like they're making their first movie. I thought, "God, it really does happen like that in Hollywood." So I would have had no control, which is why I really like doing my own projects. I don't need all those people. When there's too many people involved, it just turns into a big mess.

CRB: As a Latino filmmaker, what responsibility do you think you have? That is, as someone who's trying to operate—and survive—in a big, profit-driven, and very commercial industry?

RR: I remember hearing Edward James Olmos saying how he was disappointed because he'd made *Stand and Deliver* and no Latinos showed up to watch it. And I thought to myself, "I'm just not going to go down that road. I'm not going to make movies for people to 'appreciate.'" No one ever "appreciates" anything you do. You've got to just do something for yourself. I mean that's always where I've come from. For me it's I want to do this, this will be fun, and I'll try to make it enjoyable for a lot of people. And that's what I'll do.

As soon as you feel like you're a crusader on a mission, you'll get lost. You're doing it for the wrong reasons. You can't count on people supporting you necessarily. You can't drag people to the movies. It's just too difficult. You've got to be an entertainer first. Which is what I've always been, even when I was a cartoonist, it was always about the work and the entertainment value of whatever I was doing. I mean that's all it ever was.

I never wanted to change gears and become something else because I felt I had to be a crusader. I feel that I can accomplish more, and reach more people, by making more popular entertainment, but being conscientious about it. Not because I'm thinking, "Well, this will be nice for the Latin community." I just want to see myself and my family reflected in the work I do. I want my crazy uncles, the ones who would let me drive their trucks when I was a kid and didn't know how to drive, I want those characters in my movies. Because people have never seen that, you know?

CRB: So in your case, you'll be true to your experience, and if you're true to your experience, your ethnicity will come out.

RR: Yeah, it's going to come out naturally. Rather than forcing it. I think that one of the problems is that when Latin filmmakers get that chance to make a film, they try to do too much, and make up for all the movies that were never made before. And then it becomes too preachy. You can be much more subversive, you can be much more sly than that, and get everything you want in there. If you're just conscientious about it and try to trick people by getting them to watch something entertaining and show them something else at the same time. Slip it in the genre.

CRB: So do you go to see these films? Have you seen *Mi Familia*?

RR: I've never seen *Mi Familia*. I hear it's good. But I just wasn't interested in seeing it because it was such a specific type of family, it didn't relate to me or mine in particular. I don't feel like watching movies like those. They feel like work, like, "Oh, I have to watch it because I'm Latin." That's why I know a lot of that stuff won't be successful, because it feels like I *have* to watch that. You feel like you're on assignment to see them.

I liked *El Norte* a lot. I saw it in high school, and that's a good movie. That was great. But it's not like I really wanted to go see that one either, they made us watch it in class. It was one of the movies we were forced to see that I was actually thankful for.

CRB: One of the issues in Latino cinema today is that filmmakers are at another stage. Chicano cinema came out of a tradition thirty years ago of resistance, struggle, and politics. But now it's the children of that generation who are making films.

RR: It's a different time, a different generation. I mean when I got to L.A., I met the old-guard Chicano filmmakers. And I thought, "No wonder these guys can't get a movie made." They're so abrasive, sly, and sleazy-feeling in a way. I don't want to name names, but I didn't want to be with that group. I wanted to start a new group. And it's been great to have talent around like [Mexican-born cinematographer] Guillermo Navarro [who shot Rodríguez's *Desperado, Four Rooms, From Dusk Till Dawn,* and *Spy Kids*], [friend and Mexican-born writer-director] Guillermo del Toro, or [friend and Mexican-born director] Alfonso Cuaron. When I hear people in the filmmaking community talk about them like they're gods, that's great. That's the kind of image you want: these guys are great to work with, they're great people, and it's a different feel. The other ones act like everyone owes them something, and I don't even want to work with them.

CRB: Do you feel pressure on you, that you're trying to balance so many things—trying to be true to your roots, and trying to tell a good story, and trying to sell tickets?

RR: I've been real lucky because my whole story was one of just empowerment and telling people to just go make your own movies.

I got mad at my cousin once, when *El Mariachi* had just come out. He said he was in a film group and there was a lady teacher who said, "I don't understand what the big deal about *El Mariachi* is. What does this tell me about the Latina experience?" Like this one movie's supposed to be everything to everybody.

So I asked my cousin, "Well, what did you say? Did you get up and tell her, 'Hey, why don't you go make your own damn movie? You're a filmmaker, go make your own Latina experience film'"? And my cousin says, "No, I didn't say anything." So I tell him, "Way to go, fucker. Why didn't you stand up for me and say something?"

I mean she was teaching a class, so why don't she tell her students, "Hey, look what this one kid did all by himself with nothing. Why don't you guys go out and tell your own stories and get more movies out there?" Instead of blaming this one movie for not being everything to everybody. Why don't you find what's positive about it and spread that word? Instead of keeping yourselves in the bucket the whole time? I mean, that's ridiculous. You're a teacher and you're telling your students this? You could be giving them something positive to get out of it.

And I read another article somewhere, in a college school paper, about what a professor once said. I lost track of it, but it upset me for so long that I kept it around. I mean I felt liking writing the school and saying, "Why don't you fire this guy?"

This professor in San Jose says, the quote is actually, "So Rodríguez did the impossible . . . so what? Why didn't the other *Mexicanos* who were in the film get to follow him into the limelight? How come he was the only one?" It went on to make no recognition of the fact that a Latin had taken the bull by the horns and made his own Latin film by himself, made no attempt to inspire his students to even try to make their own films and tell their own stories. The whole thing was something to be dismissed because more people didn't get famous from the movie. I don't even think he realized I made that movie all by myself. I mean, no one does that! But instead of inspiring students, the old-guard Latinos can be so negative, just looking down on everything around them. He couldn't say one thing positive from that event to uplift his students. It's so selfish. I hate that mentality.

CRB: Tell me about your guerrilla filmmaking attitude that you used to make *El Mariachi* and runs throughout your book and the *10 Minute Film Schools*. You're constantly demystifying filmmaking.

RR: Yeah, I've always tried to tell people how it's done, that it's a lot of smoke and mirrors, and you can do a lot of stuff yourself. That frees me from worrying about making movies that are everything to everybody.

Because it's like, "Hey, you get seven grand, you go make your own movie with your own statement. And make it whatever you want. You don't have to come after me and asking, 'Why aren't you doing this and this?'" Well, why aren't *you* doing that? Get off your ass and make something. How come I have to make a movie for everybody? I'm making my own movies.

So I really don't feel that pressure. Or even try to feel that, "Well, what do I have to do for them now?" Because, I don't want to be the only one, but it's kind of like that. I am one of the only ones—still. And that's what upsets me. All the information I get out, and the guys who are using it are the non-Latinos who are running around making movies. They're the ones who are coming up to me to sign [their copy of] my book. I mean, I have so few Latinos who do that, they are mostly Anglos or different nationalities. Comparatively, I would expect a lot more Latinos to be encouraged. But maybe they're not interested in film or something.

CRB: I think a lot of people just aren't aware of how hard filmmaking is.

RR: Yeah, you have to have a real passion for it, because otherwise it's just too much work. It's so much work, I tell people, go make a film and then you'll see how much work it is and then you'll know if you really want to do it or not. Because it's a lot of work. Even *Bedhead*, I remember watching the credits for that and I was in tears, it was so much work for that little thing. *El Mariachi* was the same way. I was dead after cutting that. And that was just on 3/4" videotape, with comparatively few editing elements.

CRB: Going back to your subversion and demystifying of filmmaking, can you continue to be a guerrilla filmmaker when you're dealing with bigger and bigger budgets? Can you make a film like *Spy Kids* for $30-plus million and still adhere to the guerrilla aesthetic?

RR: Well, once I got into the business, I could see why no one believed me about doing it low budget. Because if you play by the rules, it's expensive. Now I'm a higher-profile filmmaker, and I have to hire union employees, and you want to hire better actors, and every piece of equipment is expensive, and the cost goes up. But I still find it hard to spend money, even now when I'm spending other people's money.

On this film, the studio is the one who wanted me to spend more money. On one scene, the studio heads were asking for a shot of the kids coming out of a pod, but I cut directly to the next scene. There was no need to show them getting out, it would have been just for the special effects and unnecessary, but they wanted that shot! "What's the matter?" they said. "Why are you so cheap?" And it was *their* money. So I'm even cheaper than the cost-cutting studio execs. So I can't make those real big-budget movies, because I can't justify wasting money. *Spy Kids* I can justify because it's a $100 million movie that I'm making for a fraction of that. But I made everybody work cheaper, I made the set designer work for about 1/10 of the budget he wanted, I told them try to be more creative, and it still looks great. The money just gets in the way. And now I see that I could have made it for even less.

CRB: But beyond budgets, how do you maintain your guerrilla attitude? Because when you enter the mainstream, you can change it or it can change you. How do you make studio movies and stay true to your *Mariachi,* guerrilla moviemaking aesthetic?

RR: This isn't really a studio movie. In a real studio movie, they'd make you spend all that money. They make you waste a lot of money.

And I've been going more and more in my films back to the *El Mariachi* style. I'm doing more and more of the work. On the next film, I'll probably be doing my own score. It's gotten to where I just don't want to hire anybody. I mean you're hiring people to sit around and do nothing. There's so much I can do myself, and then I keep more control. Even for *Spy Kids* I designed my own logo. They sent that job out to three companies, and they did crap. I did it on Photoshop and the studio liked it.

Rodríguez preparing a shot for Spy Kids *with Alan Cumming and Robert Patrick. (Photo by Rico Torres, courtesy of Dimension Films)*

I am my own special-effects supervisor on this film. There's four hundred effects [the finished film had five hundred] and I'm doing it all myself because on the last film I did we were paying a guy five thousand dollars a week and I ended up doing it all myself. I mean directors should learn how to do special effects because that's the way everything's going. There are so many effects, it's better to know that stuff. Special-effects supervisors didn't even exist until a few years ago, and now everybody treats them like kings and they don't even know what they're doing. They're just making up ways to do stuff, so why don't directors do that?

I want to get the studio to help me get the best talent there is. But if they can't find it, and I end up doing it in the end, then what do I need you guys for? So you realize you don't want to use a studio for a whole lot. It's distribution primarily. If you let it be a machine, and you rely on the machine, then you get in trouble. And there are a lot of directors who don't want to have to deal with this technical stuff, so they let the studios do it. They rely on the machine, then get controlled by the machine. You get the big budget that way, but you also lose a lot of your freedom.

I'm just making big independent films, that's how I look at it. They've gotten bigger and bigger, each movie is more expensive than the last, but the method has always been the same. I'm making my own movie and I get final cut, so I have final say. So there's nothing that goes in that's not OK'd by me. And you're much more willing to listen to people that way too. If the studio has comments, you say, "Sure." But you've got the final cut, so you're much more receptive and not as combative as you would be if you had to be fighting for everything because you knew they had final cut. You have the most control so you can be the most open.

CRB: When did you get final cut?

RR: With *Four Rooms*. Quentin had final cut with that, and so we all did. And once that precedent was set, then I've had it from then on. On *Dusk Till Dawn* I had final cut. On *Zorro* I was going to share final cut with Steven Spielberg. That was the protection for the studio, that it wasn't just me, but Steven too.

CRB: So will there be more *Ten Minute Film Schools*?

RR: Yeah, but I'm probably going to do them on the Internet now. I have a Web site and I'll try to give out information. And I think that'll help get more information out there. I might do classes and stuff on there.

CRB: What will you say?

RR: The same thing. You can go make a movie all by yourself if you want to! Now, with the equipment that's available, I could do the same movie, *El Mariachi,* better and cheaper. And still shoot it on film. Digitize it, then cut it on your iMac, and it would look fantastic!

[After we stopped the interview and I had turned off the tape recorder, Robert told me a story about an award he had won in 1995. It was such a good story, I wanted to use it for the end of the interview. I e-mailed him and asked him about it, and this was his reply:]

It was 1995. It was a TRAILBLAZER award at the ALMAs or the DESIs. Can't remember which. (There's a bunch of award shows.)

Here's what my diary said: "I am proud to present the 1995 Trailblazer award to Robert Rodríguez."

I went up, people got quiet when I began to talk. I said, "The Trailblazer award. This isn't the kind of award you can put up on the mantel and when your friends come over you say . . . 'see that? . . . I did that. I got an award for doing something.' "

No, this is one of those nagging kind of awards that when you see it, it makes you say, "That's what I HAVE to do over and over again."

Because you have to continue on, blazing that trail.

That's a lot of work. It's a big challenge. In fact it's too much work. I don't think I want to accept this award. It's too much of a challenge.

In fact I REFUSE to accept this award. . . . [*laughs*]
Unless everyone in this room tonight accepts the same challenge. [oohs]
Let's face it. We have to make a clear path for our children and our children's children to follow.
Here's a Trailblazer pop quiz, since everyone here tonight is going to be a trailblazer this year.
If the door into Hollywood is closed to Latinos, do you . . .
A) knock on the door and ask politely to be let inside? [everyone says no]
B) do you stage an angry protest outside and say let us in or else! [unsure response] . . .
or
C) do you kick the door open and storm in with everything you got! [cheers]
I can tell you from experience which method works best.
And if the powers that be build a wall behind that door so high that you can't climb over? Then you get a sledgehammer and break a hole in the wall, not a big hole . . . Just one big enough for you and a million of your Latino friends to follow you inside.
We are a strong people, a resourceful people, a talented and hard-working people. And we can do anything.
So, tonight . . . I'll accept this challenge.
And right back at you . . .
Thank you, God bless and good night.

Cool, huh?
Although it was a hit at the show, I felt a little later like it was a passing thing. You can't really sustain that enthusiasm when everyone else afterwards comes up and complains.
Oh, well . . . not for a lack of trying.

(Interview conducted on August 22, 2000.)

CONCLUSION

THE END OF STEREOTYPES?

So . . . where are we?

The overall picture is conflicted. As I mentioned in the Backstory section, a notable group of Latin American and American Latino filmmakers are actively producing American films. And on this front, who is to say that the most impressive anti-stereotyping and consciousness-raising Latino coup within American pop culture is not the fact that Robert Rodríguez's *Spy Kids* was the first Latino-directed film to be promoted through McDonald's Happy Meals? Furthermore, according to reports by the popular media at least, we are in the midst of a "Latino boom," with performers like Salma Hayek, Andy Garcia, Jennifer Lopez, Cameron Diaz, and Antonio Banderas among the most popular and well-paid screen stars. For his portrayal of a Mexican policeman in *Traffic* (2000)—a role in which most of his dialogue was in Spanish— Puerto Rico–born Benicio del Toro won a number of top critics awards as well as the Golden Globe and the Academy Award for Best Supporting Actor.[1]

Sadly, though, on the negative side of the ledger, recent studies commissioned by the Screen Actors Guild show that beyond these well-known superstars, the numbers of Latino actors participating in mainstream film and television are disproportionately low.[2] "Latinos," wrote SAG president Richard Masur in the initial report, "are nearly absent from movie and television screens across our country."[3]

So which is it? Are we at the dawn of a new era in which talented Latinos, taking their place in the movie business as actors, directors, writers, and producers, drive out old stereotypes? Or will the dreary pattern of negligible and negative representation of Latinos continue? A look at an earlier Latino boom may give us a better perspective and help us assess the current situation. That first Latino boom, in the 1920s and early 1930s, was in some ways an even more impressive one. It was most likely the effect of the "Latin lover craze" initiated by Rudolph Valentino in films like *The Four Horsemen of the Apocalypse* (1921) and *Blood and Sand* (1922). Valentino's screen persona—exotic and alluring, erotic and dangerous—created a demand for "Latin types" and an opportunity for an imposing roster of Latinos to find stardom in Hollywood films. In the late 1920s, for example, four Mexican-born actors were among Hollywood's biggest stars. Dolores Del Río had starring roles in a number of films, including the female lead, a Frenchwoman, in Fox's *What Price Glory?* (1926, d. Raoul Walsh), a Russian in an adaptation of Leo Tolstoy's *Resurrection* (1927), a Latina in the title role in *The Loves of Carmen* (1928), and again the lead and title role in an adaptation of Henry Wadsworth Longfellow's *Evangeline* (1929). Ramon Novarro played the title role in *Ben-Hur* (1926), one of silent film's certified blockbusters (costing a then-record $4 million), and subsequently starred in a number of films as a matinee idol. For instance, he was the romantic lead opposite Greta Garbo in *Mata Hari* (1931).

As I discussed in Chapter 4, both Gilbert Roland and Lupe Vélez rose to become noteworthy stars in the late 1920s. In the mid- to late 1920s, Roland played a series of romantic leads, beginning with his being cast as the costar in the Clara Bow vehicle *The Plastic Age* in 1925. For the rest of the silent era and into the early sound years, he was a popular leading man, starring alongside some of the foremost female stars, such as Mary Astor (*Rose of the Golden West* [1927]), Norma Talmadge (*Camille* [1927], The *Dove* [1927], *New York Nights* [1929]), and Clara Bow (*Call Her Savage* [1932]). Meanwhile, Lupe Vélez shared top billing with such established Anglo male stars as Douglas Fairbanks, Warner Baxter, Jimmy Durante, Walter Huston, and Lee Tracy.

And there were many other Latinos making their marks in the movies. Spaniard Antonio Moreno's screen acting career began in the early 1910s, and he worked his way up from small roles in some of D. W. Griffith's better-known films, such as *The Musketeers of Pig Alley* (1912) and *Judith of Bethulia* (1914), to playing romantic leads in many silent films thereafter. (He even codirected a film he starred in, *The Veiled Mystery* [1920].) In 1926 Moreno was the romantic lead opposite Greta Garbo in her second Hollywood film, *The Temptress*, and by 1930 this film veteran had acted in some 104 films.

Lupe Vélez in a publicity still. (Photo courtesy of Luis Reyes Archives)

Other, now lesser-known, Latino stars included Raquel Torres, who costarred in MGM's first fully synchronized sound feature, *White Shadows in the South Seas* (1928) and later in the Marx Brothers' *Duck Soup* (1933). The Mexican-born actress Armida starred with John Barrymore in *General Crack* in 1930, in the Dave Fleischer animated short *The Peanut Vendor* (1933), and in *Under the Pampas Moon* (1935) with Warner Baxter, as well as in many other films. Mexican Lupita Tovar costarred in numerous films between 1929 and the mid-1940s. Margo (María Marguerita Guadalupe Teresa Estela Bolado Castilla y O'Donnell) made her film debut in 1934 in Ben Hecht and Charles MacArthur's classic film *Crime without Passion* and was later seen as Maria in Frank Capra's *Lost Horizon* (1937). But for all this obvious talent, the boom was over by the mid-1930s, and as opportunities for Latino stars dwindled drastically, Hollywood cast them adrift.

By 1937, Ramon Novarro's career was finished (except for a brief resurgence in the late 1940s and early 1950s). Lupita Tovar's lasted a bit longer: she played minor characters and bit parts into the mid-1940s. Antonio Moreno stayed active, albeit in small roles, until the mid-1950s (for example, he played the Mexican *ranchero* in John Ford's *The Searchers* [1956]). Frustrated by the narrow range of stereotypical roles she was offered, Dolores Del Río returned to Mexico in the early 1940s (and became a superstar of Mexican cinema). As I pointed out in Chapter 4, Lupe Vélez was banished to B-movie limbo and eventually committed suicide. Like Moreno, Gilbert Roland managed to keep his career afloat, but, except for B-movies like *The Cisco Kid* (1949), he would never again play the romantic or heroic lead in a major American film. And adding insult to injury, Hollywood continued its stereotyping of Latinos unabated.

Gilbert Roland, early in his career, during the first "Latino boom," as the dashing, romantic leading man. (Photo courtesy of Luis Reyes Archives)

Gilbert Roland as the Cisco Kid, one of his few leading roles after the first Latino boom ended. (Photo courtesy of Luis Reyes Archives)

What happened to that first boom?

Obviously one major factor was the coming of sound. The silence of cinema allowed actors like Del Río, Vélez, Roland, Novarro, and Moreno to play characters of various nationalities as easily as they switched costumes. But sound created a new set of conventions for verisimilitude and necessitated that actors speak English clearly. For the most part, those with accents (except for a few, like Greta Garbo), were relegated to various ethnic parts or lost their film careers entirely.

But as the Latino boom ended, actors and directors from another denigrated and stereotyped immigrant group—the Irish—began their own movie boom. Why did the Irish succeed so impressively while Latinos failed so utterly? For one thing, Irish performers had two built-in advantages—they were fair-skinned and they spoke English. But no doubt the demographic reality of the United States at the time was another factor. After a half a century of heavy Irish immigration to the United States, they reached what appears to be a crucial population threshold—10 percent—in 1880. This critical population mass that the Irish held for nearly two generations before the coming of sound made it possible, I believe, for many Irish American actors to succeed in the Hollywood studio era while the Latino stars of the 1920s faded into the background.

COMPARATIVE IMMIGRATION HISTORY
AND THE 10 PERCENT THRESHOLD HYPOTHESIS

The history of the Irish in America and in the movies may provide a clue as to the viability of the current Latino boom. The studio-era "Irish boom" was, by any measure, extraordinary. Irish stars dominated the screen, and included such talents as James Cagney, Will Rogers, Buster Keaton, Spencer Tracy, Maureen O'Hara, Errol Flynn, Bing Crosby, Maureen O'Sullivan, Victor McLaglen, Pat O'Brien, Greer Garson, Margaret O'Brien, John Wayne, George Brent, George O'Brien, Gregory Peck, Gene Kelly, Walter Huston, Tyrone Power, Grace Kelly, and Mickey Rooney. To this list can be added a host of supporting players (Brian Donlevy, Sara Allgood, Barry Fitzgerald, Arthur Shields) as well as the considerable creative contributions of directors such as John Ford, John Huston, and Raoul Walsh (whose parents were Irish and Spanish).

The appearance of all this film talent can be seen as one outcome of a mass migration of Irish to the United States that began a century before sound came to the movies in 1927. Between 1821 and 1920 it is estimated that 4.35 million Irish immigrated here, and by 1880 there were more than 5 million Irish immigrants and Irish Americans residing in the United States, amounting to just over 10 percent of the total U.S. population.[4] Their percentage of the national population remained in double digits from then on. (Today, people of Irish ancestry make up roughly 16 percent of the U.S. population.[5]) Having achieved and sustained such a critical mass, the Irish dispersed geographically and socially, making their way into all walks of American life, including the world of entertainment and movies.

This large Irish American population sustained the Irish in the movies in several ways. First, once the Irish reached one-tenth of the U.S. population, they represented a significant demographic segment that wielded considerable purchasing power, no doubt making a perceptible difference at the box office. Moreover, they were a ready market for Irish stars, and one that obviously would have been sensitive to negative representation. Finally, the large number of Irish provided a sizable talent pool that was hard to ignore, no matter what the prejudices against them may have been in American society.

In terms of film content, the Irish in Hollywood affected the movies in two different but equally crucial ways. The first was that they created a space for Irish *self-representation:* the Irish experience told by Irish Americans from the Irish point of view. These overt statements of ethnic pride were exemplified by films such as Raoul Walsh's *Gentleman Jim* (1938), with Errol Flynn playing the heavyweight prizefighting champion Jim Corbett, and John Ford's *The Quiet Man* (1952) and *The Last Hurrah* (1958).

Though less ethnically obvious, a second effect of the Irish on Hollywood film content is what I would call simply *artistic expression*—the fact that the movies provided a mass-mediated arena for the display of waves of Irish talent. Popular Irish stars and directors gave the Irish a voice in the discourse of American cinematic storytelling. As I discussed in Chapter 6, John Ford became a master of the Western, and his films are now considered classics of the genre. Similarly, Gene Kelly was a superb song-and-dance man. From the perspective of sheer artistic expression, then, one of the monuments of Irish American filmmaking is *Singin' in the Rain* (1952), codirected by Gene Kelly and costarring Kelly and Donald O'Connor. Though not an explicit celebration of the Irish experience, clearly this enduring American movie classic could not have been made without the irrepressible energy and creativity of its Irish American stars.

One can imagine the effect these Irish actors and filmmakers had on audiences. Irish viewers could revel in the fact that some of their own were making an impact in the movies. For non-Irish audience members who were neutral in their feelings toward the Irish, the long line of Irish talent was just a fact of the movies. And for those who harbored anti-Irish prejudices, the pervasiveness of Irish stars and directors may well have forced some of them at least to reconsider their prejudicial views. Thus, in the discourse of Irishness in America, the many Irish stars were certainly important "voices" helping to ease and erase anti-Irish prejudice. Furthermore, the rise to box office prominence in the 1930s and 1940s of Spencer Tracy, Mickey Rooney, James Cagney, Tyrone Power, Errol Flynn, and John Wayne is surely one important indicator of the acceptance of the Irish into the American mainstream.[6]

The stereotyping of the Irish in Hollywood movies declined because

TABLE C.I

Latinos as a Percentage of Total U.S. Population

Year	Latino	Year	Latino
1930	1.1	1970	4.5
1940	1.2	1980	6.4
1950	1.5	1990	8.8
1960	2.0	2000	12.6

Source: "We . . . the American Hispanics," U.S. Department of Commerce, Economics and Statistics Administration, Bureau of the Census, 1993, 4. "Table 8: Race and Hispanic Origin of the Population by Nativity: 1850 to 1990," U.S. Census Bureau, Population Division, http://www.census.gov/population/www/documentation/twpsoo29/tabo8.html.

Note: Data for 1930 include only "Mexicans"; data for 1940 include persons of "Spanish mother tongue"; data for 1950 and 1960 include persons of "Spanish surname." Concerning the 1930 figure, even adding the population of Puerto Rico and immigrants from Latin America, the Latino percentage remains extremely low, around or just below 2 percent. The figure for 2000 is U.S. Census Bureau data reported in Charles W. Holmes, "Hispanics Outpacing Growth Estimates," *Austin American-Statesman*, March 8, 2001, A-1.

once they reached and maintained a certain fraction of the national population—the 10 percent threshold—they existed as a considerable consumer base and a substantial talent pool; they worked their way into the studio system and became key players in Hollywood.

In retrospect, it would have been extremely difficult for the Latin boom of the 1920s to be much more than a fad. After the Latin lover craze had run its ten-year course, the Latino population was too small to sustain the boom. As a glance at Table C.1 shows, the numbers of U.S. Latinos in 1930 were minuscule, far below the 10 percent threshold.

IMPLICATIONS

Today, Latinos are a statistically significant group, and if the Irish experience is any indication, it stands to reason that the Latino social and cultural infrastructure will support the current boom, making it more than a fad. So there is hope that this may indeed spell the lessening—or even the end—of the stereotyping of Latinos in American film and media.

And there are some who paint a rosier picture for Latinos behind the camera in Hollywood than is given by the depressing figures of the Screen Actors Guild report. "There is, in fact, a critical mass of Latinos forming in the industry," says producer Moctesuma Esparza, one of the first Chicano filmmakers to break in to the ranks of mainstream Hollywood producers. "The numbers are just coming to a point where people are beginning to feel like there is a community. We have the beginning of a real producing community—and that didn't exist five years ago at all."[7] And Emanuel Nuñez, a Cuban American talent agent at Creative Artists Agency, notes exactly the sort of change I traced for the Irish now occurring for Latinos. "Industries and societies evolve and change as the population evolves and changes," he says. "Hollywood is getting more Hispanic and multiracial."[8] Among the growing list of Latino producers and behind-the-camera players are Julio Caro (producer of Jennifer Lopez's *The Cell*), Elizabeth Avellan (producer of Robert Rodríguez's films), Cynthia Cidre (screenwriter of *The Mambo Kings*), screenwriter Ernie Contreras, and Alfonso H. Moreno (executive story editor on television's *The Practice*).

And as the numbers of Latino stars, writers, directors, and producers in Hollywood increase, from the Irish precedent we can see the importance and necessity of both Latino self-representation and artistic expression. Looking back on the case of the Irish gives us another perspective on the stardom of a performer like Cameron Diaz, who has never played a Latina. But Gene Kelly's dancing and singing in the rain was a positive development—I would say a triumphant one—in the history of the Irish in American cinema. Similarly, Diaz's blue eyes and incandescent smile may end up being just as pivotal in raising mainstream tolerance for Latinos as a politically contestational film like *Zoot Suit*. The point is, the Irish showed that both self-representation and artistic expression could contribute to American cinema, could add positively to the national discourse on ethnicity, and could ultimately help lessen discrimination.

The rise of Latinos in American film is wonderful, but it is not the end of stereotyping. If the 10 percent threshold marks a demographic reality and signals a turn toward more tolerant and complex movie images, two troubling facts remain. One is the downside of the 10 percent "hypothesis," the other an anomaly of the general trend. To begin with, history shows that minority groups below the 10 percent figure are extremely vulnerable to segregation, discrimination, media stereotyping, and worse. The horrific treatment of the Jews in Nazi Germany at a time when they amounted to less than one percent of the German population provides the cautionary historical example.[9]

Second, there are groups who have attained the 10 percent threshold, such as African Americans and women, who have still not achieved the kind of representational parity that I described for the Irish and that seems imminent for Latinos.[10] The failure of African Americans and women to overcome film stereotyping seems to indicate a kind of assimilation gradient. Acceptance in the mainstream occurs as the result of a complex combination of factors—demographic, social, cultural, political, discursive, historical. Apparently assimilation into the U.S. mainstream happens at the ethnic level (as the Irish example shows) before it happens at the racial one (illustrated by the failure of Black Americans to achieve the same kind of equality, acceptance, and opportunity *during the same historical period that the Irish were successfully attaining those very goals, though the population numbers of both groups were roughly the same*). And, given the fact that women are always half of the population, gender discrimination looks to be the most entrenched and most resistant to change. Said another way, Latinos may well be on the verge of assimilating and breaking stereotypes, but Black Latinos will still face a racial barrier and Latinas a sexist one.

As we near a dramatic downturn or even the end of Latino stereotyping, we need to be more, not less, vigilant. Film stereotypes are not dead, they just take on Other forms, targeting Other groups from society's margins. Knowing what we have gone through as an oppressed and stereotyped group, as we approach the center, there is only one question: How can we utilize our experience to lessen the stereotyping of Others who remain at society's fringes?

NOTES

INTRODUCTION

1. Allen L. Woll, *The Latin Image in American Film* (Los Angeles: UCLA Latin American Center Publications, 1977).
2. Arthur G. Pettit, *Images of the Mexican American in Fiction and Film* (College Station: Texas A&M University Press, 1980).
3. Gary D. Keller, ed., *Chicano Cinema: Research, Reviews, and Resources* (Binghamton, N.Y.: Bilingual Review/Press, 1985).
4. Clint C. Wilson and Felix Gutiérrez, *Minorities and Media: Diversity and the End of Mass Communication* (Beverly Hills, Calif.: Sage, 1985).
5. Chon Noriega, ed., *Chicanos and Film: Representation and Resistance* (Minneapolis: University of Minnesota Press, 1992).
6. Chon Noriega and Ana López, eds., *The Ethnic Eye: Latino Media Arts* (Minneapolis: University of Minnesota Press, 1996).
7. See, for example, the two anthologies *Latin Looks: Images of Latinas and Latinos in the U.S. Media,* ed. Clara E. Rodríguez (Boulder, Col.: Westview, 1997), and *The Birth of Whiteness: Race and the Emergence of U.S. Cinema,* ed. Daniel Bernardi (New Brunswick, N.J.: Rutgers University Press, 1996). See also the following books: Rosa Linda Fregoso, *The Bronze Screen: Chicana and Chicano Film Practices* (Minneapolis: University of Minnesota Press, 1993); Christine List, *Chicano Images: Refiguring Ethnicity in Mainstream Film* (New York: Garland, 1996); Gary D. Keller, *Hispanics and United States Film: An Overview and Handbook* (Tempe, Ariz.: Bilingual Review/Press, 1994); David R. Maciel, *El Bandolero, el Pocho, y la Raza: Imágenes cinematográficas del Chicano* (Mexico, D.F.: Cuadernos de Cuadernos, no. 5, Universidad Nacional Autónoma de México, 1994); Norma Iglesias and Rosa Linda Fregoso, eds., *Miradas de Mujer: A Bi-Lingual Anthology of Mexicana-Chicana-Latina Cinema* (Davis: Chicana/Latina Research Center at the University of California, Davis, and Tijuana: Baja California: Colegio de la Frontera Norte, 1998); Carlos E. Cortés, *The Children Are Watching: How the Media Teach about Diversity* (New

273

York: Teachers College Press, 2000); Angharad Valdivia, *A Latina in the Land of Hollywood and Other Essays on Media Culture* (Tucson: University of Arizona Press, 2000); and Chon Noriega, *Shot in America: Television, the State, and the Rise of Chicano Cinema* (Minneapolis: University of Minnesota Press, 2000).

8. See, for example, Carlos E. Cortés, "*The Greaser's Revenge* to *Boulevard Nights*: The Mass Media Curriculum on Chicanos," in *History, Culture, and Society: Chicano Studies in the 1980s* (Ypsilanti, Mich.: Bilingual Press/ Editorial Bilingue, 1983), 125–140; and "The History of Ethnic Images in Film: The Search for a Methodology," *Ethnic Images in Popular Genres and Media, MELUS, The Journal of the Society for the Study of the Multi-Ethnic Literature of the United States* 11:3 (Fall 1984): 63–77.

Rosa Linda Fregoso, "La Quinceañera of Chicana Counter Aesthetics," *Centro de Estudios Puertorriqueños Bulletin* 3:1 (Winter 1990–1991): 87–91; "The Mother Motif in *La Bamba* and *Boulevard Nights*," in *Building with Our Hands: New Directions in Chicana Scholarship*, ed. Beatriz M. Pesquera and Adela Ala Torre (Los Angeles: University of California Press, 1990), 130–145; and "*Sacando los trapos al sol* (Airing Dirty Laundry) in Lourdes Portillo's Melodocumentary, *The Devil Never Sleeps*," in *Redirecting the Gaze: Gender, Theory, and Cinema in the Third World*, ed. Diana Robin and Ira Jaffe (Albany: State University of New York Press, 1990), 307–329.

Lillian Jiménez, "From the Margin to the Center: Puerto Rican Cinema in New York," *Centro de Estudios Puertorriqueños Bulletin* 2:8 (Spring 1990): 58–69.

Christine List, "*El Norte*: Ideology and Immigration," *Jump Cut* 34 (March 1989): 27–31.

Ana M. López, "Are All Latins from Manhattan?: Hollywood, Ethnography, and Cultural Colonialism," in *Unspeakable Images: Ethnicity and the American Cinema*, ed. Lester D. Friedman (Urbana: University of Illinois Press, 1991), 404–424.

David R. Maciel, "Braceros, Mojados, and Alambristas: Mexican Immigration to the United States in Contemporary Cinema," *Hispanic Journal of Behavioral Sciences* 8:4 (1986): 369–385.

Kathleen Newman, "Steadfast Love and Subversive Acts: The Politics of *La Ofrenda*: The Days of the Dead," *Spectator* 13:1 (Fall 1992): 98–109; "Nation and Virgin as Great Performances in El Teatro Campesino's *La Pastorela: A Shepherd's Tale*," *Jump Cut* 38 (June 1993): 87–91.

Chon A. Noriega, "Chicano Cinema and the Horizon of Expectations: A Discursive Analysis of Recent Film Reviews in the Mainstream, Alternative, and Hispanic Press," *Aztlan* 19:2 (Fall 1988–1990): 1–32; "Citizen Chicano: The Trials and Titillations of Ethnicity in the American Cinema, 1935–1962," *Social Research: An International Quarterly of the Social Sciences* 58:2 (Summer 1991): 413–438; "El Hilo Latino: Representation, Identity, and National Culture," *Jump Cut* 38 (June 1993): 45–50; "The Numbers Game," *Jump Cut* 39 (June 1994): 107–111; "'Waas Sappening?': Narrative Structure and Iconography in *Born in East L.A.*," *Studies in Latin American Popular Culture* 14

(1995): 107–128; "Talking Heads, Body Politic: The Plural Self of Chicano Experimental Video," in *Resolutions: Contemporary Video Practices,* ed. Michael Renov and Erika Suderburg (Minneapolis: University of Minnesota Press, 1995), 207–228; "The Aztlan Film Institute's Top 100 List," *Aztlan* 23:2 (Fall 1998): 1–9.
Federico A. Subervi-Vélez et al., "Mass Communication and Hispanics," in *Handbook of Hispanic Cultures in the United States: Sociology,* ed. Félix Padilla (Houston: Arte Público Press, 1994), 334–350.
    9. Noriega, ed., *Chicanos and Film,* xxiv.
   10. Richard Dyer, *White* (New York: Routledge, 1997).

1. CATEGORIZING THE OTHER: STEREOTYPES AND STEREOTYPING

    1. Ashiq Ali Shah, *The Role of Impression Formation, Social Cognition, and Priming in the Development of Stereotypes* (Frankfurt: Peter Lang, 1987), 112.
    2. Walter Lippmann, *Public Opinion* (New York: Macmillan, 1922; rpt. Toronto: Free Press, 1965), 88.
    3. One of the unresolved debates about stereotyping has to do with whether stereotypes can be positive or negative, or are always negative. See, for example, Jacques-Philippe Leyens, Vincent Yzerbyt, and Georges Schadron, *Stereotypes and Social Cognition* (Thousand Oaks, Calif.: Sage, 1994), who hold that "Stereotypes can be positive" (12). In this they agree with Gordon W. Allport, in *The Nature of Prejudice* (Cambridge, Mass.: Addison-Wesley, 1954), who believed that "stereotypes are by no means always negative. They may exist together with a favorable attitude" (191). Ali Shah concisely summarizes three main views of researchers toward stereotyping as: (1) those who hold that stereotypes are "bad"; (2) those who hold that they are "not bad" but simply overgeneralizing; and (3) those who hold to the cognitive approach. See Ali Shah, *Role of Impression Formation,* 113.
    For my purposes, I will posit that stereotypes in the sense of cognitive categories are neither positive nor negative; however, stereotypes in my general definition, as prejudicial judgments, are always negative inasmuch as they generalize about a group in order to marginalize members of that group. Later, in Chapter 3, I discuss a type of "positive" stereotyping of Latinos, in the case of the Latin lover and the dark lady, which may appear to celebrate rather than debase the Latino Other but which for me is ultimately a negative, marginalizing, and divisive practice.
    4. Arthur G. Miller, "Historical and Contemporary Perspectives on Stereotyping," in *In the Eye of the Beholder: Contemporary Issues in Stereotyping,* ed. Arthur G. Miller (New York: Praeger, 1982), 28.
    5. W. G. Sumner, *Folkway* (New York: Ginn, 1906), quoted in Walter G. Stephan and David Rosenfield, "Racial and Ethnic Stereotypes," in Miller, *Eye of the Beholder,* 104–105. This definition of "ethnocentrism" is nearly identi-

cal to the meaning of prejudice cited by Clint C. Wilson and Félix Gutiérrez in *Minorities and Media: Diversity and the End of Mass Communication* (Beverly Hills, Calif.: Sage, 1985), 67–68. I use a different meaning for both terms.

6. Lippmann, *Public Opinion*, ch. 1: "The World Outside and Pictures in Our Heads."

7. See P. F. Secord, "Stereotyping and Favorableness in the Perception of Negro Faces," *Journal of Abnormal and Social Psychology* 59 (1959): 309–315, where this notion of categorical response is elaborated. "Membership in a category," writes Secord, "is sufficient to evoke the judgment that the stimulus person possesses all the attributes belonging to that category."

8. Homi K. Bhabha, "The Other Question," *Screen* 24:6 (1983): 18.

9. Richard Dyer, *White* (New York: Routledge, 1997), 16.

10. Fishman, cited in Miller, *Eye of the Beholder*, 19.

11. Several researchers have commented on this. See, for example, Wilson and Gutiérrez, *Minorities and Media*, and Ellen Seiter, "Stereotypes and the Media: A Re-evaluation," *Journal of Communication* 36:2 (1986): 14–26. Also "Different Children, Different Dreams: Advertising and Minority Families" (paper presented at the Minority Images in Advertising Symposium, DePaul University, Chicago, Illinois, April 10, 1989).

12. Several researchers have commented on the overgeneralized aspect of stereotyping, among them: Allport, *Nature of Prejudice*; E. S. Bogardus, "Stereotypes versus Sociotypes," *Sociology and Social Research* 34 (1951): 286–291; G. M. Gilbert, "Stereotypes Persistence and Change among College Students," *Journal of Abnormal and Sociology* 46 (1951): 245–254; D. T. Campbell, "Stereotypes and the Perception of Group Differences," *American Psychologist* 22 (1967): 817–829. P. R. Grant and J. G. Holmes note the assumption of out-group homogeneity in their "The Integration of Implicity Personality Theory Schemas and Stereotype Images," *Social Psychology Quarterly* 44 (1981): 107–115.

13. Here I am building on the view of researchers who have commented on the factual incorrectness of stereotypes. For example, Lippmann, *Public Opinion*; O. Klingberg, "The Scientific Study of National Stereotypes," *International Social Science Bulletin* 3 (1951): 505–515; E. T. Prothro and L. H. Melikian, "Studies in Stereotypes: III. Arab Students in the Near East," *Journal of Social Psychology* 40 (1954): 628–641. Finally, there is D. Katz and K. W. Braly's important 1933 article, "Racial Prejudice and Racial Stereotypes," *Journal of Abnormal and Social Psychology* 30 (1933): 175–193, which is the first empirical study of stereotypes. In it they say what I am claiming in this section, namely that "a stereotype is a fixed impression which conforms very little to the facts it tends to represent, and results from our defining first and observing second" (181).

14. See, for example. R. D. Ashmore and F. K. Del Boca, "Conceptual Approaches to Stereotypes and Stereotyping," in *Cognitive Processes in Stereotyping and Intergroup Behavior*, ed. D. L. Hamilton (Hillsdale, N.J.: Lawrence Erlbaum Associates), 1–35. They define stereotypes as "a set of beliefs about the personal attributes of a group of people" (16). See also A. Locksley, C. Hepburn,

and V. Ortiz, "Social Stereotypes and Judgments of Individuals: An Instance of the Base Rate Fallacy," *Journal of Experimental Social Psychology* 18 (1982): 23–42; J. Crocker, "Judgment of Covariation by Social Perceiver," *Psychological Bulletin* 90 (1981): 272–292; M. Snyder, "On the Self-Perpetuating Nature of Social Stereotypes," in Hamilton, *Cognitive Processes,* 183–212; and M. Rothbart, "Memory Processes and Social Beliefs," in Hamilton, *Cognitive Processes,* 145–181.

15. Allport, *Nature of Prejudice,* 13–14.

16. Ibid., 190.

17. See S. Asher and V. Allen, "Racial Preference and Social Comparison Processes," *Journal of Social Issues* 25 (1969): 157–166; D. J. Rox and V. B. Jordan, "Racial Preferences and Identification of Black, American, Chinese, and White Children," *Genetic Psychology Monographs* 88 (1973): 229–286; H. Greenwald and D. Oppenheim, "Reported Magnitude of Self-Misidentification among Negro Children—Artifact?" *Journal of Personality and Social Psychology* 8 (1969): 49–52; A. J. Gregor and D. A. McPherson, "Racial Attitudes among White and Negro Children in a Deep-South Standard Metropolitan Area," *Journal of Personality and Social Psychology* 68 (1966): 95–106; J. Hraba and J. Grant, "Black Is Beautiful: A Re-examination of Racial Preference and Identification," *Journal of Personality and Social Psychology* 16 (1970): 398–402.

18. Walter G. Stephan and David Rosenfield, "Racial and Ethnic Stereotypes," in Miller, ed., *Eye of the Beholder,* 110.

19. Arthur G. Miller, "Stereotyping: Further Perspectives and Conclusions," in Miller, ed., *Eye of the Beholder,* 478–479. The term "sanctions for evil" is from N. Sanford and C. Comstock, eds., *Sanctions for Evil* (San Francisco: Jossey-Bass, 1971); see also Miller, "Historical and Contemporary Perspectives," 27.

20. See Allport, *Nature of Prejudice,* 57–63, for his discussion of the violent rejection of out-groups.

21. There is a substantial body of literature that considers the long-standing anti-Semitic attitudes in Germany as leading to the Holocaust. See, for example, Bruno Bettelheim, "Individual and Mass Behavior in Extreme Situations," *Journal of Abnormal and Social Psychology* 38 (1943): 417–452; Norman Cohn, *Warrant for Genocide: The Myth of the Jewish World-Conspiracy and the Protocols of the Elders of Zion* (London: Eyre and Spottiswodde, 1967); Lucy S. Dawidowicz, *The War against the Jews: 1933–1945* (New York: Holt, Rinehart, and Winston, 1975).

22. Daniel Jonah Goldhagen, *Hitler's Willing Executioners: Ordinary Germans and the Holocaust* (New York: Knopf, 1996), 9.

23. Bhabha, "Other Question," 35.

24. Richard Dyer, "Stereotyping," in *Gays and Film,* ed. Richard Dyer, rev. ed. (New York: New York Zoetrope, 1984), 30.

25. Here again, Lippmann understood this facet of stereotyping very clearly. Stereotypes, he said, are "defenses of our position in society" (*Public Opinion,* 95).

26. Richard Dyer, *The Matter of Images: Essays on Representation* (New York: Routledge, 1993), 16.

27. Dyer, *White,* 35.

28. Michael R. Ornelas, Preface to *Beyond 1848: Readings in the Modern Chicano Historical Experience,* ed. Michael R. Ornelas (Dubuque, Iowa: Kendall/Hunt, 1993), vii.

29. Miller, "Historical and Contemporary Perspectives," 31.

30. Ibid., 27.

31. Lippmann, *Public Opinion,* 81.

32. Goldhagen, *Hitler's Willing Executioners,* 46.

33. Robin Wood, "An Introduction to the American Horror Film," in *Movies and Methods,* vol. 2, ed. Bill Nichols (Berkeley: University of California Press, 1985), 197.

34. The tripartite sociological analysis is based on Anya Peterson Royce, *Ethnic Identity: Strategies of Diversity* (Bloomington: Indiana University Press, 1982), 163–168.

35. Penelope J. Oakes, S. Alexander Haslam, and John C. Turner, *Stereotyping and Social Reality* (Cambridge, Mass.: Blackwell, 1994), 192.

36. Royce, *Ethnic Identity,* 166.

37. See Allport's discussion of discrimination and violence, especially of the conditions for physical attack on minorities (*Nature of Prejudice,* 51–65). For a discussion of violence perpetrated against Mexicans and Mexican Americans in the Southwest, see Rodolfo Acuña, *Occupied America: A History of Chicanos* (New York: Harper and Row, 1988), 118–121.

38. Wood, "Introduction to the American Horror Film."

39. Paraphrased from Oakes, Haslam, and Turner, *Stereotyping,* 85.

40. Lippmann, *Public Opinion,* 65.

41. Tzvetan Todorov, *Mikhail Bakhtin: The Dialogical Principle,* trans. Wlad Godzich (Minneapolis: University of Minnesota Press, 1984), 95, 96.

42. Sander L. Gilman, *Inscribing the Other* (Lincoln: University of Nebraska Press, 1991), 11.

43. Summarized from Sander L. Gilman, *Difference and Pathology: Stereotypes of Sexuality, Race, and Madness* (Ithaca: Cornell University Press, 1985), 16–21, and *Inscribing the Other,* 11–16.

44. Gilman, *Difference and Pathology,* 26–27.

45. Wood, "Introduction to the American Horror Film," 199.

46. Of course, the leap from individual development to social tendencies, from the analysis of the individual psyche to a cultural signifying practice, is not inconsiderable, and is one of the problematics in the application of psychological and psychoanalytical theory to texts. See Christine Gledhill's reservations about this in "Recent Developments in Feminist Criticism," in *Film Theory and Criticism: Introductory Readings,* 3rd ed., ed. Gerald Mast and Marshall Cohen (New York: Oxford University Press, 1985), 817–845.

47. Gilman, *Difference and Pathology,* 27.

48. Wood, "Introduction to the American Horror Film," 202–203.

49. For a summary of Klein's ideas and object-relations theory, see Elizabeth Wright, *Psychoanalytic Criticism: Theory in Practice* (New York: Methuen, 1984), 79–104. See also Melanie Klein, *Love, Guilt, and Reparation and Other Works, 1921–1945* (New York: Free Press, 1984), particularly "Love, Guilt, and Reparation," 306–343.

50. Laura Mulvey, "Visual Pleasure and Narrative Cinema" (1975), repr. in *Feminism and Film Theory*, ed. Constance Penley (New York: Routledge, 1988), 62.

51. Ibid., 64.

52. Ibid., 64.

53. See Chon A. Noriega, ed., *Chicanos and Film: Representation and Resistance* (Minneapolis: University of Minnesota Press, 1992), for complete texts of the following manifestos: "Ya Basta con Yankee Imperialist Documentaries!" by the Cine-Aztlán collective (275–283); "Towards the Development of a Raza Cinema," by Francisco X. Camplis (284–302); "Filming a Chicana Documentary," by Sylvia Morales (308–311); and "Notes on Chicano Cinema," by Jason C. Johansen (303–307).

54. Reprinted in *Chicanos and Film*, 3–17. Happily, Limón has continued to write about Latino film representation. See, for example, his insightful discussion of *High Noon, Giant*, and *Lone Star* in his *American Encounters: Greater Mexico, the United States, and the Erotics of Culture* (Boston: Beacon, 1998).

55. See their essays in Gary D. Keller, ed., *Chicano Cinema: Research, Reviews, and Resources* (Binghamton, N.Y.: Bilingual Review/Press, 1985).

56. Allen L. Woll, "Bandits and Lovers: Hispanic Images in American Film," in *The Kaleidoscopic Lens: How Hollywood Views Ethnic Groups*, ed. Randall M. Miller (Englewood, N.J.: Jerome S. Ozer, Publisher, 1980) and *The Latin Image in American Film* (Los Angeles: UCLA Latin American Center Publications, 1980). Allen L. Woll and Randall M. Miller, *Ethnic and Racial Images in American Film and Television: Historical Essays and Bibliography* (New York: Garland, 1987). Arthur G. Pettit, *Images of the Mexican American in Fiction and Film* (College Station: Texas A&M University Press, 1980).

57. Carlos E. Cortés, "The History of Ethnic Images in Film: The Search for a Methodology," *Ethnic Images in Popular Genres and Media, MELUS, The Journal of the Society for the Study of the Multi-Ethnic Literature of the United States* 11:3 (Fall 1984): 63–77.

58. Carlos E. Cortés, "'Who Is María? What Is Juan?' Dilemmas of Analyzing the Chicano Images in U.S. Feature Films," in Noriega, ed., *Chicanos and Film*, 74–93.

59. Carlos E. Cortés, *The Children Are Watching: How the Media Teach about Diversity* (New York: Teachers College Press, 2000).

60. Gary D. Keller, ed., *Chicano Cinema: Research, Reviews, and Resources* (Binghamton, N.Y.: Bilingual Review/Press, 1985).

61. See note 8 of the introduction for a list of these critics' articles. In addition, some of my own: Charles Ramírez Berg, "Images and Counterimages of the Hispanic in Hollywood," *Tonantzin* 6:1 (November 1988): 12–13; Charles

Ramírez Berg, "Stereotyping in Films in General and of the Hispanic in Particular," *Howard Journal of Communications* (Summer 1990): 286–230.

62. Chon A. Noriega, ed., *Chicanos and Film: Representation and Resistance* (Minneapolis: University of Minnesota Press, 1992).

63. Gary D. Keller, *Hispanics and United States Film: An Overview and Handbook* (Tempe, Ariz.: Bilingual Review/Press, 1994).

64. Berg, "Images and Counterimages of the Hispanic in Hollywood."

65. Christine List, *Chicano Images: Refiguring Ethnicity in Mainstream Film* (New York: Garland, 1996), 36.

66. Chon Noriega, *Shot in America: Television, the State, and the Rise of Chicano Cinema* (Minneapolis: University of Minnesota Press, 2000).

67. Noriega, *Shot in America*, 28.

68. Armando Rendon and Domingo Nick Reyes, *Chicanos and the Mass Media*, prepared statement with exhibits, in U.S. Congress, Senate Select Committee on Equal Educational Opportunity, *Hearings on Equal Educational Opportunity*, part 2: Equality of Educational Opportunity: An Introduction—Continued, hearings on July 30, 1970: "Effect of Television on Equal Opportunity" (Washington, D.C.: U.S. Government Printing Office, 1970), 928AH–928AR, 928AO, quoted in Noriega, *Shot in America*, 28.

69. Quoted in Noriega, *Shot in America*, 31.

70. Noriega, *Shot in America*, 31.

2. STEREOTYPES IN FILM

1. Roland Barthes, "Myth Today" (1956), repr. in *A Barthes Reader*, ed. Susan Sontag (New York: Hill and Wang, 1982), 95.

2. In "Ethnic Stereotypes," *Psychological Bulletin* 76 (1971): 15–33, J. C. Brigham referred to the trait-attribution aspect of stereotyping I am referring to here. Brigham defined an ethnic stereotype in this way: "An ethnic stereotype is a generalization made about an ethnic group, concerning a trait attribution, which is considered to be unjustified by an observer" (31).

3. Donald Bogle, *Toms, Coons, Mulattoes, Mammies, and Bucks: An Interpretive History of Blacks in American Films* (New York: Continuum, 1989).

4. The casting of feature films is one of the most important and least-recognized components of the stereotyping process in the movies. Often the casting-call sheets themselves describe the characters in stereotypical terms. As an example: while finishing this book I was introduced to a young actor who shared her frustration at this practice and then showed me a typical character breakdown for a film, *Stewart*, she was trying out for. A quick glance at the character descriptions shows that the casting office is a key player in film stereotyping. Among the characters being cast for *Stewart* were Carol, a next-door neighbor who was "white trash loud, obnoxious, funny"; Becky, a "blue-eyed, blonde all American beauty"; and Brad, "All-American jock, super handsome" (*Stewart* character breakdown sheet, Demolition Film Corp., Austin, dated February 4, 2000).

See also *Missing in Action: Latinos In and Out of Hollywood*, a report commissioned by the Screen Actors Guild and conducted by the Tomás Rivera Policy Institute (Los Angeles: Screen Actors Guild, 1999) for some pointed remarks by working Latino actors about the realities of the tryout and casting process. "The call," said one SAG actor, "was for poor white trash or Latino" (n.p.). "They said I had freckles and white skin," another Latina actor commented. "They said, 'What kind of Latin girl is going to have freckles, white skin, thin lips and blond hair?'" (n.p.). "I believe there are ignorant casting directors," another Latino SAG member remarked. "They think that Latino is Puerto Rican. We have to educate them. That is part of the reason we aren't getting anywhere" (n.p.).

Actor Vin Diesel has written, directed, and starred in a fascinating twenty-minute film, *Multi-Facial* (1994), about the vicissitudes of an actor trying out for various ethnic parts. It is available on a DVD compilation of short films, "Short 5—Diversity," DVDMAGS, Inc., a division of Quick Band Networks, distributed by Warner Home Video.

5. David Bordwell, "Space in the Classical Film," in David Bordwell, Kristin Thompson, and Janet Staiger, *The Classical Hollywood Cinema: Film Style and Mode of Production to 1960* (New York: Columbia University Press, 1985), 51.

6. Tattoos in Hollywood films have historically been indicators of foreign or class Others, generally villains, often seen, for example, on natives in adventure films or on the arms of biker, drug addict, prisoner, or poor white trash stereotypes. Though tattoos have become more socially acceptable in the last several years (probably more so *after* the release of *Falling Down* in 1993), I'd maintain that they possess different signification depending on the shade of skin on which they appear.

For poor or working-class white characters, the tattoo in films is still an indicator of Otherness, and when combined with genre, acting and costuming conventions are a routine indicator of a character's pathological villainy in prison and urban crime films. For characters of color who live in the 'hood or the barrio, as in *Falling Down*, the tattoo is as a sign of gang membership—yet another way the movies mark them as threatening Others. In contrast, for white characters within the social mainstream, tattoos are an expression of wealth, privilege, and individuality—body art.

7. See Richard Dyer, *White* (London: Routledge, 1997), esp. Chapter 3 on the photographical norm of whiteness in photography and the movies.

8. Lawrence Kasdan, *Raiders of the Lost Ark: The Illustrated Screenplay* (New York: Ballantine, 1981), 1–18.

9. Michael E. Kerr, "Chronic Anxiety and Defining a Self," *Atlantic Monthly*, September 1988, 35.

10. Murray Bowen, *Family Therapy in Clinical Practice* (New York: Jason Aronson, 1978), 400.

11. Ibid., 434.

12. Ibid., 443.

13. Ibid., 485.

14. Ibid., 445.

3. A CRASH COURSE ON HOLLYWOOD'S LATINO IMAGERY

1. Gary D. Keller, in *Hispanics and United States Film: An Overview and Handbook* (Tempe, Ariz.: Bilingual Review/Press, 1994), ch. 3, "The First Decades: Types of Characters," does a historical survey of films up to the early 1930s and comes up with a longer and slightly different list of Latino types: cantina girls; the faithful, moral, or self-sacrificing señorita; the vamp or temptress; greasers; the bandit; the bad Mexican; the gay caballero; the good or faithful Mexican; the good bad man; the Hispanic avenger; and the Latin lover. My six categories could be said to be a condensation of Keller's eleven types down to three male-female stereotype couples. In any case, as I said in Chapter 1, we both seem to be listing the same general characteristics that were—and too often still are—attributed to Latinos in American film.

2. For a discussion of the commutation test in analyzing film acting, see John O. Thompson, "Screen Acting and the Commutation Test," *Screen* 26.5 (1978): 78–90. My adaptation of the test is done for the sake of helping to determine whether the film image in question is a stereotype.

3. The marginalizing of the false female romantic interest, what might be called the "Other"-izing of her, is a standard Hollywood plot device and is certainly not restricted to Latina characters. She must be clearly devalued, and one way this is typically done is by placing her outside the mainstream norm, going from being "the other woman" to being "the Other woman." A good example of this is Jerry Maguire's fiancée, Avery (Kelly Preston), in *Jerry Maguire* (1996). She is given several characteristics that make her ultimately unsuitable for Jerry (Tom Cruise) and show her in an unfavorable light, especially in comparison with Dorothy (Renée Zellweger), Jerry's true love. First, she is unsympathetically tough, cold, and hard. Second, she is too uninhibited during lovemaking. And third, she tells Jerry in passing that she flirted with lesbianism in college. The cumulative effect of these traits is that they plainly mark her as "the Other woman," surely out of the running for Jerry, our hero.

4. SUBVERSIVE ACTS: LATINO ACTOR CASE STUDIES

1. Among them, Molly Haskell in *From Reverence to Rape: The Treatment of Women in the Movies* (New York: Holt, Rinehart, and Winston, 1974); Donald Bogle in *Toms, Coons, Mulattoes, Mammies, and Bucks: An Interpretive History of Blacks in American Films* (New York: Continuum, 1989); and Gwendolyn Audrey Foster in *Captive Bodies: Postcolonial Subjectivity in Cinema* (Albany, N.Y.: State University of New York Press, 1999). Though Richard Dyer's *Stars* (London: British Film Institute, 1979) is primarily a discursive study of stardom, its chapter on Paul Robeson is perhaps the most successful analysis of the ability of film stars to resist stereotyping.

2. Angharad N. Valdivia, *A Latina in the Land of Hollywood and Other Essays on Media Culture* (Tucson: University of Arizona Press, 2000), 93. See

also *Missing in Action: Latinos In and Out of Hollywood,* a report commissioned by the Screen Actors Guild and conducted by the Tomás Rivera Policy Institute (Los Angeles: Screen Actors Guild, 1999). For a fascinating fictional study of a performer who is caught in the stereotypical machinations of media casting practices, I highly recommend Vin Diesel's twenty-minute short film *Multi-Facial* (1994), which he wrote, directed, and stars in. It may be found on the "Short 5—Diversity" DVD, DVDMAGS, Inc., a division of Quick Band Networks, distributed by Warner Home Video.

3. Peter Krämer and Alan Lovell, "Introduction," in *Screen Acting,* ed. Alan Lovell and Peter Krämer (London: Routledge, 1999), 5.

4. Ibid.

5. See, for example, Carole Zucker's two helpful anthologies, *Making Visible the Invisible: An Anthology of Original Essays on Film Acting* (Metuchen, N.J.: Scarecrow Press, 1990), and *Figures of Light: Actors and Directors Illuminate the Art of Film Acting* (New York: Plenum, 1995).

6. Dyer, *Stars,* 151.

7. Ibid.

8. James Naremore, *Acting in the Cinema* (Berkeley: University of California Press, 1988).

9. Richard Dyer, *White* (New York: Routledge, 1997), 12.

10. I am building my idea of counterstereotyping performative excess on Kristen Thompson's notion of cinematic excess: see Kristen Thompson, "The Concept of Cinematic Excess," repr. in *Film Theory and Criticism: Introductory Readings,* ed. Leo Braudy and Marshall Cohen (New York: Oxford University Press, 1999), 487–498. In it she mentions the peculiar acting style of Sergei Eisenstein's *Ivan the Terrible* (Part 1, 1943; Part 2, 1946) as one example of cinematic excess in the film (494), but does not elaborate further.

11. Luis Reyes and Peter Rubie, *Hispanics in Hollywood: An Encyclopedia of Film and Television* (New York: Garland, 1994), 510. See Gabriel Ramírez, *Lupe Vélez: La mexicana que escupía fuego* (Mexico City: Cineteca Nacional, 1986), ch. 2, "La niña Lupe," for an account of Vélez's start in Mexico City's burlesque and vaudeville show business, 25–39. Also see Alicia I. Rodríguez-Estrada, "Dolores Del Río and Lupe Vélez: Images on and off the Screen, 1925–1944," in *Writing the Range: Race, Class, and Culture in the Women's West,* ed. Elizabeth Jameson and Susan Armitage (Norman: University of Oklahoma Press, 1997), 475–492. See also Carmen Huaco-Nuzum, "(Re)constructing Chicana, Mestiza Representation: Frances Salomé, España's *Spitfire* (1991)," in *The Ethnic Eye: Latino Media Arts* (Minneapolis: University of Minnesota Press, 1996), 260–274. The essay is an analysis of a film by Chicana experimental filmmaker Frances Salom, España in which Vélez plays a central part. See also, of course, España's film. For a brief mention of Vélez, see Antonio Ríos-Bustamante, "Latinos and the Hollywood Film Industry, 1920–1950s," *Americas 2001* 1:4 (January 1988): 8–9. Also, there is Floyd Conner's *Lupe Vélez and Her Lovers* (New York: Barricade Books, 1993), 1–19. Finally, there is a useful listing of female screen performers of color: Maryann Oshana's *Women of Color: A Filmography*

of Minority and Third World Women (New York: Garland, 1985), which includes a film-by-film listing of all of Vélez's films with abbreviated cast and crew credits and a one-paragraph plot summary.

12. For example, Vélez commands only four sentences in Annette Kuhn and Susannah Radstone's *Women in Film: An International Film Guide* (New York: Fawcett, 1991), 235, 237. The only scholarly book-length study of Vélez is Gabriel Ramírez's in Spanish. In English there is Floyd Conner's more sensationalistic work.

13. Ana M. López, "Are All Latins from Manhattan?: Hollywood, Ethnography, and Cultural Colonialism," in *Unspeakable Images: Ethnicity and the American Cinema*, ed. Lester D. Friedman (Urbana: University of Illinois Press, 1991), 412.

14. Sharon Smith, "The Image of Women in Film: Some Suggestions for Future Research," in *Feminist Film Theory: A Reader*, ed. Sue Thornham (New York: New York University Press, 1999), 16.

15. I quote the passage at length to make the point that Latinos continue to provide the dominant society with material for laughs, even decades after their death. The scene in question is between Roz and Frasier:

ROZ: Ever heard of Lupe Vélez?

FRASIER: Who?

ROZ: Lupe Vélez. The movie star in the thirties. The Mexican Spitfire. Her career hit the skids so she decided to take one final stab at immortality. She figured if she couldn't be remembered for her movies, she'd be remembered for the way she died. And all Lupe wanted was to be remembered. So she plans this lavish suicide. Flowers, candles, silk sheets, white satin gown, full hair and makeup, the works. She takes an overdose of pills, lays on the bed and imagines how beautiful she's going to look on the front page of tomorrow's newspaper. Unfortunately, the pills didn't sit well with the enchilada combo plate she sadly chose as her last meal. She stumbles toward the bathroom, trips and falls head first into the toilet. And that's how they found her.

FRASIER: Is there a reason you're telling me this?

ROZ: Yeah. Even though things may not happen like we planned, they can work out anyway.

FRASIER: Remind me again how it worked out for Lupe, last seen with her head in the toilet?

ROZ: All she wanted was to be remembered. *(beat)* Will you ever forget that story?

Quoted from "The Good Son," created and written by David Angell, Peter Casey, and David Lee, in David Angell, Peter Casey, and David Lee, *The Frasier Scripts* (New York: Newmarket, 1999), 24–25.

This reference is similar in tone and content to the chapter on Vélez's suicide (titled "Chop-Suicide") in Kenneth Anger's *Hollywood Babylon* (New York: Dell, 1975), 230–239. Conner writes that there are two accounts of Vélez's suicide. One was that she was found dead in her bed by her housekeeper, and the other was the more lurid version recounted by Anger and "Frasier" (228–230). Gabriel Ramírez gives the first, less sensational, account (*Lupe Vélez*, 15).

16. "Mexican Spitfire," *Leonard Maltin's Movie and Video Guide, 2000 Edition* (New York: Signet, 1999), 901.

17. López, "Are All Latins from Manhattan?" 413. Rodríguez-Estrada also says that Vélez's roles became more and more stereotypical as her career progressed, and similarly sees Carmelita as a marginalized and stereotyped figure in the *Mexican Spitfire* films ("Dolores Del Río and Lupe Vélez," 483–484).

18. See Charles Ramírez Berg, "Stereotyping in Films in General and of the Hispanic in Particular," *Howard Journal of Communications* 2:3 (Summer 1990): 286–300. Some of this material was reconceptualized and appears in Chapters 1 and 3 of this book.

19. Among them are J. Robert Bren, a writer and producer from 1934 to 1955; José Luis Tortosa, an actor and writer who scripted some of Hollywood's Spanish-language films in the 1930s; and Julio De Moraes, apparently Brazilian, who was credited with the story for *The Veiled Woman* (1929).

20. Reyes and Rubie, *Hispanics in Hollywood*, 483–486.

21. One notable exception to the rule of Roland dressing in this way but avoiding the Latin lover role was in *The Racers* (1955), in which he and Kirk Douglas play Italian(!) car drivers, and Roland's character is the happy-go-lucky seducer.

22. Reyes and Rubie, *Hispanics in Hollywood*, 402–403.

23. I am greatly indebted to my wife, Cecilia Arroyo Berg, M.A., C.C.C./S.L.P., a superb speech pathologist and therapist (and a beautiful one too!), for help in analyzing José Ferrer's voice.

24. Angharad N. Valdivia, *A Latina in the Land of Hollywood*, ch. 5, "A Latina in the Land of Hollywood: Transgressive Possibilities," 105.

25. Ibid., 97.

26. Ibid., 101.

5. *BORDERTOWN*, THE ASSIMILATION NARRATIVE, AND THE CHICANO SOCIAL PROBLEM FILM

1. Peter Roffman and Jim Purdy, *The Hollywood Social Problem Film: Madness, Despair, and Politics from the Depression to the Fifties* (Bloomington: Indiana University Press, 1981), viii.

2. Roffman and Purdy, *Hollywood Social Problem Film*, 252–256, 264–267, and 158–162.

3. Richie Pérez, "From Assimilation to Annihilation: Puerto Rican Images in U.S. Films," *Centro Bulletin* 2:8 (Spring 1990): 8–27.

4. In deciding which films to include, my sole criterion was that the film's narrative had to focus on the prejudicial treatment of Mexican Americans in the United States. On that basis, several other films—all fascinating for their por-

trayal of Mexican Americans—were considered but finally excluded. The films I omitted were *Border Incident* (1949, d. Anthony Mann), *Ace in the Hole* (1951, d. Billy Wilder), *Touch of Evil* (1958, d. Orson Welles), and *Requiem for a Heavyweight* (1962, d. Ralph Nelson).

5. *Salt of the Earth* is probably the one of this group most written about; see Michael Wilson and Deborah Silverton Rosenfelt, *Salt of the Earth* (Old Westbury, N.Y.: Feminist Press, 1978) for the screenplay, a detailed commentary, a critique of the film, memoirs of some of the principals, and other documents. Also see director Herbert Biberman's *Salt of the Earth: The Story of a Film* (Boston: Beacon, 1965), as well as Ruth McCormick, "*Salt of the Earth,*" *Cineaste* 5 (Fall 1972): 5–55, and Tom Miller, "*Salt of the Earth* Revisited," *Cineaste* 13:13 (1984): 30–36.

Chon A. Noriega's "Citizen Chicano: The Trials and Titillations of Ethnicity in the American Cinema, 1935–1962" is an excellent study of these films from a sociohistorical and political perspective; see *Social Research: An International Quarterly of the Social Sciences* 58:2 (Summer 1991): 413–438.

On other of these films, see, for example, Gary D. Keller, "The Images of the Chicano in Mexican, United States, and Chicano Cinema: An Overview," in Gary D. Keller, ed., *Chicano Cinema: Research, Reviews, and Resources* (Binghamton, N.Y.: Bilingual Review/Press, 1985), 13–58. In the same collection, see Linda Williams, "Type and Stereotype: Chicano Images in Film," 59–63, and Carlos E. Cortés, "Chicanas in Film: History of an Image," 94–108. Also Keller's more recent *Hispanics and United States Film: An Overview and Handbook* (Tempe, Ariz.: Bilingual Review/Press, 1994), esp. 127–135.

Also see Allen L. Woll's works on Hispanics in film: "Bandits and Lovers: Hispanic Images in American Film," in *The Kaleidoscopic Lens: How Hollywood Views Ethnic Groups,* ed. Randall M. Miller (Englewood, N.J.: Jerome S. Ozer, Publisher, 1980); *The Latin Image in American Film* (Los Angeles: UCLA Latin American Center Publications, 1980); and Woll and Miller, *Ethnic and Racial Images in American Film and Television: Historical Essays and Bibliography* (New York: Garland, 1987). Also, Arthur G. Pettit, *Images of the Mexican American in Fiction and Film* (College Station: Texas A&M University Press, 1980).

6. I am indebted to Steve Carr for coining the term "assimilation narrative."

7. Robin Wood, "Symmetry, Closure, Disruption: The Ambiguity of *Blackmail,*" in *Hitchcock's Films Revisited* (New York: Columbia University Press, 1989), 243.

8. Laura Mulvey, "Afterthoughts on 'Visual Pleasure and Narrative Cinema' inspired by *Duel in the Sun,*" in *Feminism and Film Theory,* ed. Constance Penley (New York: Routledge, 1988), 69–79.

9. Julia Kristeva, "La femme, ce n'est jamais ça," *Tel Quel* 59 (Fall 1974): 24, quoted in Toril Moi, *Sexual/Textual Politics: Feminist Literary Theory* (New York: Methuen, 1985), 164. Translated by Moi.

10. Robert Warshow, "The Gangster as Tragic Hero," in *The Immediate Experience* (1948; repr. New York: Athenaeum, 1971), 133.

11. Teresa L. Ebert, "The Romance of Patriarchy: Ideology, Subjectivity, and Postmodern Feminist Cultural Theory," *Cultural Critique* 10 (Fall 1988): 39.

12. Robin Wood, "The American Nightmare: Horror in the 70s" and "Normality and Monsters: The Films of Larry Cohen and George Romero," chs. 5 and 6 in *Hollywood from Vietnam to Reagan* (New York: Columbia University Press, 1986).

13. Wood, *Hollywood from Vietnam to Reagan,* 78.

14. Laura Mulvey, "Visual Pleasure and Narrative Cinema" (1975), repr. in *Feminism and Film Theory,* ed. Constance Penley (New York: Routledge, 1988), 62.

15. It is worth noting that both of these films were made by blacklisted filmmakers, and that their departures from the norm should not be taken as either accidental or coincidental.

16. Mulvey, "Afterthoughts," 70.

17. See Pettit, *Images of the Mexican American,* ch. 7.

18. To a certain extent, José Limón and Rafael Pérez-Torres have begun this work. See Limón's *American Encounters* (Boston: Beacon, 1999), esp. 119–124, and Pérez-Torres's article, which does not see the film as ultimately progressive: "Chicano Ethnicity, Cultural Hybridity, and the Mestizo Voice," *American Literature* 70 (1998): 153–176.

To my mind, the most sustained study of *Giant* by a Chicano author to date is Tino Villanueva's book-length poem, *Scene from the Movie "Giant"* (Willimantic, Conn.: Curbstone Press, 1993). It sensitively and vividly captures the experience of watching the film for Chicanos growing up in the 1950s, myself included. In my case, I watched it in the mid-1960s, when I was in high school, with my Mexican mother, who had seen the film when it was first released in 1956. Just before the fight scene, she leaned over to me and whispered, "Pay attention to this." I did, and it is not too much to say that it affected my entire life. It is one of the reasons I am teaching and writing about films all these years later.

19. Mulvey, "Afterthoughts," 70.

20. Richard Dyer, "Judy Garland and Gay Men," in *Heavenly Bodies: Film Stars and Society* (New York: St. Martin's, 1986), 141–194. See also Robin Wood, "Star and Auteur: Hitchcock's Films with Bergman," in *Hitchcock's Films Revisited,* 303–335.

21. Mulvey, "Afterthoughts," 70. Work on early Black spectatorship provides a useful culture-based model for Chicano and ethnic film reception. See, for example, Jane Gaines, "The Scare of Shame: Skin Color and Caste in Black Silent Melodrama," *Cinema Journal* 26:4 (Summer 1987): 3–21; and Adrienne Lanier-Seward, "A Film Portrait of Black Ritual Expression: The Blood of Jesus," in *Expressively Black: The Cultural Basis of Ethnic Identity,* ed. Geneva Gay and Willie L. Baber (New York: Praeger, 1987), 195–212. Carlos Muñoz Jr. reveals how Chicano scholarship itself has oscillated between assimilation and separatism since the 1930s; see "The Quest for Paradigm: The Struggle for Chicano Studies," in *Youth, Identity, Power: The Chicano Movement* (London: Verso, 1989), 127–169.

6. THE MARGIN AS CENTER: THE MULTICULTURAL DYNAMICS OF JOHN FORD'S WESTERNS

1. Robin Wood, "'Shall We Gather at the River?' The Late Films of John Ford," *Film Comment* 7:3 (Fall 1971): 12.

2. Michael Dempsey, "Ford: A Reassessment," *Film Quarterly* 28:4 (Summer 1975): 5–9. Ford's stereotyping, Dempsey felt, was a major flaw in his oeuvre that could be neither ignored nor explained away. Though Ford "wants to 'do right,'" wrote Dempsey, "he cannot escape his own innate condescension" toward Native Americans, Asians, and African Americans, who are trivialized and stereotyped in film after film (7).

3. See also Brian Henderson's "*The Searchers*: An American Dilemma," *Film Quarterly* 34:2 (Winter 1980–1981): 9–23, repr. in *Movies and Methods: An Anthology*, vol. 2, ed. Bill Nichols (Berkeley: University of California Press, 1985), 429–449; Angela Aleiss, "A Race Divided: The Indian Westerns of John Ford," *American Indian Culture and Research Journal* 18:3 (Summer 1994): 167–186; Jim Weigert, "John Ford and the Indians," *Media Educators Association Journal* (1979): 10–13; Kirk Ellis, "On the Warpath: John Ford and the Indians," *Journal of Popular Film and Television* 8:2 (1980): 34–41.

See Lee Lourdeaux's *Italian and Irish Filmmakers in America: Ford, Capra, Coppola, and Scorsese* (Philadelphia: Temple University Press, 1990) for a treatment of the Irishness of Ford's cinema. See also Joseph McBride's "Half Genius, Half Irish," in *John Ford,* ed. Joseph McBride and Michael Wilmington (London: Seeker and Warburg, 1974), for a nice analysis of the cultural duality in Ford. On Ford's depiction of Irish male drinking, see Stephanie Demetrakopoulos, "John Ford's Irish Drinking Ethos and Its Influence on Stereotypes of American Male Drunks," *Midwest Quarterly* 32:2 (Winter 1991): 224–234. On the religious aspect of Ford's films, see Paul Giles, "The Cinema of Catholicism: John Ford and Robert Altman," in *Unspeakable Images: Ethnicity and the American Cinema,* ed. Lester D. Friedman (Urbana: University of Illinois Press, 1991), 140–166.

Finally, Tag Gallagher's thorough study, *John Ford: The Man and His Films* (Berkeley: University of California Press, 1986), deals with Ford's portrayals of Native Americans and defends Ford's films against charges of racism and intolerance.

4. Ella Shohat, "Ethnicities-in-Relation: Toward a Multicultural Reading of American Cinema," in Friedman, ed., *Unspeakable Images,* 216.

5. In the main, I will employ a critical method pioneered by Ella Shohat, Robert Stam, Hamid Naficy, Teshome H. Gabriel, and other multicultural film critics. See Shohat's "Ethnicities-in-Relation" and her "Gender and Culture of Empire: Toward a Feminist Ethnography of the Cinema," in *Otherness and the Media: The Ethnography of the Imagined and the Imaged,* ed. Hamid Naficy and Teshome H. Gabriel (Langhorne, Pa.: Harwood Academic Publishers, 1993), 45–84; and Ella Shohat and Robert Stam, *Unthinking Eurocentrism: Multiculturalism and the Media* (New York: Routledge, 1994).

For more examples of this type of criticism, see, for example, the other articles in the anthologies mentioned above, as well in Chon A. Noriega, ed., *Chicanos and Film: Representation and Resistance* (Minneapolis: University of Minnesota Press, 1992); Chon A. Noriega and Ana M. López, eds., *The Ethnic Eye: Latino Media Arts* (Minneapolis: University of Minnesota Press, 1996); bell hooks, *Black Looks: Race and Representation* (Boston: South End Press, 1992) and *Reel to Real: Race, Sex, and Class at the Movies* (New York: Routledge, 1996); and Mark Winokur, *American Laughter: Immigrants, Ethnicity, and 1930s Hollywood Film Comedy* (New York: St. Martin's Press, 1996).

6. Andrew M. Greeley, *That Most Distressful Nation: The Taming of the American Irish* (Chicago: Quadrangle Books, 1972), 120.

7. See Charles Maland, "From Aesthete to Pappy," in Gaylyn Studlar and Matthew Bernstein, eds., *John Ford Made Westerns: Filming the Legend in the Sound Era* (Bloomington: Indiana University Press, 2001), 220–254.

8. Or, in Neal Gabler's view, Hollywood's America was the Jewish moguls' *conception* of the American mainstream's utopian view of itself. It was driven, according to Gabler, by a desire to assimilate "so ruthless and complete that they cut their lives to the pattern of American respectability as they interpreted it"; see Gabler, *An Empire of Their Own: How the Jews Invented Hollywood* (New York: Anchor Books, 1988), 4.

9. John Ford was not the only Hollywood filmmaker close to his immigrant roots. Many first- and second-generation Americans rose to top creative positions during the studio era. Frank Capra (born in Sicily) and Elia Kazan (born in Turkey of Greek parents) both came to the United States as children. Many other directors, among them F. W. Murnau, Ernst Lubitsch, Fritz Lang, Billy Wilder, Fred Zinnemann, Erich Von Stroheim, Charles Vidor, Rex Ingram, Alfred Hitchcock, and Charlie Chaplin, emigrated here from Europe. Most of the heads of the major studios—Carl Laemmle, Adolph Zukor, William Fox, Louis B. Mayer, Harry Warner—arrived in the United States in their youth. (Warner's three younger brothers, Albert, Sam, and Jack, were born in the United States after their parents emigrated from Poland: see Gabler, *Empire of Their Own*, 120–127.)

But much of the cinema these filmmakers produced was "naturalized," in both the ideological (dominant ideas made invisible as common sense) and culturally transformative (an alien made into a citizen) meanings of the term. Of this group, Chaplin's cinema is probably the most culturally ambiguous (his Tramp was upwardly mobile, though Chaplin's films criticized a dehumanizing system) and thus the most like Ford's. And though it is true that some of these directors contested the status quo (Lang, Hitchcock, and Wilder, especially), their films tended to elide ethnicity from their critique. As a result, many of the characters in their films seemingly possessed no ethnicity at all. Thus, for Capra it was Mr. Smith who went to Washington; for Wilder, the ethnically nondescript Joe Gillis who made the fateful turn into the driveway on Sunset Boulevard; and for Lang, the culturally neutral Eddie Taylor who ran for his life in *You Only Live Once* (1937). In contrast, Ford's characters were, as Tag Gallagher says, "always distinctly characterized as representative of a specific culture. There is no confusing a Boston Wasp with an Irish-American or Swede" (Gallagher, *John Ford*, 478).

10. Gregory H. Nobles, *American Frontiers: Cultural Encounters and Continental Conquest* (New York: Hill and Wang, 1997), xii.

11. A distinctive element of Ford's Westerns is that he takes pains to distinguish between the segregated white ethnics and the assimilated mainstream, and shows the built-in antagonism between the two groups. When depicted in most other Westerns, this animosity plays out as a class battle that pits the sod-busters against the large ranchers. In Ford, as I have said, immigrant ethnicity is almost always foregrounded.

12. Of course, some of Hollywood's classical-era cinema was similarly suspicious, and sometimes explicitly critical, of the mainstream's dominant ideology—the cinema of Orson Welles (*Citizen Kane* [1941], *The Magnificent Ambersons* [1942]) and Fritz Lang (*Fury* [1936], *You Only Live Once* [1937]) provides powerful examples. But Welles's and Lang's characters were generally class rather than ethnic Others. Ford's outsiders were defined by more than one marginalizing marker—class *and* ethnicity at a minimum, and sometimes race or gender as well. See also Peter Lehman's article, "How the West Wasn't Won," in Studlar and Bernstein, *John Ford Made Westerns*, 132–153.

13. McBride, "Half Genius," 21.

14. Quoted in Gallagher, *John Ford*, 254.

15. The character's name is Ford's homage to Mexican director Emilio Fernández and Mexican cinematographer Gabriel Figueroa, both of whom assisted him in the making of *The Fugitive* (1947). Fernández was his assistant producer, Figueroa his cinematographer.

16. Demetrakopoulos, "John Ford's Irish Drinking Ethos." See also Lane Roth, "Ritual Brawls in John Ford's Films," *Film Criticism* 7:3 (1983): 38–46.

17. As Dr. Kersaint (Thomas Mitchell) asks the sullen governor (Raymond Massey) in *The Hurricane* (1937), "Is there any law against dancing and singing when your heart is happy?"

18. See Carl Witke, "Militia, Fireman, and Police," ch. 6 in *The Irish in America* (Baton Rouge: Louisiana State University Press, 1956).

19. Witke, "Militia, Fireman, and Police," 136; see also the documentary *The Irish in America* (1997), produced by Rhys Thomas for A&E Productions. Myles Keogh, mentioned in *She Wore a Yellow Ribbon* as a friend of Nathan Brittles, serves as a historical example of the Irish immigrant who signs up to be a U.S. soldier. As in the film, the real Myles Keogh died with Custer at the Little Bighorn.

20. In Ford's *The Hurricane* (1937), the importance of a uniform is made explicit when Terangi (Jon Hall) remarks to his wife (Dorothy Lamour), "What a difference a cap makes! In Tahiti . . . I'm just the same as a white man." In this regard, the point of *The Hurricane* is to illustrate how violently the colonizers respond to the perceived threat of a native presuming to act as an equal.

21. In Peter Bogdanovich's *John Ford* (Berkeley: University of California Press, 1968), 86, there is the following exchange:

In *Fort Apache,* do you feel the men were right in obeying Fonda [Lieutenant Colonel Thursday] even though it was obvious he is wrong and they were killed because of his error?
Yes—he was the Colonel, and what he says—goes; whether they agree with it or not—it still pertains. In Vietnam today, probably a lot of guys don't agree with their leader, but they still go ahead and do the job.

22. McBride, "Half Genius," 109. Tag Gallagher echoes the sentiment; see *John Ford,* 253–254.

23. Ford sought military service twice. As a young man, he applied to the U.S. Naval Academy but was rejected. Later, when the United States entered World War I, he volunteered for naval duty. This time, bad eyesight caused his rejection.

24. A point that is superbly demonstrated in *The Long Gray Line* (1955), which celebrates the military even as it criticizes it for shutting out and ignoring Marty Maher (Tyrone Power), who is clearly shown by the film to be not only a good soldier but a better man than many who attended West Point.

25. "My sympathy was always with the Indians," said John Ford. "Do you consider the invasion of the Black and Tan into Ireland a blot on English history? It's the same thing, all countries do the same thing. There's the British doing it, Hitler doing it, there's Stalin. Genocide seems to be a commonplace in our lives" (Gallagher, *John Ford,* 254).

26. As Jane Tompkins puts it, "An Indian in a Western who is supposed to be a real person has to be played by a white man" (*West of Everything: The Inner Life of Westerns* [New York: Oxford University Press, 1992], 9). Michael Wood noted a similar pattern in the portrayal of Blacks by whites in the movies. "There is obviously some murky principle at work that says that we can recognize dignity in blacks only when white folks dress up and lend a bit of dignity to them" (Michael Wood, *America in the Movies* [New York: Basic Books, 1975], 133–134).
In his films, Ford further revised the ethnic casting rule so that when an Indian character is singled out, the peaceable and humane ones tend to be portrayed by Native Americans (Chief Big Tree in *Drums along the Mohawk* and *She Wore a Yellow Ribbon,* Inclán in *Fort Apache,* Jim Thorpe in *Wagon Master*), the savage and violent ones by whites (Henry Brandon in *The Searchers* and *Two Rode Together*). Woody Strode's playing a Native American in *Two Rode Together* and a Mongolian warrior in *Seven Women* (1965) is an instance of Ford's adhering to Hollywood's minorities-can-play-any-ethnicity rule (and doing something he did throughout his career—giving an old friend some work).

27. Among many other roles, Miguel Inclán played, for example, the villain in the film that made Dolores Del Río a star upon her return to Mexican cinema from Hollywood, *María Candelaria* (1943), then played the heroic cop-on-the-beat in the urban melodrama *Salón México* (1948). (Both films were directed by Emilio Fernández.) Inclán was also featured in the role of the blind man in Luis Buñuel's *Los Olvidados* (1950).

28. Armendáriz, who began working in Mexican films in 1935, was one of

the best-known and most popular Mexican leading men. He gained fame by teaming with Dolores Del Río in several films directed by Emilio Fernández. In 1945 he won the Mexican film industry's Best Actor Award (for his performance in *La Perla*, Fernández's adaptation of John Steinbeck's *The Pearl*), and he won another in 1953.

29. What Tompkins calls "That yipping sound on the sound tracks that accompanies Indian attacks" (*West of Everything*, 9).

30. I am reading the ending of *The Searchers* as Ethan's exclusion because, while it is true that he does stop short of entering the Jorgensens' house, it is also true that he is not invited in. Furthermore, the door closes on him as he walks away. This interpretation is different from those of scholars who, like Brian Henderson, see the ending as Ethan's "self-exclusion" (Henderson, "*The Searchers*," 447). Maybe it is a mutual isolation.

31. One can see how Ford would be attracted to the cultural assimilation plot of Sinclair Lewis's novel *Arrowsmith*, which he filmed in 1931. The in-or-out cultural plot of *Arrowsmith* is similar to *Young Mr. Lincoln*'s, but it concludes with Dr. Arrowsmith (Ronald Colman) doing exactly the opposite of Lincoln. Arrowsmith must decide between fame, wealth, and recognition as a scientist at an elite research institute, or service as a physician to the needy (immigrant Italians in the urban East, Swedes at the margin, and the Black natives in the West Indies). Like Lincoln, he also loses a woman (his wife, played by Helen Hayes) who serves as the margin's conscience. But Arrowsmith is able in the end to do what Lincoln could not: reject the mainstream's definition of success and the comely temptress (Myrna Loy) who comes with it. *Arrowsmith* allows Ford to rewrite Lincoln's story, only with a more palatable cultural resolution. In this revised version, a marginal protagonist achieves (actually, redefines) mainstream success without assimilating and without compromising his ethnic values.

32. There are other Ford characters who withdraw from America. Sean Thornton (John Wayne), in *The Quiet Man* (1952), leaves the United States in search of his ethnic roots. So do Donovan (again Wayne) and company in *Donovan's Reef* (1963), a wonderfully multicultural (and countercultural) film that discloses Ford's continuing loss of faith in the American mainstream, to the point that a far-flung retreat seems the only viable ethnic alternative.

7. IMMIGRANTS, ALIENS, AND EXTRATERRESTRIALS: SCIENCE FICTION'S ALIEN "OTHER" AS (AMONG *OTHER* THINGS) NEW HISPANIC IMAGERY

1. In this chapter I will use the capitalized form "Alien" to designate the science fiction movie creature, and the lowercase form "alien" to designate immigrants.

2. Vivian Sobchack summarizes a few of the more interesting speculations about the Alien Other in *Screening Space: The American Science Fiction Film* (New York: Ungar, 1987), 36, 47.

3. Judith Hess Wright, "Genre Films and the Status Quo," *Jump Cut* 1 (May–June 1974): 1, 16, 18; repr. in *Film Genre Reader,* ed. Barry Keith Grant (Austin: University of Texas Press, 1986), 46.

4. Peter Biskind, *Seeing Is Believing* (New York: Pantheon, 1983), 111. Jim Naureckas, "Aliens: Mother and the Teeming Hordes," *Jump Cut* 32:4 (1986).

5. Sobchack, *Screening Space,* 241.

6. Peter Fitting, "Count Me Out/In: Post-Apocalyptic Visions in Recent Science Fiction Film," *CineAction!* 11 (winter 1987–1988): 42–51.

7. Robin Wood, "An Introduction to the American Horror Film," in *Movies and Methods,* vol. 2, ed. Bill Nichols (Berkeley: University of California Press, 1985), 199.

8. Ibid., 199–200.

9. Ibid., 201.

10. James Stuart Olson, *The Ethnic Dimension in American History,* vol. 2 (New York: St. Martin's, 1979), 206. "Growth of a Nation," *Time,* July 8, 1985, 34–35, gives a figure of 8.8 million for the period.

11. Otto Friedrich, "The Changing Face of America," *Time,* July 8, 1985, 26–27.

12. U.S. Department of Justice, Immigration, and Naturalization Service, *1985 Statistical Yearbook of the Immigration and Naturalization Service,* 176.

13. Olson, *Ethnic Dimension,* 379. For the *bracero* program, see Wayne A. Cornelius, *Mexican Migration to the United States: Causes, Consequences, and U.S. Responses* (Cambridge: Massachusetts Institute of Technology, Center for International Studies, 1978), 18; Leonard Dinnerstein and David M. Reimers, *Ethnic Americans,* 2d ed. (New York: Harper and Row, 1982), 93; Olson, *Ethnic Dimension,* 384–385. On the 1965 Immigration Act, see Leonard Dinnerstein, Roger L. Nichols, and David M. Reimers, *Natives and Strangers: Ethnic Groups and the Building of America* (New York: Oxford University Press, 1979), 258–259; Olson, *Ethnic Dimension,* 384.

14. U.S. Department of Justice, *1985 Statistical Yearbook,* 166–169; 178–179.

15. Dinnerstein and Reimers, *Natives and Strangers,* 112.

16. Anya Peterson Royce, *Ethnic Identity: Strategies of Diversity* (Bloomington: Indiana University Press, 1982), 163–167.

17. Ibid., 160.

18. John Higham, *Patterns of American Nativism, 1980–1925* (New Brunswick, N.J.: Rutgers University Press, 1955), 3–4, 9.

19. *The Poems of Emma Lazarus,* vol. 1 (Boston, 1889), 202–203, quoted in Higham, *Patterns,* 23.

20. "Congress Clears Overhaul of Immigration Law," *Congressional Quarterly Almanac,* 99th Congress, 2d Session, 1986, 61–67, provides a good description of the features of the law and a concise outline of its congressional history.

Interestingly, one of the major obstacles preventing a quicker passage of the bill was a capitalistic dilemma emblematic of the larger, contradictory nature not just of immigration reform but of the whole immigration question in this country. In the hopes of discouraging the entry of undocumented aliens by making it harder for them to find work in the United States, one of the goals of the bill was to provide tougher legislation to punish Americans who hired undocumented aliens. But at the same time the law had to find a way to placate Western growers, who for decades (since the end of the *bracero* program in 1964) had depended on undocumented workers to pick their crops. The built-in advantages for the growers—a cheap, reliable, and disposable labor pool—were clearly jeopardized by the new legislation. To ensure the bill's passage, the growers had to be assured that the new law would allow them to maintain an adequate workforce.

21. Fredric Jameson, *The Political Unconscious* (Ithaca, N.Y.: Cornell University Press, 1981), 20.

22. Claude Lévi-Strauss, "The Structural Study of Myth," quoted in Thomas G. Schatz, *Hollywood Genres* (New York: Random House, 1979), 262.

23. Fitting, "Count Me Out/In," 48.

24. See, for example, Walter G. Stephan and David Rosenfield, "Racial and Ethnic Stereotypes," in *In the Eye of the Beholder,* ed. Arthur G. Miller (New York: Praeger, 1982), 106.

25. Wright, "Genre Films," 47–48.

26. Wood, "An Introduction to the American Horror Film," 203.

27. Sigmund Freud, *The Interpretation of Dreams,* trans. and ed. James Strachey (New York: Avon, 1969), 175.

28. Ibid., 177–178.

29. Ibid., 301.

30. Higham, *Patterns,* 162.

31. Sander L. Gilman, *Difference and Pathology: Stereotypes of Sexuality, Race, and Madness* (Ithaca: Cornell University Press, 1985), 15–21.

32. Ibid., 21.

33. Mark Winokur, "Improbable Ethnic Hero: William Powell and the Transformation of Ethnic Hollywood," *Cinema Journal* 27 (1987): 12.

34. Anders Stephanson, "Regarding Postmodernism—A Conversation with Fredric Jameson," *Social Text* 17 (Fall 1987): 43.

35. Francis A. Walker, quoted in Higham, *Patterns,* 143.

36. Earlier in the film another Replicant asks Deckard the same question. Right before he tries to kill Deckard, Leon pauses for a moment to ask, "Painful to live in fear, isn't it?" It is at this point that Rachel kills Leon and saves Deckard's life.

37. Naureckas, "Aliens," 1.

38. Sobchack, *Screening Space,* 297.

39. Arthur G. Miller, "Stereotyping: Further Perspectives and Conclusions," in Miller, ed., *In the Eye of the Beholder,* 479–480, 483.

40. Ibid., 481.

41. Herbert Kelman, quoted in ibid., 481.

42. Ibid., 480.

43. Siegfried Kracauer, *From Caligari to Hitler* (1947; repr. Princeton: Princeton University Press, 1974), 32.

44. Sobchack, *Screening Space,* 229, 289.
45. Gilman, *Difference and Pathology,* 240.

BACKSTORY: CHICANO AND LATINO
FILMMAKERS BEHIND THE CAMERA

1. The best account to date of the birth and evolution of Chicano cinema is Chon A. Noriega's *Shot in America: Television, the State, and the Rise of Chicano Cinema* (Minneapolis: University of Minnesota Press, 2000). Other summaries of Chicano and Latino film history and criticism may be found in *Chicanos and Film: Representation and Resistance,* ed. Chon A. Noriega (Minneapolis: University of Minnesota Press, 1992), specifically in Noriega's Introduction, xi–xxvi, and his essay "Between a Weapon and a Formula: Chicano Cinema and Its Contexts," 141–167. For Chicano film history in relation to Hollywood and Mexican cinema, see Gary D. Keller's Introduction to the essays he edited in *Chicano Cinema: Research, Reviews, and Resources* (Binghamton, N.Y.: Bilingual Review/Press, 1985), 13–58, and more recently, chapter 7, "The Emergence of U.S. Hispanic Films," in his *Hispanics and United States Film: An Overview and Handbook* (Tempe, Ariz.: Bilingual Review/Press, 1994).
2. Compare these with the aims of Third Cinema as elaborated by Teshome Gabriel in *Third Cinema in the Third World: The Aesthetics of Liberation* (Ann Arbor: UMI Research Press, 1992). For a critique of Gabriel's formulation of Third Cinema in the Third World, see Julianne Burton's "Marginal Cinemas and Mainstream Critical Theory," *Screen* 26:3–4 (1985): 2–21.
3. Lillian Jiménez, "Moving from the Margin to the Center: Puerto Rican Cinema in New York," 22–37, and Ana López, "Greater Cuba," 38–58. Both in *The Ethnic Eye: Latino Media Arts,* ed. Chon A. Noriega and Ana López (Minneapolis: University of Minnesota Press, 1996).

8. *EL GENIO DEL GÉNERO:* MEXICAN AMERICAN
BORDERLAND DOCUMENTARIES AND POSTMODERNISM

1. A note on my family's names: For some reason that none of his children have been able to explain to me, my maternal grandfather broke with Spanish tradition regarding his name; he called himself Jesús Morales Ramírez, with Ramírez being the family name, not Morales. Thus my mother was baptized Hortensia Ramírez. When she married my father, she called herself Hortensia Ramírez Berg. Wishing to acknowledge both my Mexican and my German heritages, I adopted my mother's maiden name as a middle name and call myself Charles Ramírez Berg.
2. Pat Mora, *Chants* (Houston: Arte Publico Press, 1982), 52. See also a poem by the historian Oscar J. Martínez, "Chicano Borderlander," in his *Border People: Life and Society in the U.S.–Mexico Borderlands* (Tucson: University of Arizona Press, 1994), 116–117.

3. Cherríe Moraga, *Loving in the War Years: Lo que nunca pasó por sus labios* (Boston: South End Press, 1983), 32.

4. Linda Hutcheon, *A Poetics of Postmodernism: History, Theory, Fiction* (New York: Routledge, 1989); see ch. 4, "Decentering the Postmodern: The Ex-Centric," 57–73.

5. Moraga, *Loving in the War Years*; Gloria Anzaldúa, *Borderlands/La Frontera: The New Mestiza* (San Francisco: Spinsters/Aunt Lute, 1987); Guillermo Gómez-Peña, *Warrior for Gringostroika* (St. Paul, Minn.: Graywolf Press, 1993) and *The New World Border* (San Francisco: City Lights, 1996).

6. Anzaldúa, *Borderlands*, 87.

7. Craig Owens, "The Discourse of Others: Feminists and Postmodernism," in *Postmodern Culture*, ed. Hal Foster (London: Pluto Books, 1985), 59. Note: *Postmodern Culture* was originally published as *The Anti-Aesthetic* (Townsend, Wash.: Bay Press, 1983).

8. See, for example, José David Saldívar, *Border Matters: Remapping American Cultural Studies* (Berkeley: University of California Press, 1997).

9. Thomas Docherty, Introduction to "Periphery and Postmodernism" section, in *Postmodernism: A Reader*, ed. Thomas Docherty (New York: Columbia University Press, 1993), 445.

10. I am purposely omitting Nestór García Canclini from my list of Chicano postmodernist critics because, first, he is not Mexican American and, second, the postmodern condition he is analyzing is Latin American, which, it seems to me, is quite different from the Mexican American postmodernism I am arguing for in this chapter. True, some of his theoretical positions are closely related to my project here, most specifically the synthesis of the intellectual trends of Pierre Bourdieu and Antonio Gramsci. However, I tend to agree with Renato Rosaldo, who wrote in the foreword of the English translation to *Culturas híbridas* that "García Canclini's analysis of tradition and modernity may prove difficult for readers in the United States to apprehend." I would add that for Mexican Americans the difficulty in grasping and applying García Canclini's argument is doubled, excluded as they are from both the U.S. and the Latin American mainstream. See Rosaldo's foreword in García Canclini, *Hybrid Cultures: Strategies for Entering and Leaving Modernity*, trans. Christopher L. Chiappari and Silvia L. López (Minneapolis: University of Minnesota Press, 1995), xiii.

11. José E. Limón, *Dancing with the Devil: Society and Cultural Poetics in Mexican-American South Texas* (Minneapolis: University of Minnesota Press, 1994), 106.

12. Ibid., 111.

13. Hal Foster, "Postmodernism: A Preface," in Foster, ed., *Postmodern Culture*, ix–x. My thanks to Doug Kellner for clarifying the two postmodernisms and for referring me to Foster's work.

14. Toni Morrison, quoted in *Modernism/Postmodernism*, ed. Peter Brooker (London: Longman, 1992), 213.

15. Cornel West, "An Interview with Cornel West," in Brooker, ed., *Modernism/Postmodernism*, 214, 217.

16. It could be argued that what I am describing in really a postcolonial rather than a postmodern theoretical position. There is certainly a postcolonial/ Mexican American postmodernism overlap. A number of postcolonial characteristics *are* postmodern: anti-imperial resistance being a key one, and a notion of hybridization.

Though it may well be that what Bill Ashcroft, Gareth Griffiths, and Helen Tiffin suggest in *The Empire Writes Back: Theory and Practice in Post-Colonial Literatures* (London: Routledge, 1989), namely, that what is called postmodernism from the developed world's viewpoint is, from the postcolonial standpoint, postcolonial, I tend to think there is a significant difference. The deciding factor for me is the array of specific characteristics that taken together are distinctly postmodern (and are found in these documentaries and in the Mexican American experience): heterogeneity, hybridization, and the contradictory "both . . . and" stance, all three hallmarks of what Anzaldúa called the "new *mestiza* consciousness" (in ch. 7: "La conciencia de la mestiza/Towards a new consciousness," Anzaldúa, *Borderlands*, 77–91); the ironic, questioning regard for the past; the use of and subversion of traditional forms; and, in Gloria Anzaldúa's words, a tolerance for ambiguity (79).

In the end, I see Mexican American postmodernism not as a sort of postmodern postcolonialism but as a real postmodernism that stretches back to—and is in part defined by—Mexican Americans' experience under colonialism.

17. Saldívar, *Border Matters*, 9.

18. Américo Paredes, *A Texan-Mexican Cancionero: Folksongs of the Lower Border* (Urbana: University of Illinois Press, 1977), xiv.

19. Due to the constraints of space, I decided to limit my focus to film and not to add Chicano videos to this list. However, a longer and more comprehensive study of Mexican American postmodern documentaries would list such postmodern Chicano video documentaries as Louis Hock's *The Mexican Tapes: A Chronicle of Life outside the Law* (1986), a series of four one-hour videos on the lives of Mexicans living in the San Diego area; and Willie Varela's *Thanksgiving Day 1991* (1993; 36 minutes), which investigates the aesthetics and ethics of producing video documentaries on the U.S.–Mexico border. Both are available for rental or purchase from the Video Data Bank at the School of the Art Institute of Chicago, 112 S. Michigan Ave., Chicago, Illinois 60603, (312) 345-3550; fax (312) 541-8073.

20. A close variation on this line is articulated as a joke by Ned Nederlander (Martin Short) in *¡Three Amigos!* (1986), after he and his buddies (Chevy Chase and Steve Martin) are confronted by a *bandido* (Alfonso Arau) and his gang in a small Mexican village. When they discover that the Mexicans' guns are firing real bullets, Ned's response is, "What am I doing in Mexico?"

This, in turn, is a variation on a line that Eddie Cantor says once he finds himself in Mexico impersonating a famous *torrero* from Spain in *The Kid from Spain* (1932): "Oh, why did I ever have to come to Mexico?"

21. For another account of the cinematic treatment of the border from a different perspective, see David Maciel, *El Norte: The U.S.–Mexican Border in*

Contemporary Cinema (San Diego: Institute for Regional Studies of the Californias, San Diego State University, 1990). Maciel deals with both Hollywood and Mexican films' treatment of the border. For a detailed analysis of the border in Mexican cinema, see Norma Iglesias, *Entre yerba, polvo y plomo: Lo fronterizo visto por el cine mexicano* (Tijuana: El Colegio de la Frontera Norte, 1991). Iglesias shows that, over the years, the Mexican border film has centered on various themes. From the 1930s to the 1960s, for example, Mexican border films were primarily *charro* or *vaquero* movies (Westerns) or dealt with emigration to the United States. Since 1970, however, Mexican films set on the border have tended to deal with either emigration or drug trafficking. See her tables 3 and 4, p. 48. For an analysis of 1970s Mexican border films as cautionary tales depicting the dangers of emigrating to *el norte*, see my *Cinema of Solitude: A Critical Study of Mexican Film, 1967–1983* (Austin: University of Texas Press, 1992), 196–200.

22. Saldívar, *Border Matters*, x.

23. Ali Behdad, "INS and Outs: Producing Delinquency at the Border," *Aztlán* 23:1 (Spring 1998): 109.

24. Both U.S. society in general and the Latino community in particular were ambivalent with regard to NAFTA. According to surveys, about 50 percent of Latinos opposed the treaty. In the U.S. Congress, the Hispanic Caucus was divided. When it came time for a vote, most of the Mexican American members (from California, Texas, Arizona, and New Mexico) voted for NAFTA, while most of the Cuban and Puerto Rican representatives (from New York, Florida, Illinois, and New Jersey) voted against it. See Magalí Muriá, "Mexico, Latinos, and NAFTA: The Increasing Role of Mexican Americans in Trade Policy," *The Arizona Report* 2:1 (Spring 1998): 5–6.

25. *Out of Ireland* (1994), produced by American Focus; *The Irish in America* (1997), produced by Rhys Thomas for A&E Productions; *The Irish in America: Long Journey Home* (1998), produced by Jane West.

26. Rodolfo Alvarez, "The Psycho-Historical and Socioeconomic Development of the Chicano Community in the United States," in *The Mexican American Experience: An Interdisciplinary Anthology,* ed. Rodolfo O. de la Garza, Frank D. Bean, Charles M. Bonjean, Ricardo Romo, and Rodolfo Alvarez (Austin: University of Texas Press, 1985), 40–44.

27. Rafael Pérez-Torres, "Refiguring Aztlán," *Aztlán* 22:2 (Fall 1997): 21.

28. Limón, *Dancing with the Devil*, 112.

29. See Charles Jencks, *What Is Postmodernism?*, 4th ed. (London: Academy Editions, 1996).

30. Charles Jencks, "The Emergent Rules," in Docherty, ed., *Postmodernism: A Reader*, 289.

31. Gloria Anzaldúa, "La Conciencia de la Mestiza: Towards a New Consciousness," in *Making Face, Making Soul/Haciendo Caras: Creative and Critical Perspectives by Women of Color,* ed. Gloria Anzaldúa (San Francisco: Aunt Lute Foundation Books, 1990), 379.

32. Gómez-Peña, *Warrior for Gringostroika*, 39.

33. From notes taken from remarks made by filmmaker Louis Hock, during

a question-and-answer session after the screening of *La Mera Frontera*, April 6, Society of Cinema Studies Conference, San Diego, California.

34. Anzaldúa, *Borderlands*, 73.

35. Because Portillo is such a rich and provocatively imaginative filmmaker, there has been a significant amount of critical writing on her work. All of it is fascinating and worthwhile, though none from quite the same postmodern and genre perspective I am discussing here. See, for example, Rosa Linda Fregoso, "Chicana Film Practices: Confronting the 'Many-Headed Demon of Oppression,'" in *Chicanos and Film Representation and Resistance*, ed. Chon A. Noriega (Minneapolis: University of Minnesota Press, 1992), 168–182. Also, Fregoso's "Sacando los trapos al sol [Airing Dirty Laundry] in Lourdes Portillo's Melodocumentary, *The Devil Never Sleeps*," in *Redirecting the Gaze: Gender, Theory, and Cinema in the Third World*, eds. Diana Robin and Ira Jaffe (Albany: State University of New York Press, 1999), 307–330, which includes an insightful interview with Portillo on that film. See also Fregoso's *The Bronze Screen: Chicana and Chicano Film Culture* (Minnesota: University of Minnesota Press, 1993), particularly ch. 5. Also see Kathleen Newman, "Steadfast Love and Subversive Acts: The Politics of *La Ofrenda*: The Days of the Dead," *Spectator* 13:1 (Fall 1992): 98–109. Finally, Chon A. Noriega comes at Portillo's work from the point of view of his study of television and film industrial practices and Chicano filmmaking in *Shot in America: Television, the State, and the Rise of Chicano Cinema* (Minneapolis: University of Minnesota Press, 2000), esp. 186–194.

36. Jencks, "The Emergent Rules," 282.

37. Gómez-Peña, *New World Border*, 70.

38. Limón, *Dancing with the Devil*, 108.

39. Ibid., 116–117.

40. Four important manifestos are reprinted in *Chicanos and Film: Representations and Resistance*, ed. Chon Noriega (Minneapolis: University of Minnesota Press, 1992): Cine-Aztlán's "Ya Basta con Yankee Imperialist Documentaries!" (1974), 275–283; Francisco X. Camplis's "Toward the Development of a Raza Cinema" (1975), 284–302; Jason C. Johansen's "Notes on Chicano Cinema" (1979), 303–307; and Sylvia Morales's "Filming a Chicana Documentary" (1979), 308–311. See also filmmaker Jesús Salvador Treviño's "Chicano Cinema," *New Scholar* 8 (1982): 167–180, and "El desarrollo del cine chicano," *Hojas de cine: Testimonios y documentos del nuevo cine latinoamericano*, vol. 1: *Centro y Sudamérica* (Mexico City: Fundación Mexicana de Dineastas/Universidad Autónoma Metropolitana, 1988), 277–284.

41. The Mighty Zebra, *Calypso from the Virgin Islands* (RCA LPM-1169). The Mighty Zebra sang all the numbers and wrote most of them. Among my favorites were "Men Smart—Women Smarter," the antiimperial "Englishman's Diplomacy," and the Spanish-language merengue, "Al Compás del Merengue." As I play it today, I am still amazed by its wit and imaginative wordplay; furthermore, it strikes me how much calypso is an antecedent to rap. The lyrics were certainly adult fare for the time (mid-1950s), and I remember cousin Leo, Lulu's brother, concerned that a parochial school fourth grader owned and lis-

tened (hundreds of times) to music with overt—but very clever, inventive, and funny—sexual references. I heard Leo, twelve years my elder, ask Aunt Chita if she'd listened to the record before she gave it to me. "No," she replied. "Why—should I have?"

42. Dag Hammarskjöld, *Markings* (New York: Knopf, 1964), 55.

9. ETHNIC INGENUITY AND MAINSTREAM CINEMA: ROBERT RODRÍGUEZ'S *BEDHEAD* (1990) AND *EL MARIACHI* (1993)

1. See the summary of Chicano film history in the Backstory section and the notes on other histories of the movement.

2. Charles Ramírez Berg, "Ya Basta con the Hollywood Paradigm!—Strategies for Latino Screenwriters," *Jump Cut* 38 (June 1993): 96–104.

3. Personal interview with Robert Rodríguez, March 10, 1992, Austin, Texas. Rodríguez also told this story on *Late Night with David Letterman* (NBC, February 26, 1993).

4. Quoted in Chon Noriega, "Cafe Orale: Narrative Structure in Born in East L.A.," *Tonantzin* 8:1 (February 1991): 17.

5. Armond White, "The New Players: Hollywood's Black Filmmakers Observe the Rules of the Game," *Emerge* (August 1992): 42.

6. Both films are available on the *El Mariachi* video, laser disc, and DVD, and on a special edition DVD containing both *El Mariachi* and Rodríguez's *Desperado* (1995). This double-feature DVD also contains Rodríguez's shorts on how to save money in filmmaking, *10 Minute Film School* (on how he cut corners while making *El Mariachi*) and *10 More Minutes . . . (Anatomy of a Shootout)*, on how he did the same on *Desperado*. Both are distributed by Columbia/TriStar Home Video, 3400 Riverside Drive, Burbank, California 91505, (818) 972-8686.

7. Charles Ramírez Berg, *Cinema of Solitude: A Critical Study of Mexican Film, 1967–1983* (Austin: University of Texas Press, 1992); see ch. 5, "Women's Images, Part II: The Feminine Revolt—From La Malinche to La Llorona to Frida," esp. 77–96.

8. See Norma Iglesias, *Entre yerba, polvo y plomo: Lo fronterizo visto por el cine mexicano* (Tijuana: El Colegio de la Frontera Norte, 1991), 48, 55. See also David R. Maciel, *El Norte: The U.S.–Mexican Border in Contemporary Cinema* (San Diego: Institute for Regional Studies of the Californias, San Diego State University, 1990), 45–51.

9. In terms of identifying these films, Moisés Viñas, in his comprehensive index of nearly a century's worth of Mexican film, *Indice Cronológico del Cine Mexicano, 1896–1992* (Mexico: Dirección General de Actividades Cinematográficas, Universidad Nacional Autónoma de México, 1992), does note the "type of production," that is, video or film, for this recent type of film. Where he indicates video as a category, however, it is unclear whether he means that

these recent films were initially released on video (whether shot on film or video) or that they were initially shot on video. Furthermore, he gives this information on a film-by-film basis and does not provide any comprehensive tally of the number of such video films.

10. This information is summarized from Iglesias, *Entre yerba, polvo y plomo*, 42–88, and Maciel, *El Norte*, 3–6.

11. Marilyn D. Mintz, *The Martial Arts Films* (Rutland, Vt.: Tuttle, 1983), 219.

12. John Lent, *The Asian Film Industry* (Austin: University of Texas Press, 1990), 100. See also brief mentions of Hong Kong's martial arts cinema in Chiao Hsinng-Ping's "The Distinct Taiwanese and Hong Kong Cinemas" and Jenny Kwok Wah Lau's "A Critical Interpretation of the Popular Cinema of China and Hong Kong," both in *Perspectives on Chinese Cinema*, ed. Chris Berry (London: British Film Institute, 1991), 155–165 and 166–174, respectively. See also Li Cheuk-To, "Popular Cinema in Hong Kong," in *The Oxford History of World Cinema*, ed. Geoffery Nowell-Smith (Oxford: Oxford University Press, 1996), 704–711. Finally, two book-length studies: Stephen Teo's *Hong Kong Cinema: The Extra Dimension* (London: BFI, 1996) and David Bordwell's *Planet Hong Kong: Popular Cinema and the Art of Entertainment* (Cambridge: Harvard University Press, 2000), esp. part of ch. 2, "Two Dragons: Bruce Lee and Jackie Chan," 49–60, and ch. 3, on the history of Hong Kong cinema.

13. From another perspective, John J. Donohue has isolated some different narrative elements, such as type of warrior, what he fights for and against, and what resolution is arrived at. See his *Warrior Dreams: The Martial Arts and the American Imagination* (Westport, Conn.: Bergin and Garvey, 1994), esp. 53–69.

14. David J. Graper, "The Kung Fu Movie Genre: A Functionalist Perspective" in *Culture and Communication: Methodology, Behavior, Artifacts, and Institutions*, ed. Sari Thomas (Norwood, N.J.: ABLEX, 1987), 154.

15. Mintz, *Martial Arts Films*, 69–73. See also Donohue, *Warrior Dreams*, 50–51.

16. Steve Neale, "Questions of Genre," *Screen* 31:1 (spring 1990): 46.

17. Robin Wood, "*Rancho Notorious*: A Noir Western in Colour," *Cine-Action!* 13–14 (Summer 1988): 84. See also Wood's "Ideology, Genre, Auteur" in his *Hitchcock's Films Revisited* (New York: Columbia University Press, 1989), 288–302, esp. 292, where Wood states that the attempt to treat genres as discrete "is one of the greatest obstacles to any fruitful theory of genre."

18. See Neale, "Questions of Genre"; see also Steve Neale, *Genre* (London: British Film Institute, 1980), and Thomas Schatz, *Hollywood Genres: Formulas, Filmmaking, and the Studio System* (New York: Random House, 1981).

19. Personal interview with Robert Rodríguez, March 10, 1992, Austin, Texas; Rodríguez on *Late Night with David Letterman* (February 26, 1993).

20. Neale, "Questions of Genre," 56.

21. Graper also sees the Hong Kong kung fu martial arts genre as conservative, though for a slightly different reason. In an analysis of how these films are received by lower-class American audiences, Graper concludes that they

"function to keep this [lower-class] audience member in his socially defined position and help to maintain the existing social class structure" (*Kung Fu Movie Genre*, 157).

22. Judith Adler Hellman, *Mexico in Crisis*, 2d ed. (New York: Holmes and Meier, 1983), 112–115. See also Debbie Nathan, *Women and Other Aliens: Essays from the U.S.–Mexico Border* (El Paso, Tex.: Cinco Puntos Press, 1991), 20. Both authors point out that the majority of the *maquiladora* workers are women.

23. Robert Rodríguez on *The Today Show* (NBC, February 26, 1993).

CONCLUSION: THE END OF STEREOTYPES?

1. Benicio Del Toro joins three other Latinos who have won acting Academy Awards. José Ferrer was the first, in 1950, for Best Actor in the Stanley Kramer production of *Cyrano de Bergerac*. Anthony Quinn won two awards for Best Supporting Actor: one for his role as Emiliano Zapata's brother in Elia Kazan's *Viva Zapata* (1952) and the other for playing Paul Gauguin in Vincente Minnelli's *Lust for Life* (1956), a role in which he appeared on screen for only nine minutes. Rita Moreno won her Best Supporting Actress award in 1961 in the role of Anita in *West Side Story*.

2. Harry P. Pachon, Louis DeSipio, Rodolfo O. de la Garza, and Chon Noriega, *Missing in Action: Latinos In and Out of Hollywood* (Los Angeles: Tomás Rivera Policy Institute, 1999). See also the same researchers' follow-up study, *Still Missing: Latinos In and Out of Hollywood* (Los Angeles: Tomás Rivera Policy Institute, 2000).

3. Pachon et al., *Missing in Action*, "President's Letter," unnumbered page.

4. "The Irish Immigration to America—Some Highlights," American Irish Historical Society Web page, http://www.aihs.org/History/history10.htm.

5. Marlita A. Reddy, ed., *Statistical Record of Hispanic Americans*, 2d ed. (New York: Gale Research, 1995), Table 77, "Population Distribution by Reported Ancestry of Ethnic Group, 1990," 123.

6. See Tino Balio's discussion of Hollywood film stars of the 1930s based on their ranking in exhibitors' polls in Chapter 6, "Selling Stars," of his *Grand Design: Hollywood as a Modern Business Enterprise, 1930–1939* (New York: Scribner, 1993), esp. 147–152.

7. Quoted in Lorenza Muñoz and Greg Braxton, "An Accent on Progress," *Los Angeles Times*, January 6, 2001, F-1.

8. Ibid.

9. Daniel Jonah Goldhagen, *Hitler's Willing Executioners: Ordinary Germans and the Holocaust* (New York: Knopf, 1996), 42.

10. Using the "10 percent threshold" for African Americans is somewhat perplexing. When looking at their numbers, as seen in Table N.1, one finds that African Americans were a larger group than the Irish in 1880 and were nearly at the 12 percent level at the dawn of the twentieth century. However, their num-

African Americans as a Percentage
of Total U.S. Population

Year	African Americans	Year	African Americans
1860	14.1	1940	9.8
1870	12.7	1950	10.0
1880	13.1	1960	10.5
1890	11.9	1970	11.1
1900	11.6	1980	11.7
1910	10.7	1990	12.1
1920	9.9	2000	13.0
1930	9.7		

Source: "We . . . the American Blacks," U.S. Department of Commerce, Economics and Statistics Administration, Bureau of the Census, 1993, 4. "Table 1: Population by Age, Sex, and Race and Hispanic Origin," U.S. Census Bureau, Current Population Survey, March 2000, Racial Statistics Branch, Population Division, http://www.census.gov/population/socdemo/race/black/pp1-142/tabo1.txt.

bers, as a percentage of the total U.S. population, steadily decreased from 1860 to 1950. They did not *reach and sustain* the 10 percent level again until 1950.

That, despite their numbers, they did not assimilate in the same way and at the same time as the Irish is understandable. The African American experience is far different from that of any other immigrant group, because of the necessity of overcoming slavery, oppression, and racism.

This is not the place for an extended debate on the state of African American images in films, but although many negative images persist, there are some hopeful signs. One of the most optimistic is the large number of African American writers, directors, and stars who are working on both sides of the camera in Hollywood cinema and are not relegated to separate and unequal minority cinemas, such as the "race movies" of the period 1920 to 1950. Furthermore, it is noteworthy that the breakdown in 1950 of the kind of parallel movie industry that the race pictures represented coincided with the upturn in the Black population to the 10 percent level. And, of course, it was in the 1950s that the civil rights movement began to make its deepest inroads.

INDEX

Above the Law (1988), 228
Acting in the Cinema, 88–89
Affairs of Annabel, The (1938), 96
African Americans: "buffalo soldiers,"
   139; representation in John Ford's west-
   erns, 135–136, 139, 146, 147, 148;
   stereotypes, 39, 271
Against All Odds (1983), 199
Agar, John, 139
Agueda Martinez (1977), 186
¡Alambrista! (1977), 186
Alegres de Terán, Los, 201
Alien (1980), 83, 153, 158, 163, 176
Aliens (1986), 153, 158, 167, 176–179,
   180
Allen, Woody, 102
Allgood, Sara, 267
All the King's Men (1949), 111
Alonso, María Conchita, 76
American cinema: usage explained, 7
American Me (1992), 187
Anaconda (1997), 83, 188, 189
Angeli, Pier, 84
Anglo: usage explained, 7
Anima (1989), 186
Annabel Takes a Tour (1938), 96
anti-Semitism, 21, 24, 27, 270–271. See
   also stereotypes
Anzaldúa, Gloria, 192–193, 196, 204, 207
Apocalypse Now (1979), 49
Arau, Alfonso, 72, 73, 188
archetype, 54–56, 57. See also stereotypes
Archuletta, Beulah, 134
Arizmendi, Yareli, 206, 210
Armendáriz, Pedro, 84, 136, 141, 142
Armida, 264
Arnaz, Desi, 71
Arquette, David, 248
Arquette, Rosanna, 69

Arrival, The (1996), 9
Artenstein, Isaac, 187, 198, 205
Arteta, Miguel, 188
assimilation narrative, 113–116
Astaire, Fred, 80
Astor, Mary, 263
Aurora Encounter, The (1986), 158
Avellán, Elizabeth, xi, 243, 270
Avila, Carlos, 187

Baca, Jimmy, 187
Bacon, Lloyd, 166
Bad and the Beautiful, The (1952), 98,
   99, 100
Badge 373 (1973), 31, 68
Badham, John, 154
Baker, Carroll, 134, 148
Bakhtin, Mikhail, 28–29
Ball, Lucille, 96, 97
Ballad of an Unsung Hero (1983), 198,
   205, 206, 207, 217
Ballad of Gregorio Cortez, The (1982),
   187
Banderas, Antonio, 76, 247, 248, 249,
   250, 262
Bandido (1956), 100
bandido stereotype: 19, 31, 32, 37, 38,
   39, 40, 41, 43, 66, 73, 83, 159, 166,
   172, 173, 182; analyzed 1–2, 39–41;
   cinematic sign, 17, 39–41; contrasted
   with Mexican history, 17–18; described,
   1, 68–69; dictator variant, 85, 102–
   105; as futuristic bandolero, 169, 182;
   José Ferrer's subversion of, 102–105;
   moral traits, 41; Raúl Julia's evasion of,
   105; in Treasure of the Sierra Madre,
   85. See also stereotypes
Barbarosa (1982), 98, 100
Barrymore, John, 264
Barthes, Roland, 38

305